Life's a Trip... expect Falls!

A GUIDE TO LIFE & OTHER THINGS BY

Mike Moody

outskirts press

Life's a Trip...Expect Falls!
All Rights Reserved.
Copyright © 2019 Mike Moody
v4.0

The opinions expressed in this manuscript are solely the opinions of the author and do not represent the opinions or thoughts of the publisher. The author has represented and warranted full ownership and/or legal right to publish all the materials in this book.

This book may not be reproduced, transmitted, or stored in whole or in part by any means, including graphic, electronic, or mechanical without the express written consent of the publisher except in the case of brief quotations embodied in critical articles and reviews.

Outskirts Press, Inc.
http://www.outskirtspress.com

Paperback ISBN: 978-1-9772-0343-4

Cover Photo © 2019 Kevin Van Hyning. All rights reserved - used with permission.

Outskirts Press and the "OP" logo are trademarks belonging to Outskirts Press, Inc.

PRINTED IN THE UNITED STATES OF AMERICA

Table of Contents

Introduction i

CHAPTER ONE
    "Acting Out…" 1

CHAPTER TWO
    Collecting Bottles 3

CHAPTER THREE
    Billy Ray and the Midnight Ride 7

CHAPTER FOUR
    The "Smoking" Tree 17

CHAPTER FIVE
    First Kiss 21

CHAPTER SIX
    Wrecking a Romance (and a car at the same time!) 26

CHAPTER SEVEN
    The Wrecking Crew 32

CHAPTER EIGHT
    Hell's Angels Approaching! 37

CHAPTER NINE
    "Let's Make a Deal!" 43

CHAPTER TEN
  A Serious Breach of Etiquette 48

CHAPTER ELEVEN
  You're In The Army Now. 51

CHAPTER TWELVE
  The Chicken Family 70

CHAPTER THIRTEEN
  "Happy" Days Were Here Again 75

CHAPTER FOURTEEN
  In the Swim. 84

CHAPTER FIFTEEN
  Hitting the Road (And Other Things That Get in the Way) . 89

CHAPTER SIXTEEN
  The Governor's Night Out (With C'nelia) 115

CHAPTER SEVENTEEN
  Moving On and Starting Over 122

CHAPTER EIGHTEEN
  Life in a Fairy Tale. 131

CHAPTER NINETEEN
  Janice's Lesson ("the girl from Grenada") 137

CHAPTER TWENTY
  Celebrating "Stewardess-ship" 142

CHAPTER TWENTY-ONE
  A Job or a Career? 147

CHAPTER TWENTY-TWO
  A Good Doctor is Hard to Find 168

CHAPTER TWENTY-THREE
  The End of the Road. 176

CHAPTER TWENTY-FOUR
    Remembering Friends 191
CHAPTER TWENTY-FIVE
    The Road Is Long 212

Failure is simply the opportunity to begin again, this time more intelligently.

– Henry Ford

I have not failed. I've just found 10,000 ways that won't work.

– Thomas A. Edison

ACKNOWLEDGMENTS AND SPECIAL THANKS

To my beautiful daughters, Ashley and Crystal,
who have always had faith in me,
especially as I have struggled to be a "writer"

To my sweet and precious granddaughters,
MaKayla Michele and Vox Vivienne
who taught me how to love unconditionally

To my incredible sister, Jean,
who has protected me since Day One

To my parents, John and Lillie,
who, with the help of God, gave me life

To Dana Stephens, my unofficial "art director,"
who rescued me at the last minute and provided inspiration
for the "front cover"

To Daniel Clark, Ph.D. and Marnie Dillon, Psy.D.,
who believed in me and took a chance on me when no one else
would and who taught me the true meaning of compassion and
professionalism

And to the many unforgettable friends and family
who refused to laugh at me when I fell (failed)
and cheered me on every time I got back up

Introduction

I wrote a book several years ago, entitled *Mules in The Fast Lane*, which included a collection of things I remembered growing up in a small Southern town and the lessons I had learned along the way. I failed to include some really funny (poignant?) stories that came to mind later. I thought it would make sense to start with some "leftovers" as a sort of segue, if you will, to this book. But first, a little history lesson.

My formative years took place in a small town called Luverne in Crenshaw County, Alabama, except for a short stint in Phoenix City, across the river from Columbus, Georgia when I was still in diapers. My daddy got a job working for the "Triple A" (something to do with agriculture, I believe) and got transferred over there, so we stayed with one of Daddy's first cousins, Alice Moody Wyrosdick, and her husband, Troyce. That job didn't last very long, so we moved back to the farm outside of Luverne, near what I now refer to as "The Moody Compound" on Gin Creek Road. My parents eventually bought an old country store (sometimes called a "Mom and Pop" store) at the corner of Highways 331 and 10, about two miles north of town. The intersection formed a sort of triangle, so that's what we called it…"The Triangle." That's where I grew up…literally.

I won't say I was pampered as a child, but there was definitely some doting going on as I was growing up, especially on my mother's part. Despite this, I can't say I learned to be really very positive about the future. I think this was partly due to my angel mother's "realism" in dealing with my father. Although I no longer dwell on the fact that he was a heavy drinker (dare I say, hopeless alcoholic) for many years, I do believe this impacted my mother's somewhat defeatist attitude at times.

For the majority of my childhood, almost everything we planned in the way of activity—other than work at The Triangle (e.g. movies, nights out, trips to relatives', school extracurricular activities, etc.)—was tempered by a dark cloud of uncertainty (fear) that Daddy wouldn't make it home when the appointed time came. His job as an insurance salesman required much driving, as he worked a "debit," which meant he not only sold the policies, he also collected monthly premiums (i.e. money) from the buyers.

Two-car families were virtually unheard of back then (except for some of the "rich people" who lived in town), so early on, when it came to travel outside The Triangle, we were totally at the mercy of Daddy and his drinking binges. There would be many nights as a toddler, I would perch myself on the curb and fantasize that the next car would be Daddy. And that he would be happy to see me…and safe…and sober. But he rarely was…sober, that is. Most times, I would become too weary to wait him out, or bedtime or sleepiness would overtake me, with the inevitable call from my mother that it was time to come in. Strangely though, I never lost hope that he would come as promised, despite my mother's assurances to the contrary. I remember her feeble attempts at being positive about these scenarios, but once in a while, I would overhear her say something like, "I guess it's just not meant for us to ever have anything nice," because she knew Daddy would usually "drink it away."

I didn't know anything about budgets at the time, but I doubt any of the money Daddy earned on his insurance job ever made it home. Sometimes Mother would simply pass it off with the most positive view she could muster at the time: "Well, we just have to expect the worst and hope for the best." I eventually passed this advice on to my own children, who called my mother "Granny" and my father "Big Daddy."

As the years passed, we found this philosophy helpful in getting through the hard times, hoping that the best (or at least better times) would be coming soon. Although it wasn't immediate, it did finally happen. Several incidents occurred prior to the infamous date that led up to my father successfully ending his drinking career. The abbreviated story is told that, one day my father came to my mother with one of his many "bottles" in his hand, to which he had affixed a piece of tape and on which he had written the date, October 18, 1975. He quietly and solemnly announced, "Lillie, this is my last drink," and handed the bottle to my mother. And, indeed it was.

To my father's credit, he never took another drink of alcohol, and gave us almost 17 wonderful years of sobriety. He made up for the time lost, and then some. Even my mother's death eight months prior to his, couldn't drive him back to the bottle. Unfortunately, Daddy was so overcome with grief, he tragically took his life October 7, 1992.

Exactly five years later on October 7, 1997, my granddaughter (Granny and Big Daddy's great granddaughter), MaKayla Michele Moody was born. On that day, I finally understood my mother's admonition to "expect the worst…and hope for the best."

Still, being more of a pragmatist/realist than a Norman Vincent Peale positivist, I struggled with positive thinking. That said, sometimes things would often happen that made me wonder if I should make it a practice to think more in the positive direction.

So, back to the original admonition to "expect the worst and hope for the best," I began to compare it with the biblical tenet that "…all things work together for good to them that love God…" (KJV, Romans 8:28). I struggled with whether God was really trying to tell me something or whether it was just "coincidence."

My daughter, Ashley, has been mostly in the positive camp, usually believing that things will work out if one has the patience to wait it out.

So, when she finally decided at around age 38 to think about having children after vowing to never do so, we all thought, "O.K., this is a positive thing." My younger daughter, Crystal, wasn't so sure, because, by this time, her daughter, MaKayla, was going through those difficult mid-teen years.

Nevertheless, Ashley's husband, Joel, was called in to complete the decision, and preparations began in earnest in September of 2009. However, by the end of April of 2011, positive thinking began to take a hit as the rabbit lived on. Joel subjected himself to fertility testing, testing positive, which, in this case, was a negative, and Ashley was later diagnosed with endometrial cancer. The cancer was so aggressive, there was no time to harvest eggs and the prognosis so grim, that a complete hysterectomy was ordered. All this was followed by months of brutal chemotherapy, baldheadedness, nausea, time missed from work, and a rethinking of ever having a baby.

But, in true Ashley fashion, hoping for the best (at this point, we wouldn't allow ourselves to even consider the worst), Ashley got busy. After her first round of chemo, Ashley began her search for wigs. They say that one loses most of the warmth from one's body through the head (which is, of course, why we have hair!), and facing possible chemo into the winter months in Boston, she wasn't looking forward to a cold bald head!

If a daughter can be more beautiful without hair, Ashley was the one to prove it. By September of 2011, Ashley was totally bald. I flew to Boston to spend some time with her during chemo, drive her to appointments, and help out around the house, and one memorable incident stands out in my mind. We had gotten home after a rather nauseating chemotherapy session and, exhausted, Ashley told me she was going to try to get some rest, and headed for her bedroom. Overall, her treatments were going well, and I wasn't too worried about her; nevertheless, after a couple of hours, I decided to check on her. I quietly opened her bedroom door and could see that she was sleeping soundly. For just a moment, I went back in time and was looking at my sweet little baby in her crib with no hair! The lump stuck in my throat as I gently closed the door and slipped away. Wanting to "stay strong" for Ashley, I maintained a positive persona for the rest of that week. As I was still employed, I eventually returned home to Montgomery, leaving her in the capable hands of her husband. Ashley slowly recovered from the cancer and the devastating effects of chemotherapy, and was able to return to work.

But, positivity took another hit when, in October of 2013, Joel was diagnosed with lung cancer. He had surgery to remove part of his right lung on November 6, 2013, less than two years after Ashley's final chemotherapy session. Joel's cancer was puzzling to all of us, as he had been a lifelong tobacco teetotaler. Both Ashley and Joel had played in "rock" bands for a number of years, and we wanted to believe that "second-hand" smoke was the culprit. Still, we were all having a hard time finding anything positive in any of this.

Then slowly, things took a turn for the better. Good news finally came when Ashley got the report from her oncologist: cancer free! Then Joel got the report from his doctor in December of 2013. No more cancer! And time to pick up where the talks about family—including a baby—had been put on hold.

Being about 1200 miles from Boston, I wasn't privy to the discussions that took place leading up to the phone call from Ashley. The decision had been made—again—to have a baby. *How would this be possible*, I asked. *It's called surrogacy*, Ashley explained. This time, negativity begins to take hit, after hit, after hit, as Ashley and Joel take us on their journey over the next several months. Finding an egg donor, finding a surrogate, finding a doctor to "implant," finding time to do it all…the list goes on.

And, once again, Granny's admonition held fast (at least the part about hoping for the best). On July 10, 2014, Vox Vivienne Reader became part of our family at 10:35 P.M. It might be a stretch to make a point here, but a couple of things have since been pointed out to me that made me rethink (again!) that maybe positivism really is the best policy. Vox's surrogate mother's name was Ashley, and Crystal pointed out that, numerically expressed, Vox's birthday is 7-10, making it the mirror image of my only other granddaughter, MaKayla's birthday: 10-7. It makes a skeptic like me wonder… coincidence or "positive" confirmation? You decide.

Anyway, back to those "leftovers" I promised earlier.

CHAPTER ONE

"Acting Out..."

Throughout high school, I found myself in a lot of "plays" (not the football kind), having a reputation as the "class clown." I often ended up in some sort of production when the teachers felt a need to put one on. I rarely volunteered, but rather would be drafted by peers or teachers who would state, "Oh, we'll get Mike to do it. He's crazy (or a nut, or funny, etc.)."

There was one such production I remember vividly. (I think it was the Beta Club "skit" which we performed every year at the Beta Club Convention in Birmingham.) Our science teacher, Mrs. Fuller was one of the teachers in charge of directing this particular skit. We had rehearsed for weeks, and it was finally time for the dress rehearsal, the final performance to be presented to the entire school prior to the trip to Birmingham. Needless to say, we were all quite nervous, but there was one funny (dare I say…embarrassing…?) incident in the crucial opening scene. Anyone who has ever performed on stage at my high school, remembers the heavy, thick, velvety curtains that had to be pulled to reveal the full stage. Just before the opening scene, Mrs. Fuller was scurrying around, making sure everyone was in their designated places. I was the Master of Ceremonies—looking all spiffy in my suit and tie, just before the soon-to-be-pulled heavy curtain was drawn, and Mrs. Fuller was standing to my right, both of us facing our expectant audience. Apparently, the curtain opened so fast, it caught her (and me) off guard and nearly knocked her down. As she stumbled backwards (attempting to avoid being seen by the audience, as she was not part of the actual production), she wildly flung her left arm back, grabbing at whatever she could to keep from taking a pratfall and grabbed me squarely in my groin!

    Miraculously, we both recovered quickly enough for her to exit stage left undetected and for me to continue the opening performance without a hitch (no pun intended) and with a broad grin on my face! I'll never forget the "roar of the greasepaint and the smell of the crowd," and the incident was never mentioned by the only two people who knew of it. Mrs. Fuller was definitely a "class act!"

CHAPTER TWO

―――⁂―――

COLLECTING BOTTLES

ON SEPTEMBER 24, 1968, CBS debuted a program on Sunday nights called "60 Minutes," which has become one of that network's longest-running shows. As popular as it has been, I can't say that I remember the content of a single episode. What I do remember, however, was the colorful character featured at the end of each show from 1978 to 2011. His name was Andrew Aitken "Andy" Rooney. The thing most people remember about old Andy was his penchant for making seemingly insignificant things suddenly seem important. His bushy eyebrows were reminiscent of United Mine Workers Union leader John L. Lewis, and he frowned into the camera with such intensity, the viewer dared not look away lest he be chastised for not paying attention. His little part of the show, "A Few Minutes with Andy Rooney" lasted only about five minutes, but its content was as colorful as Rooney himself. He would typically start his feature with the familiar question, "You know what bothers me…?" At first you might think, "Who cares," but before the feature was over, you found yourself saying, "Yeh…right…!"

One episode made an especially poignant impression on me because it dealt with a tiny copper disc called a penny and how its value had changed over the years. Part of the segment made the point that the penny had become so insignificant that people no longer stopped to pick one up if spotted on the street. Rooney even cited a study that had been done to prove his point.

It made me start thinking about my own experiences with the lowly penny, and growing up during a time when it meant a lot to have one. One of the first things I learned to do growing up in our little Mom and Pop store was how to "make change" and "count back" the money when a customer made a purchase. Pennies were (and still are) an integral part of that counting, although the counting is now usually done with computers, with the money being handed back in a wad rather than verbally and meticulously repeated back for accuracy.

People of my generation undoubtedly remember "penny candy," two-for-a-penny cookies, and the infamous "penny deposit" on returnable Coke bottles. (At that time, of course, "Coke" meant any carbonated beverage.) That penny deposit was very important for a number of reasons. For one (although we didn't think so much about it at the time), it aided in recycling bottles. It also made it possible to make a little extra money, if you had a few left-over bottles around the house or under the car seat. Why, back in the day, it was almost considered a capital offense to not return a returnable bottle!

Now to the real reason for my explaining the importance of a penny, and how I came to realize that a person's character could be judged by how much they valued it. My lesson began one night as a young teenager (probably 15 or so) when I was asked to "go riding" with some friends. Being always aware of how much money we *didn't* have, I was constantly looking for ways to, not only save it, but also to make a little here and there. This particular night, there was the usual crowd I hung out with in the car, but also a sweet pretty girl named Martha (who I secretly had a crush on...uh...well, along with most of the other girls in our little town). I had never "gone riding" with Martha, probably because I saw her and her family as being in a somewhat higher socioeconomic status than mine. Although it wasn't stated outright, being in the "class" I was, we "knew our place" and we rarely associated with the upper class. I probably made more out of it at the time than anyone else, but nevertheless, with Martha in the car, I was painfully aware that I was in the presence of someone special and "classy."

Martha's mother was one of my favorite teachers in high school, so I knew Martha was from "good stock." Having become a Christian at age 11, I was happy to later have "Miss Sara" as a teacher, especially first thing in the morning, because she always started class with Bible reading and prayer. (Mind you, this was a public school, but this practice was not uncommon—and often expected—before secular humanism invaded the schools.) But, I was actually intrigued with Martha's family for another reason. They were all physically attractive people. Miss Sara, Martha, and her older sister, June, looked exactly alike and were absolutely beautiful in my mind! O.K., I liked her dad, too, although I was a little intimidated by his quiet, confident manner.

Back to that night in the car. Here I am in the back seat with Princess Martha (and who knows who else…). Being sort of a class clown and naturally happy-go-lucky, I was always looking for "different" ways to have fun. Somehow the notion came to me that we should look for bottles! (What else would you do for fun on a Saturday night in a small town, right?) My reasoning was that I could enlist my friends to collect these rare treasures, then I could take them back to The Triangle to help defray the cost of operation. What a great plan! Before I knew it, and to my delight, the treasure hunt was on! Full speed ahead! Something sparkling up ahead! Screech to a halt! Scoop up the bottle and dash away! We were having unheard-of-fun!

But then something strange happened. After several frantic minutes of collecting, I noticed that the number of bottles in the back seat floorboard didn't seem to add up. It seemed as though I was collecting many more bottles than were actually there. It never occurred to me (until now) that Martha might be taking advantage of little ol' me and my awkward (underclass) nature. To confirm my suspicions, at the next stop, I hung back a couple of extra seconds, and looking over my shoulder, I caught Martha red-handed, throwing the bottles out the other door faster than I could scoop a new one up!

Needless to say, my stock in Martha went down that night. Although they all considered it good-natured fun, I was secretly humiliated and felt betrayed, but worse, stupid for letting myself be taken advantage of. But in true class clown form, I laughed heartily, and no one was the wiser. Of course, I later forgave "Princess Martha," and was thrilled when she married a cousin of mine years later. All in the family!

CHAPTER THREE

BILLY RAY AND THE MIDNIGHT RIDE

I REALIZE THAT, in this "modern age," it's not politically correct to point out the distinct differences between boys and girls (male and female, men and women) and to hold the view that the intimate (sexual) kind of love is possible only between two people of opposite gender. That said, I still believe that most people, even today, would find the idea of two teenage boys "sleeping" together freaky at best.

Not so when I was 16 and one of my best friends, Henry, and I wanted to get an early start on the weekend. The best way to do that, as we saw it, was for Henry to spend the night with me. I've told many stories over the years about The Triangle. Although it seems kinda strange now, back when we moved there in 1947, I thought it was normal to actually live in a store. I mean, we worked there all the time, so why not just live there, too? My daddy had some crude living quarters added onto the store, and we later turned the attic into some bedrooms so my sister and I could have some privacy.

The bedrooms were rather small, and there wasn't room for

anything extra, like a cot, for example. So, when Henry came over, there was nowhere else for him to sleep except in the bed with me. That didn't really matter though, because we had decided ahead of time that we were not going to stay cooped up in my bedroom for long. Adventure was calling!

Earlier that (Friday) night, Henry and I had attended the local high school football game. I had been fortunate enough to get "Lizzy," our old '53 Chevy, for Henry and me to ride around in, and life was good. Henry was fairly active in sports and had played football, but this particular game was not one he played in. That left the two of us free to get into as much trouble as we wanted to after the game. ("Trouble" in those days usually meant us chasing girls who had boyfriends, then us being chased by the boyfriends.)

Anyway, there was one menacingly tough guy in our school named Billy Ray Hardway. Billy Ray had his own circle of "friends" he hung out with, none of whom you wanted to mess with. They were the kind who swaggered around in pegged pants and jeans and a pack of cigarettes rolled up in the sleeve of their T-shirt. Billy Ray was at the game that night, and Henry and I had had a run-in with him as the game ended—something to do with the way we parked the car—and after some heated words, we went on the lam, hoping that Billy Ray wouldn't hunt us down and blacken our eyes!

We thought nothing more about it as we enjoyed the after-game activities at Ed's (the preferred hangout), the Dairy Dream, and Miller's Skating Rink. By the time we made it home to The Triangle, my folks were already in bed, so we silently crept up the stairs to my bedroom in the attic, still not ready to call it a night.

After some discussion about what to do the rest of the night, one of us came up with a great idea. I'm not sure if it was Henry or me who came up with it, but obviously very little thought had gone into the plan. The Patsaliga (pronounced Pat-suh-LAG-ee) River Bridge was probably a mile or so down the road, so we decided to see if anything was going on at the Oil Well gas station on the other side of the bridge.

I'm sure it was after midnight, which made the adventure even more daring. Heck, things were kind of dying down, and we weren't ready for that! Time for some action!

When we think back on it now, it really was a stupid idea, but certainly at face value not very dangerous either. After all, by this time, most people in our sleepy little town were sawing logs anyway. There was a big mimosa tree outside my bedroom window, providing the perfect "quiet" escape from our otherwise dull night. Of course, we probably would have made less noise and could have just quietly snuck out the way we came in, but that wouldn't have made nearly as interesting a story to tell our friends the following Monday morning at school. We had to create real adventure, so to make the whole thing more stupid, we decided to climb out the bedroom window, shimmy down the mimosa, drop down to ground level, and stealthily head out for the Patsaliga! Henry didn't want to mess up his "good pants," so he borrowed a pair of my jeans just in case we had to fight some wild hogs… or something. We're talkin' fun!

It didn't take long to make it out the window, the most time taken deciding (arguing?) about who would go first. *Go ahead, Henry. Nah, you go ahead, Mike. You know the roof better than I do. (Really…?)* With each trepidatious inch, the tension grew. *Have you ever noticed how slippery a roof can be after midnight when you're trying to be quiet so as to not wake your soundly sleeping parents? And…I didn't realize how high up we were until I looked down from the roof…Gulp!*

I landed on the ground first (thankfully, on my feet), followed closely by my partner in crime. It's funny how paranoid a couple of teenage boys can get when trying to pull a fast one on some (hopefully) unsuspecting parents. The second Henry's feet hit the ground, he thought he "heard" something!

"What was that?" he grunted, trying to stifle his fear.

"What? What was it?"

"You didn't hear it?"

"No! What! What was it?"

"I don't know! I thought..."

"What did it sound like...?"

"It sounded like...uh...I dunno!"

By this time, I think we both realized we'd never make it to the Patsaliga if we didn't pull ourselves together. Huddling in fear and peering into the darkness, we agreed to move on, hoping that what we "heard" wasn't my parents on their own scouting mission. I knew my daddy had a collection of guns and probably wouldn't have hesitated to use one of them if he thought somebody was trying to break in!

Half walking, half running, we finally made it to the bridge. Reality began to set in, as we started to take inventory of the situation. The bridge looked a lot longer than we remembered it, especially when you're standing at one end in the midnight darkness! Then it hit us. *You know, this might be a little dangerous. I mean, after all, it was Friday night. A lot of nuts on the road, right?*

We just hadn't thought it through. We'd seen the Patsaliga up close a couple of times when we went fishing down there. We probably even looked up at the bridge. But we'd never seen it from this angle, and suddenly it was daunting...and dark!

Neither of us wanted to let the other know we were "chicken," though, and started kidding each other about it. I don't remember who started it, but the dialogue went something like this: "Hey, you wanna go, or not?" What are you waitin' for? Let's go!"

Of course, after the initial adrenaline-fueled anticipation, it was somewhat anticlimactic as we strode up to the Oil Well. *Dark. Nobody there. Quiet. Dull. What are we doing here?* After a couple minutes kicking rocks, shuffling feet, and trying our best to salvage an incredibly dull situation, we decided to head back to The Triangle. And this is where things got interesting.

Although it's not a straight shot from the Patsaliga Bridge to the curve at Rusty Furr's house, it was possible to see a good ways up the road past The Triangle on a clear day. Problem was, this was not a clear day; it was the middle of the night! And dark! And scary! But, as I said, neither of us wanted to show how chicken we were.

We had gotten about a third of the way back across the bridge (again, half walking, half running) when straight ahead, just coming out of the curve, we saw headlights!

Decision time! Do we run for cover back to the Oil Well, or do we race those headlights to the other end of the bridge? Panic! More paranoia! What if we don't make it? What if we never see our friends again? What if...? What if it's Billy Ray Hardway?! Oh, no! The phantom!

We had to get a hold of ourselves! This is silly, we thought. Let's just amble our way toward home, and just ignore the car (or whatever it was) speeding toward us. Suddenly, we were running at warp speed toward The Triangle, which seemed a hundred miles away! The closer we got to the end of the bridge, the closer the looming car. At one point, Henry lost a shoe, causing me to shoot past him at the speed of light.

"Hey, wait! Stop! Mike...I can't find my shoe!" *Who's worried about a shoe,* I thought, as I did a U-turn and raced back to help Henry find it. Loafers were popular at the time, and in his speed, Henry had apparently slung it off, several yards away toward the edge of the bridge. Everything went into slo-mo...I could see Henry leaning down, teetering toward the rim. *He must have found it! Too late!* It was every man for himself. Hopping on one foot and slipping the loafer on the other one, Henry never skipped a beat. He passed me before I could reach him, going the other way! Another U-turn!

Huffing and puffing, we barely beat the phantom car to the end of the bridge. The plan was to shuffle past the car and pretend that nothing was out of the ordinary, that we were just out for a midnight stroll. Suddenly it didn't make sense to be shuffling, as the headlights blinded us, maybe 20 feet away. I think we were holding each other's hand as we sailed over the guard rail, rolling and sliding down the embankment toward the chilly Patsaliga!

It was only the patch of level ground at the bottom that stopped our descent. Due to our vast experience in counterinsurgency, we managed to roll over, tugging on the grassy knoll as we came to a screeching halt. We looked at each other in terror as we realized the car had stopped directly above us! It seemed like a scene from an alien invasion movie, complete with an eerie glow, dust and fog shrouding the ominous black car.

As we peered upwards, it was evident that the car had now come to a complete stop. We could hear the engine rumbling faintly. We imagined that we heard "people" talking. Trying painfully to not attract attention, I whispered to Henry, "Why don't we just crawl back up to the road and...you know...just kinda walk away like we didn't notice they were there?" I knew it sounded stupid. *I mean, how could they not know we were there? Weren't they racing us to the end of the bridge? Did they have guns? Had they just robbed a bank? Were they federal fugitives? Oh, God...was it BILLY RAY??* It was paranoia on steroids!

Incredibly, Henry thought my idea was a good one. Then he came up with another good suggestion that really made sense. "Let's just pretend we don't even see 'em," he suggested. Nodding in agreement, we slowly climbed up toward the light and what we hoped wouldn't be our doom. It couldn't have taken more than thirty seconds, but it felt like an eternity.

All seemed to be going well, and somehow in our wisdom, we must have thought that, if we didn't look toward the car, maybe "they" wouldn't see us either. We were so close, we could feel the heat from the engine as we scrambled over the guardrail. Out of the corners of our eyes, however, something just didn't seem right. *What was that? Did we see something? Was that a car door opening?* To shuffle (again) or to run? That was the question.

Then, from the direction of the car came a weak but foreboding voice, "I'm gone git them boys!" *OH, NO! BILLY RAY HARDWAY!* Henry and I didn't have to ask each other if we should run. We were already doing it! At least he'd have to shoot us in the back, we thought. No time to look back; that would take too much time. *How did this happen? Why didn't we just go to bed like normal people? Dooooom!*

After running for what seemed like 10 miles, I decided it was time to work out another plan. Since we were sure we were dealing with Billy Ray Hardway, we had to think smart. By this time, we realized we'd outrun him (because we were still alive), but of course, he surely had his buddies up ahead, waiting to ambush us. We had to trick them by leaving the main road and circling around in the pasture that bordered the highway. We're now in full survival mode. We would do whatever we had to do to escape the evil empire!

Henry liked the plan, so we climbed the barbed wire fence and hunkered down so as not to be detected from the main highway (which is probably where Billy Ray's henchmen were patrolling), the tall bahia grass stinging our faces. And once again, the race was on!

Panic and adrenaline would alternately infect us as we made the circle back around to The Triangle and ultimately safety. Henry would surge ahead, then I would overtake him and take the lead. We could see The Triangle as we sped through the field. Henry was the football player, so I was glad to have him take the lead. He sort of inspired me with his athleticism, I guess. We were making really good time. But then, disaster!

Henry was about eight or ten yards ahead of me, when suddenly he disappeared! *Argh! Ohh!* I heard him scream. Almost immediately, it hit me (literally) why Henry had "disappeared." I ran into the same barbed wire fence at an angle, but stopped short of falling over it like Henry did! It had literally torn his (my) jeans up! And as barbed wire fences usually do, it actually tore up his thighs too. *Wow! Can anything else go wrong tonight?*

Now we really did have to get home. With Henry hobbling in pain and me worried sick that I might be blamed for the whole thing, we had one more hurdle to cross. The pasture was divided into smaller sections, with the main fence surrounding the entire field. The outside fence was much taller, and we had to climb it to get back to the main road that bordered The Triangle.

The final terror hit us as we started to swing our feet over the top of the fence. It looked like all of the lights were on at The Triangle! More panic ensued as we sprinted for home. We figured that, although my parents might be upset with us, at least they'd protect us from Billy Ray Hardway! We'd deal with their punishment later.

However, as we approached The Triangle, we realized that what we thought were lights on was actually lights from the nearby Amoco Station reflecting in the windows of The Triangle! Relief! We began to feel like we'd spent the whole night in a bipolar treatment center!

We never debated whether to climb back up the Mimosa to get back to my bedroom. It seemed a moot point at this stage, what with Henry's wounds and all. Until we got inside, we didn't know how bad it was. Opening the side door at The Triangle, we paused to consider whether to go back upstairs and try to forget the whole thing, or to "fess up" and tell my parents what we had done. By this time, Henry was almost in tears, so we decided it would be better to just come clean and tell all. Besides, we still weren't sure who that was in that darn car and why they wanted to "git them boys."

In addition to having several guns, my daddy was also an ambulance chaser and liked nothing better than to get involved anywhere there was excitement. As we tapped on their bedroom door, we realized that my parents had slept through the whole thing and probably would never have found out what happened if Henry hadn't flown into that fence!

"Huh…what? What is it," we heard my mother say. Daddy was a pretty sound sleeper (and may have actually had a little to drink before he hit the hay), so we had to shake him out of his slumber. With all the lights on now, we told them the whole story, including our suspicions about Billy Ray Hardway.

Well, that's all Daddy needed to jump out of bed and get ready to roll! We had to wait for Mother to patch Henry up, which took about five or six Band-aids. The blue jeans, however, didn't fare as well. I think we threw them away that night.

Anyway, off to town we go, with Henry and me giving Daddy the play-by-play in graphic detail. But, by the time we got back to the Patsaliga, there was no sign of the black car...or Billy Ray Hardway, and Henry and I were beginning to wonder if it had all been a bad dream.

Daddy didn't want to give up though, seeing as how we'd gotten him up out of a sound sleep (a miracle), so we rode on downtown to the police station, our eyes peeled for the now infamous black car. Somehow, Daddy missed the turn to the police station, but Henry and I looked down the side street where it was, and almost in unison, hollered, "There it is! There's the car!"

Daddy screeched on the brakes, slammed 'er in reverse, and sped down to the station. As we pulled up beside the black car, Daddy looked at Henry and me and warned us, "Y'all stay right here. I'm gone go find out what's goin' on."

I've thought about that night probably a thousand times since then. All I can say is, when we heard "the rest of the story," it wasn't nearly as dramatic or scary as our imagination had made it out to be. According to Daddy, the black car belonged, not to Billy Ray Hardway, but to a local gas station employee named Guy Olson. Guy was a fella about Daddy's age who was well known for his occasional partying behavior, especially as the weekend approached. Apparently, he and his girlfriend (we'll call her Erlene) had been out at Bodiford's Pool, a hangout for the older crowd up Highway 331. Bodiford's Pool was actually a swimming pool with a concession stand the whole family would frequent during the day, but on weekends the liquor would flow and people like Guy would imbibe and sometimes get in trouble. The story goes that Guy and Erlene had almost made it home when they got into an argument, causing Guy to pull out the nearest Coca Cola bottle and start beating her senseless. It wasn't clear if she or Guy was driving. It must have been Erlene, because we figured that, as they approached the Patsaliga River, she saw "somebody" on the bridge and decided to stop and "get help."

We figured out that she must have stopped the car just as Henry and I sailed over the guardrail. Undoubtedly, they were both rather plastered and Erlene being groggy from the whaling, they waited for us to surface as the car idled at the edge of the bridge. So…it wasn't Billy Ray, but rather Erlene we heard say in her raspy, liquor-infused voice, "I'm gone git them boys." Mystery solved.

    We never found out what happened to either Guy or Erlene after that night. I didn't really care; I just knew that I would never cross the Patsaliga Bridge on foot *ever again*!

CHAPTER FOUR

THE "SMOKING" TREE

I'M SURE THAT, in any small town back in the day, there were probably kids in high school who were known to be "fast." At one time, this term meant those kids undoubtedly smoked a cigarette or two on the sly, maybe got hold of a beer from their Uncle Bert's stash, and might even have engaged in a little hanky-panky with the opposite sex if the truth be known.

Those kinds of kids and that sort of thing was sort of overlooked though, and they didn't really have to worry about NBC or CNN showing up on their doorstep hoping to expose the scandal and ruin their lives forever. It was just accepted that these were the "fast" kids and, more than likely, they would grow out of it (or maybe not).

Looking back on those days, I find it incredible how "advanced" our high school was to have provided a special place for kids who smoked! It was called "the smoking tree."

I've seen "the media" demonize many things, then go back and forth with other things such as cigarettes, alternately condemning those who used them, then advertising them, and then trying to come up with ways to "help" people not use them! There were catchy slogans and jingles, like Brewton Snuff: "Brewton, Brewton, got more pep than e'er before; Brewton, Brewton, sure as shootin'; you're the snuff that I go for!" Arthur Smith was a popular country/bluegrass musician who once pitched Tube Rose Snuff, proclaiming in his characteristic Southern twang, "It calms me down and keeps me feeling fine all day long!"

I remember movies (before "Technicolor" was popular) that were in black and white, and it was almost weird to sit through one and not see someone smoke a cigarette. Later, it became popular to hate cigarettes, and for a while, Hollywood made a bunch of movies where you'd be hard pressed to find a single smoker. Of course, things like bloody murders, beatings, cursing, and violence of all kinds have not only become acceptable but have progressively gotten worse as the digital age has made such scenes all the more "real-looking."

As a young tyke, working at The Triangle, I sold plenty tobacco products to anyone who had the money to purchase them. There was no law (nor stigma) against selling cigarettes or other tobacco products to children. Usually when children bought such items, it was understood they were buying them for their Uncle Bert or their daddy. (My maternal grandmother, Myrtle, actually dipped snuff.) And we didn't think anything about it. I remember one of the few vacations we ever took when I was a child, driving up into Tennessee and Kentucky and looking at the fields of tobacco growing in their natural "state." Daddy stopped at the edge of one of the fields and tore off some leaves and we brought them back to The Triangle to hang up in a corner to show to our customers. Most of them had probably never seen anything like that.

I could name all of the snuff, chewing tobacco (plug and pouch), cigarettes, cigars, roll-your-own, and knew the prices of all of them. In the chewing genre, we had "plugs" (a bunch of tobacco leaves mashed flat into a sort of hard block) like Bull of the Woods, Brown's Mule, and Day's Work, to name a few. If you were a dipper, we had Garrett,

Tube Rose, and even one called "Dental" snuff. Beech Nut was a pouch full of "shredded" tobacco. And who could forget "Prince Albert in a can." The popular joke of the day was to call a store and ask, "Do you have Prince Albert in a can?" The answer would usually be, "Yes," prompting the caller to shout, "Well, you better let him out; he's gonna suffocate in there (or some other inane declaration)!"

All that said, it was understood that it was still unacceptable for kids to smoke, dip, or chew (at least before a certain age). Which makes the "smoking tree" phenomenon all the more incredible. It was a huge oak tree ("water oak" I think they called it), providing abundant shade year 'round. It was at the back of the high school, close to the street and sort of in front of the gymnasium. I'm not sure if it was ever "officially" designated as a "smoking area," but it was where the few "fast" kids gathered to enjoy a smoke at recess.

However, there was an incident one afternoon that caused the smoking tree's stock to go down considerably. It was in early spring on a beautiful sunny day, and the crowd had started to gather under the shade.

The puffing was becoming considerable when suddenly the sky darkened (which seemed strange, since it was an amazingly clear day). The darkening was accompanied by a fluttering sound which increased to a dull roar as a throng of blackbirds descended on the tree. True, there had been sightings of birds before in the smoking tree, but nothing of this magnitude. Within seconds, the din became almost deafening as the mighty oak began to groan under the weight of the feathered hoard. Normally, little attention was paid to the smoking tree, and most of the other students simply ignored the tree and the smokers. At first, the delighted smokers were intrigued with their winged guests, but what happened next shocked everyone.

Initially, it started slowly, with a drop or two here, a "spattering" there. Suddenly, the realization hit (no pun intended) that this wasn't the beginning of a rain shower. Oh, it was a shower all right. But it wasn't rain!

For some strange reason, every bird in that tree had decided to take a bathroom break! And within seconds, cigarettes were extinguished en mass, sending those "fast" students running for cover. Er, well, actually it was the opposite. They were running *from* the cover! But it was too late. Who could have known that a bunch of blackbirds could be so full of (expletive deleted)!

I'm not sure how many students went home early that day. I think I can safely say that, for the rest of the day, there were no smokers in our school. I also heard that several students made the decision to stop smoking that day. The last time I looked, that oak tree was still there, a constant reminder of the day Chicken Little's warning came true.

CHAPTER FIVE

First Kiss

Most of us who had a TV during the 70's, at some time or other, watched Richie Cunningham and "The Fonz" invade Al's and talk about—well, whatever teenage boys talked about at the local "hangout." I'm not sure if every small town in America had an "Al's" during that time. I do know that we had one in Luverne, way before the Al's of Happy Days was a twinkle in Hollywood's eye.

Ed Turner owned the one we had in Luverne, and named it, appropriately, "Ed's." I guess signs must have cost a lot of money back then, because Ed didn't have one. Didn't matter anyway. Everybody knew where Ed's was. It was on the outskirts of town, out on the Troy Highway, and you could identify it by the throng of cars driven by slick-haired boys and an occasional non-steady-going cute girl, especially on Friday and Saturday nights.

Ed didn't advertise either. He didn't have to. Understand, this was a small southern town in the 50's, and if somebody sneezed on the north side of town, the whole town knew about it before the sneezer could pull the hanky out to wipe his nose. Besides, there was only one

TV station 50 miles away (and no cable, of course), and there was one 50,000 watt AM radio station (also 50 miles away) with the call letters WBAM, and appropriately called "The Big Bam." Anyone who had a radio within a hundred to a hundred and fifty mile radius of the state capital can recall that infernal cannon going off (the big bam) virtually every time the disc jockey opened his mic. At night, there were a couple of "clear channel" AM stations in far away places like Chicago (WLS; Dick Biondi was the man!), Nashville (WLAC), or Cincinnati (WCKY). There was the local newspaper in Luverne, named The Luverne Journal (of course), but it was reserved for important advertisers, and things like church social announcements, weather reports, and corn and hog prices.

In spite of its seemingly insignificance in the minds of our parents and the overall scheme of things, Ed's was Mecca for every teenager and teenager wannabe in Crenshaw, and sometimes surrounding, counties. It was *the* place you had to be on Friday and Saturday night. It did have a little competition from the "Dairy Dream" and Miller's Skating Rink, but they were basically stopping-off places until you made it to Ed's. It was the Red Carpet, the Grand Prix, the Academy Awards, the Crème de la Crème. In short, it was Nirvana. You could get food there, but everybody knew why everybody else went to Ed's. It was to socialize! Business got so good, Ed had to knock out a wall and make it bigger, because on a good night, you couldn't even get to the juke box, much less see it or hear it. After the expansion, you could actually dance in there and move your feet without stepping on somebody else's!

But, if the truth be known, the real action was often in the parking lot. (There weren't any markings. You just parked wherever you could, and hoped you didn't get blocked in or block somebody else in!). Depending on the designated curfew, most kids went to Ed's after the drive-in movie, for one last ditch effort to smooch with their squeeze!

Some of us, however, who were too young or otherwise socially delayed, used the venue of Ed's to dream and fantasize about scoring that first kiss. And so it was for me one warm spring evening with Peggy.

The night had come and almost gone. My "love affair" with Peggy had started at the beginning of the school year when she and the rest of the "Glenwood crowd" came to Luverne High School from their school about seven or eight miles away. Glenwood School went through the ninth grade, so there was always a "fresh crop" of kids in the tenth grade when they transferred to Luverne, and it invariably included the occasional beauty queen. This year it was Peggy, and she was an immediate hit at our school. Her skin was flawless, her hair like spun silk, eyes that were truly the window to my soul, and lips straight from a Revlon commercial.

Maybe it was because I felt so small around her, but Peggy seemed exceptionally tall and slender, and she wouldn't just walk; she would *glide*. Bobby Darin recorded a song that year called "Dream Lover," and I was convinced he had recorded that song just for me (and Peggy). I was sure, as he was closing out the song, that he clearly sang, "Peggy, don't make me dream alone..." (He was actually saying "Baby...")

But...I digress. The Glenwood crowd (of which Peggy was a star member) had taken over Ed's this particular night, and boy after lucky boy had had the privilege of being near darling, sweet, beautiful, nearly perfect Peggy. Everyone except awkward, socially inept, hopelessly-in-love, nearly retarded little ol' me. My friend, Joe Lester—around 14 years old at the time and a year or so younger than me—had bummed a ride to Ed's from Glenwood with his older sister, Ressie, along with a carload of other Glenwood desirables. Joe and Ressie's father was a fairly well-to-do businessman, and Joe had the confidence and personality of Dale Carnegie. Everybody liked Joe. Being from a rural background, he had learned to drive while still in diapers, but this particular night, Ressie was doing the driving. I had bummed a ride with my older sister, Jean, and as the night drew to a close, I began looking for a ride home. As I wandered the parking lot, the Red Sea parted, and God, in the form of my good buddy, Joe, offered me the ride. I knew that Peggy had come with Joe and Ressie, and until this precise moment, I hadn't felt that I was any closer than 10 miles from Peggy. And now...I was going to be in the same car with her! It was a '55 Chevy, four-dour sedan with bench seats and ample room for at least the five or six original passengers that made it to Ed's that night.

As we approached the car, my mind went into overdrive. *Where would I sit? Where would Peggy be sitting? How close would I be to her?* If my luck held out (it usually didn't), I would be in the back seat with Peggy—along with perhaps four or five others. Maybe it was just my imagination, but I still believe I heard the Hallelujah Chorus as Peggy opened the back door for me.

I have to say at this point that only a few of my closest confidants knew of my deep abiding love for Peggy. Somehow, Peggy must have found out, and I began to sense conspiracy. "Get in, Mike," she purred.

I had used my legs my entire life (at least since reluctantly giving up the practice of being toted by my mother until the ripe old age of 15 months), but at this moment, my muscles spontaneously atrophied. Incredibly, however, there I went, into the back seat already occupied by three Glenwood boys and Peggy wedged among them.

To further describe the sardinely-packed bodies, I was placed supine, legs (the paralyzed ones) and feet crammed into Joe's lap, and the rest of my helpless body struggling for composure. My head ended up literally in the lap of luxury, and my fevered brow being stroked by the hands of an angel. The Hallelujah Chorus repeated itself as I pretended to attempt a getaway from the clutches of my "dream lover."

As the overly-packed Chevy's creaky frame adjusts to the load and eases out of the parking lot, Peggy casts her magic spell. "I think I need to kiss you good night!" *Wait… is it possible to hear velvet?* More pretend struggling. More Hallelujah Chorus. Too late! My eyes blur as Peggy's lips meet mine for one glorious nanosecond. All feeling leaves my body, except for my burning lips, as I suddenly realize the kiss had missed its mark. "Wait!" Peggy giggled. "That one was in the air. I need to give you another one!" And this time, it was the real deal!

I'm told that, if one could arrange the 26 letters of the alphabet into all the possible combinations, the number of combinations would approach infinity. But no such combination of letters or words could have described the bliss of that moment. I could make up stories attempting to describe what happened after that kiss, that night. But they would all be fiction and conjecture, as any memory following that magic moment would have been anticlimactic.

When I finally came to—probably three minutes later—I was exiting the Chevy, and my spirit was floating me up the stairs to my bedroom. I stared at my quivering lips in the mirror for several minutes before collapsing into bed.

Although Peggy and I never developed a serious relationship, she unexpectedly sent me a get well card as I was recovering from cancer 45 years later. We later visited and renewed our friendship, and she later remarried. I don't think Peggy ever realized the impact she—and that first kiss—had on me. She—and it—opened up a whole new world for me. She gave me the confidence to see myself as worthy of sharing an intimate moment with another, as an awkward, unsure teenager, and 45 years later as a frail, recovering cancer survivor. Hers was truly the kiss I built a dream on.

CHAPTER SIX

WRECKING A ROMANCE (AND A CAR AT THE SAME TIME!)

WHAT'S INTERESTING TO me is that, with all the modern technology, varied advanced degrees offered by fancy universities, and even bloated government assistance to "help" people, one thing that has not been improved on that much since I was 13 is the process whereby a young person learns how to drive (a car, that is).

Driver's Ed in my day consisted of a crash course (no pun intended) on a hot summer afternoon in a cow pasture on my uncle's farm. (See Chapter 43 entitled "My First Cattle Drive" in my book, *Mules in The Fast Lane*.) The vehicle of choice (actually, there was no choice to it) was Uncle Vernon's 1940-something International Harvester pickup truck with "three on the column." For you city slickers, that's a manual transmission (as opposed to an automatic) with three gears, the gear shift lever for which was located on the steering column rather than in the floor(board) as in most modern hot rods of today.

After said crash course at age 13, I took on a whole new personality with the unmitigated confidence on a Mario Andretti. I honestly believed I was a better driver than anyone else who had come before me. Imagine the cockiness two years later after my first kiss and I had started dating (usually "double-dating" because I couldn't legally drive until age 16). My parents had gotten my sister and me a used '53 Chevy Bel Air I called "Lizzy," which I courted the girls in. And what a chariot Lizzy was!

I'll never forget the first time I saw Lizzy. My sister, Jean, and I had heard our parents talking about getting a "second car" so Mother wouldn't have to chauffeur us around everywhere. It would also give my sister and me a little more independence and freedom. We were all stoked up waiting for Lizzy's owner to bring her out to The Triangle for a viewing, but for some reason he didn't show up. Tired of waiting for the owner, we were headed out to the "walk-in" (movie theater) for a relaxing night at the "picture show." We were approaching the Patsaliga Bridge when, all of a sudden, Lizzy blazed by us going the other way! I had never heard my sister utter a cuss word before that day, but in her excitement, she obviously forgot the rule about cussing and shouted out, "Oh, there's our d**n car!" Ordinarily, a tongue lashing would have followed such verbalization, but instead, everything came to a screeching halt! We all lunged forward as Daddy slammed on the brakes, and Jean and I screwed our necks around to see if Lizzy had also braked. Lizzy's owner must have seen Daddy slam on the brakes too. Apparently they were as eager to sell Lizzy as we were to buy her, as we both executed precision, choreographed U-turns right there on the spot!

I don't remember too much about the deal itself, but I do remember worrying about what Mother was going to do about that cuss word my sister had just blurted out. I also knew that our lives were going to change forever.

And thus began my "love affair" with Lizzy and the important part she would play in my teen years. I had no idea *how* important until I noticed friends I didn't even know I had coming out of the woodwork, asking for rides to here and there, asking if they could come over (if we would pick them up), and suddenly just wanting to 'hang out." All because my sister and I "had our own car!" I didn't really mind, though, because I had plenty of friends anyway.

A couple of years later, I realized that my good friend, Henry, seemed to have an endless supply of friends and female cousins that he would steadily introduce me to. He was almost a year older and already had his driver's license. Problem was, he didn't have a car or access to one like I did, which meant that he was one of my best resources for chauffeuring me out of the yard until we got out of sight of my parents. Henry's mother would bring him over to my house so we could hang out (drive out), and one day we devised a great little plan. Once we were down the road a-ways (with Henry driving), and without wasting any time stopping the car, we'd just switch positions, one of us sliding over or under the other without missing a beat and barely slowing down. Then *zoom!* Off we'd go, seeking adventure (and girls)!

One day after picking a mess of figs down in the country at Mr. Wilson King's place, we decided to go see Henry's cousin, Emily (who lived in Pensacola, but was visiting more cousins in the thriving metropolis of Glenwood, population 136, a mere seven-plus miles from my house). After I'd gotten over the heartbreak of Peggy never giving me a second glance after that first kiss, I had recently fallen in love with her and her with me, so we kinda "had this thang goin" to the delight of my good friend, Henry, seeing as how he was the one who had "fixed us up" in the first place. (It seems that when I start recalling the "good ol' days, I revert back to the redneck vernacular.)

Anyhoo, it didn't take long to get to Glenwood, and by the time we got there, we were ready for a hearty drink at the artesian well (known as "the flowin' well by the town folk) smack dab in the middle of town. Somebody had put a spigot on it years before I found out about it, and the crystal clear water that came bubbling out of it was the best thirst-quencher around. After drinking our fill of that cool refreshing treat, it was time to go a-courtin' over to Emily's house.

We knew that all we had to do was show Emily our chariot, and she would be rarin' to go! It was time to ride, and within seconds, we were speeding down a dusty dirt road, headed back to the county seat (population 2,000) to show off my new squeeze, Emily, to all my jealous buddies. It was safer (from a not-getting-caught-driving-without-a-license standpoint) to take the back roads, and besides, it was a whole lot more fun. We didn't have to deal with that infernal traffic!

We'd gotten about half way back to civilization (if you could call it that) when suddenly Emily implored, "Hey, let me drive!" Intrigued, I inquired, "Do you know how?" "Well…no," she declared in a tone that also said, "Does that matter?"

"O…K…well, I'll teach you!" Seemed easy enough, I thought, failing to recall my difficulty in the cow pasture training course two years earlier. "Have you ever driven a car before?" I probed. With mounting excitement, Emily snickered seductively, "Nooo…!"

Scene II: I was sure my expert driving would impress Emily out of her mind, not to mention my macho but gentle driver's ed teaching technique. Eager to get closer to Emily's steamy warmness (it was July, I think), I stopped the car and let her take the wheel. Back in those days, none of the cars had bucket seats, so it was not uncommon to have three people in the front seat, although it was against the law to have more than three. So, with Emily's eyes glued on the road and mine glued on her (Henry was riding shotgun), I sidled closer and thus began Emily's first (and last, as it turned out) driving lesson.

Truth be known, Emily was no more interested in learning how to drive than I was in teaching her. She was the same age as me but apparently only felt the need to impress me that she was just as mature as I was. (Yeh, right!) After a mere 10 seconds of lurching and jerking, (which felt like hours), the wind was whipping through the old '53 Chevy—and our hair—like a Southern tornado! There was no stopping us now, as we went literally racing down the road at breakneck speed (probably a bad choice of words in retrospect).

Now, I'm not much of a mathematician, but I do know that if you take three crazy teenagers, add one hot summer day, plus one speeding

'53 Chevy with all four windows down, factor in a sudden drop in elevation (as in flying off a dirt road hill), *and* one unexpected curve in the road, it can only add up to disaster.

No, it didn't total the car, but the results were just as devastating. (Remember a second ago, I said something about flying? Well, here's where it happened.) We could call this Scene III.

Funny how things can happen so fast, yet seem like slow motion. *Me grabbing the steering wheel, attempting to jerk us out of the ditch, Henry screaming as he tried to stomp on the brakes (that's right, from the other side of the car...), and Emily in a trance, completely out of control.* No seat belts, no air bags, no power brakes, but somehow, after cleaning out the ditch on the left side of the road with the Chevy (except for the huge root of that tree coming out of the bank that tried to come through the windshield), we came to a very dusty stop. Although it was a hot day, we were all frozen in place, staring straight ahead, wondering how it all came to this tragic end. After prying Emily's frozen fingers from the steering wheel, I noticed a tiny spot of blood in the middle of her forehead, the miniscule shard imbedded there being the only reminder that there was once a windshield where it came from. Fortunately, it was only a flesh wound, and the only sympathy I could muster was for poor ol' Lizzy. "Oh...my...car..." I croaked. I don't remember much conversation after that, except trying to explain to the nearby farmer with the tractor and rope how we managed to clean out that ditch so neatly.

Somehow Emily got home—I don't remember how—but I do remember the scene (Scene IV?) with me and good ol' Henry, and my mother coming out the front door to survey the damage. It wouldn't be accurate necessarily to say that my mother wore the pants in our family, but it would be safe to say that she was the one who worried the most about the bills. And this was definitely going to be a bill! But incredibly, other than the shattered windshield, the only other damage the old Chevy sustained was a pulverized left fender and a missing hubcap. Well...I didn't count the 8,000 scratches on the left side.

Anyway, after much wailing and gnashing of teeth (and some time passing to get over the shock and humiliation—not to mention the loss of my true love, Emily), it was time for a makeover. And, believe it or not, my mother let me decide what color to paint the poor thing, as well as how to solve the problem of the missing hubcap. I chose drab Army green because it seemed to fit the old clunker's personality, and because I recalled it being one of the two colors I remembered by number (21) from the paint-by-number kit I enjoyed as a much younger child. The other number was 22 (chartreuse green), but I think I remember being overruled on that one.

The hubcaps, however, were a different matter, because, back in the day, it was hard to find just one hubcap to fit three others; you had to buy the whole set. We didn't want to spend the money on four new "standard" hubcaps, and besides, we'd have to wait several weeks to have them ordered from the "Chevrolet Place." "Spinner" hubcaps were popular on hot cars of the day, but again, the cost was prohibitive. I finally settled on some cool spun aluminum "moon" hubcaps, cheap and easily obtainable. I knew I was right in choosing these, because I was the only kid in school who had them. I was further validated in my choice when, in 1972, The Statler Brothers immortalized those snazzy wheel covers in their song about the good ol' days, entitled "Do You Remember These?" It goes something like this: "Moon hubcaps, and loud heel taps, and 'he's a real gone cat.' Ah, do you remember that?"

All I can add to "that" is "How could I forget?!"

CHAPTER SEVEN

THE WRECKING CREW

I'VE OFTEN MADE the statement that my mother was an angel from heaven. To my way of thinking, my sister, Jean, wasn't far behind her and had made it her mission early on to take care of me, come what may. I've already told the story of my first day in school (see Chapter Two in my book, "Mules in the Fast Lane," entitled "School Days") for proof of my sister's goodness.

All that said, there was one incident that involved my mother which made me rethink her perfection. Let me make it clear, however, that it wasn't really her fault, so technically, she still remains perfect in my eyes. Before getting to her incident, though, I need to confess to one of my own. And this one *was* my fault.

To say that a teenager's life is dramatically changed when he or she gets a driver's license would be an understatement. I know, that in my case, it meant freedom! As much as I loved my mother, at times, she worked a little too hard at being a mother, and would be what some would call a "hovering" parent. Not in a negative or meddling, intrusive kind of way, but sort of like

"You-probably-can't-do-this-yourself-so-I'll-just-do-it-for-you" kind of way. Being what she considered a good parent meant, basically, doing *everything* for me. So, as I grew up, I began to feel a need to assert my independence, if you will. My bicycle, for example, gave me the freedom to be on my own, out in the pasture, down the road, or wherever I could take the two-wheeled marvel, away from my protective mother's gentle but sometimes over-protective presence. At age 14, I had a friend named Sammy who got a "motor scooter," the amazing thing about which was that you didn't have to peddle it, especially up hills! Anyway, I had to skip that phase because my mother's protective ways saw this motorized bicycle as a threat to my safety, so I never got one. My first car, however, was a different story. (Yep, the one I named "Lizzy" and the one my true love, Emily, later wrecked.)

My sister, being two years older, got her driver's license before me. Our parents had made a deal with a local guy to buy Lizzy, which they thought would be a perfect "starter" car for my sister and me, as it was old(er), not fancy, it was practical (a stick shift and therefore less expensive overall), and it had an AM radio (a must for any up-and-coming teenager). It turned out that the term "starter" was somewhat ironic, seeing as how it often wouldn't crank and had to be (when available) parked on a hill and pushed off to get the darn thing going!

But, that was the price we paid for a "second car," and we felt fortunate to have it. As I really got deep into the dating scene, however, I got to be pretty good at conning my daddy out of his much newer and nicer, candy apple red, four door hard top, Pontiac Bonneville on date nights (usually Saturday, but sometimes Friday night and Sunday afternoon too). That outstanding vehicle was what we would later call a "chick magnet." For the purpose of this story, I'll just called it "Big Red." It reminded me of the 1955 hit song by Charlie Ryan, "Hot Rod Lincoln." One of the lines went like this: "It's got a 4-barrel carb and dual exhaust, four livin' gears that can really get lost!" But the one I really liked was "Everything went fine up the Grapevine Hill; we was passin' cars like they were standin' still!" I didn't really know too much about cars back then (and still don't), and I wasn't sure Big Red had any of the amenities the Hot Rod Lincoln did, but I knew it definitely had a *passing gear!* I had discovered it by accident when I took it out to show my friends how fast it would go. One of my buddies must have known a little more about cars than I did, and he yelled, "Hit the passin' gear!" I had no idea what he meant, so he elaborated, "Mash the gas real hard!" Once I had discovered that luxury, I also discovered I had lead in my right foot, and speed became almost an addiction. I will say, however, that I did use it sparingly, usually just to impress the girls, or my male buddies. Or when I wanted to show up Bob Preston.

Bob was a quiet but tough farm boy who liked to push his weight around. He played every sport that was available in school, and all of us weaklings thought he must have been born with his Charles Atlas physique. He was a good-looking guy with short, jet black hair, and I would usually tremble at his sight. Unless, that is, I was with my own buddies, and I was driving Big Red.

My friends, Charles and Henry, and I had the displeasure of running into Bob at Miller's Skating Rink one Saturday night. If you didn't have a date (and for some reason, this particular night, we didn't), the drill was always the same. As we've established, the three main attractions in town were Miller's, The Dairy Dream, and Ed's, and we'd spend the entire night driving from one to the other, trying to scare up some excitement. However, we weren't expecting the excitement caused by Bob and a bruiser buddy of his in their ragged pickup truck.

Things were getting dull at the rink, so my two buddies and I decided it was time to high tail it over to Ed's on the other side of town (maybe three miles away). I don't think it was planned, but Bob and his buddy apparently decided to leave about the same time headed for the same destination. As we pulled out of the gravel parking lot, Bob pulled out in front of us. And I may have been imagining it, but it seemed to me that Bob tried to intentionally "scratch off" and spray gravel all over the front of Big Red's beautiful grill! Wellll, now, I couldn't have that, could I? Especially knowing that I had a passing gear just waiting to show off for ol' Bob. He must've sensed my indignation and began alternately pumping his brakes and speeding up, just to aggravate me! By the time we approached the (at that time) one and only red light in town, that passing gear was burning a hole in my foot, as Bob screeched to a halt, almost as if trying to make me hit his rear end!

With engines rumbling and tempers flaring, it seemed to take longer than usual for the light to change. *Green light!* Suddenly, Bob peeled rubber with me in hot pursuit, looking for a chance to show him who was boss! It took only a few seconds, and as we approached the county court house on our right and the street widened, I veered to the left and hit the passing gear! Here again, I don't know if it was intentional, but in the next split second, as Big Red shot half way around the old pickup, headlights illuminating its interior, Bob did the unspeakable. He turned left in front of me! The crash sickened me as Big Red's right fender succumbed to the pickup's running board and curled neatly up over the right front tire. We both ended up on the left side of the street, perched on some city slicker's front lawn. The passing gear had done its job…just not fast enough.

As the smoke cleared, I was reminded of another hit record by the Platters, "Smoke Gets in Your Eyes," leaving me crying like a (16 year old) baby and vowing to never use that passing gear again.

With that horrible experience still ringing in my memory, not to mention the humiliation of the wreck itself, the fact that I disappointed my parents, made me have second thoughts about ever driving again.

The paint was barely dry when my mother asked me to ride with her to Uncle Willie and Aunt Rebie's house one Sunday afternoon, way back in the country. It had rained the day before, but we didn't know how muddy the roads were until we turned off the asphalt and started to slide. Mother was actually a pretty good driver, and had she known the condition of the road, she probably would have taken Lizzy instead of Big Red. But it was too late to turn back. It looked as though we were going to make it without too much difficulty, because overnight, deep ruts had been carved into the road by a good number of other cars and trucks. Anyone who has driven on muddy (red dirt) roads after a rain knows that the key is to stay in the ruts, if possible. Apparently, however, fate had other plans. We were approaching Snuffy Smith's place when, out of nowhere, a local farmer came barreling over the hill, straight toward us! I think I'd have to say that Mother chose the lesser of two evils when she quickly veered left to avoid the head-on and plowed into the ditch, this time curling Big Red's left fender up over the left front tire!

Angel that she was, my mother kept her cool through it all, and eventually was able to maneuver the Bonneville out of the ditch and on to Aunt Rebie's house. I could tell it upset her though, because I saw her discreetly wipe a tear before we drove up into the yard.

I remember thinking that she didn't cry nearly as much as I did when I wrecked Big Red!

CHAPTER EIGHT

HELL'S ANGELS APPROACHING!

I ALWAYS SECRETLY admired the guys who lived in town, because a good many of their families had more than one car and actually lived in brick houses. You see, in my mind, farmers (and anybody else who didn't live in town) didn't live in brick houses. The mighty brick was so revered, that even the lowly outhouse was elevated in stature when it was applied to one of them. Let me explain.

Most people (at least those who lived in New York City) probably didn't realize that, when the popular Commodores (from Tuskegee, Alabama) recorded their hit song "Brick House" in 1977, they were actually referring back to a popular, but totally crude expression about a girl who had a good physique. Don't ask me how such a nasty expression came to apply to a beautiful girl, but it did. It went something like this: "Wow! She's built like a brick (s**t) house!" I never used the expression myself, because I respected my mother too much, and I viewed it as disrespectful to all girls. I guess even the rapidly evolving music industry at the time thought it was too risqué, so they dropped the nasty four letter expletive. Of course, we all see where the music (and movie) business has descended to since then, not only with that word, but most all of the other four letter words - and then some - being common fare.

But, I digress. The fact that we didn't live in a brick house and had only one car hadn't weighed too heavily on my mind until my sister, Jean, came of driving age at 16, two years ahead of me. It made sense to buy Lizzy for Jean and me to drive around in, since my daddy was always on the road selling insurance and my mother was always "keeping store." Daddy put a lot of miles on a car, so he bought a new one every three years at around 100,000 miles. We could always tell when it was "time to trade," because back then, when a car had 100,000 miles on it, the odometer tripped back over to "zero!"

The day we finally got Lizzy, in my mind, our socio-economic status shot up! Now I could compete, or at least measure up to my "city friends," who lived in brick houses (and had two cars). Silly, I know, because our "city" had only about 2,000 people, and we lived only about two miles out of town.

But there was one such "city" guy I really admired for his suave, debonair manner. My friend, Stanley, was one of those "jocks" that everybody liked. All the boys wanted to be his friend, and all the girls wanted to go out on dates with him. In my mind, Stanley was a real "Casanova." My ego was always boosted a bit when he wanted to hang out with me, so naturally, I was thrilled when he started dating my sister. I started dating his sister, Becky, at the same time, which got to be a lot of fun. It was a popular custom to "double date" at the time, and since Jean was older than the rest of us, and before I got my license, she would haul the three of us around, with Stanley up front with her and Becky in the backseat with me. Lizzy was definitely paying for her keep!

Eventually, both of those relationships ended amiably, and Stanley and I remained friends. He had, of course, had his pick of all the other girls in town, and by the time he started dating "Jill" (who lived in Greenville, about 20 miles away), I had already gotten my driver's license and had inherited partial ownership of Lizzy. In any typical small Southern town in the late 1950's and 60's, boys usually had a limited dating pool, and I had often commented that, once you dated the five or six girls in town, you had to go out of town if you wanted to date somebody new!

It was on a Sunday afternoon toward the end of the school year, and Stanley and Jill were on the verge of breaking up (again). So a couple of my buddies and I decided we'd take Stanley over to Greenville and help him "get over" Jill by shopping around for some new girls for all of us. One guess as to who was elected to take their car on our eagerly anticipated hunting expedition. Little ol' me…and Lizzy.

This was OK with me, because I was always glad to show off my driving skills. But, as noted previously, Lizzy was sometimes an embarrassment and would often "die" at the most inopportune times, and we were always keeping an eye out for a convenient hill to park her on just in case she needed a shove to get her started. Lizzy was equipped with only the bare essentials compared to the modern marvels of today. Some of the amenities Lizzy didn't have were air conditioning, power steering, power brakes, power seats, power windows, steel-belted radial tires, cruise control, leather (bucket) seats, air bags, seat belts (I could go on and on…).

But what she did have, by golly, was ample room for four (or more) young testosterone-charged teenage boys and an AM radio that would pick up one 50,000 watt rock and roll station during the day!

Now, at this point, our focus was not so much on Lizzy as it was on our mission. After the approximately 30-minute drive to the happy hunting grounds of Greenville, we were all confident in our ability to flush out game!

Unfortunately, however, what we ended up flushing out was definitely not the game we had in mind. We were probably 15 to 20 minutes into our expedition when suddenly there they were, engines roaring, chrome shining, and long hair flapping in their own breeze—two larger than life, home grown, redneck bikers—and they were headed straight for us! Somehow Lizzy now seemed enormously inadequate, as I'm sure we were all convinced that, even if she could outrun these two hot shots, it would only be a matter of time before they would corner us and rip Lizzy and her occupants apart with their bare hands. Not a pretty sight.

Nevertheless, we pretended to be as tough as they looked and, as the cat and mouse game began, we stealthily locked our respective doors, and prayed for guidance from above.

Although it was still early spring, the weather was already heating up ol' Lizzy's un-air conditioned interior as the chase became even hotter! It seemed that, no sooner did we think we'd lost them, they would appear out of nowhere, as sinister and menacing as ever. *Zoom! Zoom!* With each near-fatal brush with the James Dean wannabes, our anxiety grew. Since I was the "designated driver" of Lizzy, I somehow felt responsible for the safety of my safari-mates, and I began to plan an exit strategy to end this nightmare.

We had slowed down to about 20 miles an hour over the posted speed limit in the neighborhood Stanley had led us to where Jill was supposed to be when the opportunity presented itself. Checking my rear view mirror, I saw the two Hell's Angels approaching! Side by side they rode in perfect unison, looming larger in my rear view. With heart pounding, and as pride overtook reason, my diabolical plan began to materialize. It would be over in a split second. My idea was to teach these hoodlums a lesson by suddenly slamming on Lizzy's brakes as they were in hot pursuit, causing them to panic, screeching their tires as they slid toward her rear end and narrowly averting disaster. This would, of course, cause them to learn a valuable lesson (that of not harassing fun-loving out-of-towners) and to retreat in shame and disgrace, never to bother us again. I would, of course, be a hero for coming up with such a brilliant idea, and my buddies (especially Stanley) would be laughing and slapping me on the back in congratulatory affirmation, and we would go home bragging to the home folks about our successful hunting trip to Greenville.

As you might imagine, it didn't turn out quite that way. In order to understand what actually did happen, I offer the following slow-mo replay of the action: The part about me slamming on brakes went great. But then, as my buddies lurched forward, eyes bugging from surprise (and later disbelief), Hell's Angel Number One (the one on the left) slammed into Lizzy's rear end with the force of a Sherman Tank. *Crash! Crunch! Tumble! Rumble! Clatter! Boom! Uugghh!* The impact caused Number One to hurtle over Lizzy's trunk, past the rear window, up to the top of her roof, then roll sideways, finally coming to rest with a resounding, need I say, sickening, thud adjacent to her left rear wheel.

Number Two had been somewhat luckier. Prior to impact, Number One had been conversing with Number Two, squinting in his direction, while Number Two had his eyes straight ahead on the target (bad choice of words…). Fortunately for Number Two, he was able to barely miss Lizzy's rear end, zooming between her right side and the street curb and screeching to a halt several yards ahead of the fray!

In stunned silence, the four of us (well, three actually) sat motionless, trying to figure out what had just happened. Their first thought being *What the H****, and mine being *Oh, no, I have just killed a guy.* Stanley was the first one to speak (of course) and to take charge of the situation. Something like, "I guess we better get out and see what happened." As we slowly opened our doors and (in slow motion) made our way to Lizzy's left rear wheel well, we all wondered if we should abandon Lizzy and run, or stay and face the music. Then we saw movement! Number One was alive! *Oh, no, that only meant we were dead!* Apparently his left ring finger had taken the brunt of the crash, and was the only thing we saw bleeding. It, and the other nine fingers were encircling the top of his head, apparently checking to see if it was still attached. His rear end was crammed against the tire, with his feet and legs (still intact) resting on the side of the car, pointing straight up to heaven!

Again, Stanley was the first to speak. Surveying Number One for signs of life, he bravely asked "Hoss Man, are you hurt?" Hoping for a positive response, we waited for what seemed like eternity. Finally, with eyes fluttering, Number One growled, "Hoss Man, Hell!"

At that moment, I'm sure we all looked like the Little Rascals awaiting a chase by the Wild Man of Borneo as he came to life! By this time, Number Two had made his way back to the crowd and (still in slow motion…and maybe in a fog) began helping his partner-in-survival up, searching for his motorcycle's battery, which had been knocked off by the crash.

To be totally honest, I don't remember too much after that. As the adrenaline subsided, all I wanted to do was to get out of Greenville alive! The only thing I do remember (and vividly) was driving lickety-split out of town after one or two more circles around Jill's neighborhood and seeing the most beautiful sight I had ever seen: Those two Hell's Angels flying past us (alive and well) and disappearing in my rear view mirror!

CHAPTER NINE

"Let's Make a Deal!"

One would think one would learn a lesson fairly quickly if it caused enough "pain." However, that wasn't the case with me and my "reckless driving." Aside from the normal "learning curve" mishaps and the not unusual occasional fender benders during the teen years, I had always thought that I was your typical driver. Until I looked around and noticed that I was the only one at age 20 who had his driver's license suspended.

I could chalk it up to learning to drive in my uncle's pasture in an old (manual transmission) pickup truck at age 13, or having a sister who started driving two years before I did, or maybe being the last one in my class in high school to get a driver's license. It could have been any number of factors that didn't make any sense. The reality was that, from the start, I detested all traffic laws. I guess I figured I was such an excellent driver that the rules didn't apply to me. My reasoning was, if you're in a hurry, ignore the speed limit. If there's no one coming, run that red light! In short, as long as you don't hurt anybody or don't have a wreck (or get a ticket), what's the big deal, right?

By the time I graduated from college, I had already gotten several tickets for speeding and reckless driving. (That's not as bad as it sounds; if you were speeding faster than a certain speed, the charge of "reckless driving" would be levied, so in my mind, it wasn't really "reckless," just really fast.) I always blamed the large number of tickets I got on the fact that, after getting my first job, I had bought a shiny new 1964 red Chevelle convertible. I was sure "the law" singled me out because I had made it look and sound like a "fast" car, with spinner hubcaps, double scavenger exhaust pipes and lowered back end for extra "thrust." In secret, I had installed a "cut out," which meant a hole cut in the manifold pipe before it went into the muffler, with a short pipe welded on. It was done "in secret" because it was actually against the law due to the excessive noise it made, especially when accelerating. But, in my mind, it was a "chick magnet" and something I had to have on my car. The cut out had a screw-on cap that could be taken off when out in the country (and not within earshot of law enforcement) and screwed back on when danger lurked.

Although I knew there was something called "suspension" of your license, I didn't worry about it that much, because the state was supposed to send you a letter "warning" you that, if you got any more such tickets, your license would be suspended.

I had come home for Christmas break and felt like a big shot around town. My parents were glad to see me, but even though it was a holiday, The Triangle never closed (except when we went to bed), and there was always work to be done. One such job was to deliver groceries to folks out in the country who didn't have cars. I didn't really mind the "work" because it meant I could drive my car and show it off to the "home folks!"

It was early afternoon on Christmas Eve, and the weather had been threatening rain, but the temperature was tolerably cool. I had loaded up an order of groceries for delivery to the Seawright's house about a half mile down a dirt road off the main highway just a little north of the store.

I had made the delivery and was headed back to The Triangle. I was approaching Highway 331 and eased up to the pavement, carefully looking both ways before pulling out onto the main drag. There was a straightaway to my right, and it was calling my name, the Chevelle's engine rumbling with anticipation. However, it was Christmas Eve, and I wanted to spend time with the family, so I decided I'd better go left.

There was a curve probably a hundred yards away, which was nicely banked and ideal for trying out souped-up convertibles. I eased onto the asphalt in first gear, and as soon as all four tires were on pavement, I floored my right foot, jerking the clutch out in one beautiful move. *Waaahhh! Second gear! Third gear!* Approaching the curve, I hit fourth gear as I banked left, feeling the pull down on the bucket seat. What a ride!

Instinctively, I glanced up in my rearview, and my heart sank. *Flashing red lights! Crap! Where did he come from?!* It was too late anyway. I was caught in the act! I was only a quarter mile from The Triangle, so I didn't even brake, just let off the gas and coasted into the yard, with the Highway Patrol in hot pursuit!

I dutifully reached for my wallet as Mayberry's finest ordered me out of the car. There was no need to protest, as I knew Barney had me dead to rights. I thought about how this wasn't going to be my best Christmas. But the worst was yet to come.

Three months later, the "notice" arrived from the Department of Public Safety. I was ordered to turn in my driver's license immediately! No warning. No letter. I had four years of (licensed) driving under my belt, and I was back to square one. And the bad news is that I had quit my job a month earlier. With The Triangle as my "home base," I had been looking diligently for a job, which was now going to be much more difficult. I was stuck. But I had a plan.

After a couple of months bumming rides, applying for jobs posted in the "want ads," and feeling generally helpless, I asked Daddy if he'd take me to the Department of Public Safety in Montgomery to plead my case and beg for my license back. He agreed. My license suspension was for 90 days, and I had less than a month left, but I was literally going stir crazy, so I figured I didn't have anything to lose by trying.

The Department of Public Safety was adjacent to the state capitol building downtown, and to say I was a little nervous as we walked into the office would have been a huge understatement. I had made the appointment ahead of time, so we were ushered into a small office and got right down to business.

"What can I do for you, Mr. Moody?" the gentleman asked.

"Well, I wanted to talk to you about getting my driver's license back," I responded. I then explained to him that I had graduated from college and was looking for a job and further pointed out how difficult this was without a driver's license. I let him know that I realized how reckless I had been (a great choice of words, considering some of the charges) and that I felt I had learned my lesson.

The man listened carefully to my plea and without verbally responding slowly opened a folder he had brought in. I recognized my license as he slowly laid it on the desk in front of him and slid it toward me with his index finger.

"Here's your license, Mr. Moody," he said, staring intently at me.

This is going to be easier than I thought, I said to myself as I leaned forward.

"You can have it back," he said, almost teasingly. "But…let me tell you this. You can also leave it here, and you'll get it back in another month." Obviously, he had done his homework on me. He knew I wasn't due to get the license back for another month, and I could tell he was ready to deal.

"You can take your license with you right now," he continued, "but if you do take it, in exchange, I'm going to put you on probation for two years." His tone became even more somber. "And if you so much as sneeze at a red light in those two years, I will take your license back, and I can't tell you if you will ever see it again."

Something told me he wasn't kidding. The silence was deafening, and I could feel the sweat trickling down my forehead.

"What'll it be, Mr. Moody; it's your decision. Do you want your license now or not?"

The choice was excruciating, but I knew I had come too far to back out. I felt like I was on "Let's Make a Deal" and Monty Hall was waiting for my answer. "I'll take the license!" I blurted.

And thus ended my reckless driving career. For the next two years, I drove like a saint. If the speed limit was 35, I went down to 30. If I approached a green light, I slowed down as soon as I saw it, not waiting for it to turn yellow. I could feel the tension behind me at each intersection with a stop sign. No more "rolling stops" for me. Horns would blow, tires would screech, and people would curse. But my resolve never wavered. *I was not going to get another ticket and risk losing my license again!*

I'm not saying I became the perfect driver. I am saying I've had a driver's license in my wallet ever since that day I appeared on "Let's Make a Deal." Lesson learned!

CHAPTER TEN

A Serious Breach of Etiquette

I'M SURE THERE must be other people who have, at one time or another, had that nagging feeling of doubt and uncertainty when they started something new…like a job or something that would prove they weren't doubtful or uncertain. They say that two of man's greatest fears are fear of failure and fear of the unknown.

Well, I gotta tell you, I've always had a heaping helping of both. I also have to say, however, that one of my strong points has always been an uncanny ability to "fake it 'til I make it." But the caveat on that is, if you get caught faking it, revealing that you really don't have any idea what you're doing, well, that just does not turn out well.

One of my least fond memories of one of my most embarrassing experiences was shortly after I got a life-changing job at the University of Alabama working in Broadcast Services. Since I had first seen a "television set," my dream had been to work in that exciting profession in some form or fashion, and needless to say, I was very apprehensive about doing a good job and "proving myself."

Apparently it was the custom for Dr. Jensen, the head of the Department of Broadcast Services to have a "cocktail party" in September (the official beginning of the school year) to welcome new employees and have them meet and greet other staff members. Dr. Jensen (I could never remember his first name) had been department head long enough to establish his reputation as a very capable leader, but also a crude and profane man who couldn't utter a complete sentence without a half dozen cuss words in the mix. His boss was the dean of the department, a crotchety old man who was meaner than Jensen. Everybody just referred to him as "Dean Morton." I don't think anybody knew his first name either. My direct supervisor was a man named Frank Blodgett, a nice humble man who knew how to treat people and give them criticism without demoralizing them. Blodgett answered to Graydon Ausmus, a snappy-dressing, dapper 50-ish, average (in appearance) kind of guy who was an expert at bridging the gap between "upper management" and us peons at the bottom.

Shortly after accepting the job at Broadcast Services, (my future wife) Andrea and I had begun dating. So, it seemed natural that I would ask her to accompany me to the party. *This is where my acting abilities will come in really handy,* I thought.

We intentionally arrived at the gala a little late, hoping that others we had met previously would already be there. I was somewhat nervous but was counting on my acting abilities to get me through the night without sticking my foot in my mouth in the presence of all the dignitaries who would be there. Being a life-long committed teetotaler because of my father's alcoholism, I knew I wouldn't even be able to sip on a drink to calm my nerves. And Andrea had her own problems with social anxiety, so no support there.

We'd been mixing and mingling for probably 30 minutes or so, and doing quite well actually, when a familiar face appeared at the door. Graydon Ausmus entered the room in typical natty fashion, followed about five steps behind by an unsteady, doddering, much older-looking lady who I assumed was his mother.

"Hey, Mr. Ausmus," began my self-assured greeting, and turning toward my date, "I'd like you to meet Andrea." I had taken charge and felt certain that it was going to be a great evening, with me ultimately looking like the super newcomer I was trying to portray. By this time, the old lady had made her way to Mr. Ausmus's side.

Turning to her, and with the confidence of a Dale Carnegie, my greeting seemed appropriate. "And this must be your mother," I confidently announced.

Suddenly, as in a movie, a hush fell over the congregation. And just as suddenly, I was naked, as Mr. Ausmus icily replied, "…No…this is my wife…"

My life was over. That moment was undoubtedly the most cringeworthy of my life. Two weeks following that incredibly awkward incident are totally erased from my memory. I was so mortified that I have absolutely no memory of anything happening after that.

I guess the good news is that I didn't lose my job.

CHAPTER ELEVEN

You're In The Army Now

No one would dispute that the 1960's were a turbulent time, especially if one had worked on a college or university campus. A lot of changes were taking place, some for the better, some for the worse. For me personally, the changes were horrendous, and their effects continued to impact me for years to come. I was learning exponentially that things were not the way I thought they would be when I "grew up." To start with, I thought, you know, after the education part (high school and/or college), I'd get started with my life as a responsible adult, maybe play a little, maybe work a lot, maybe get married, maybe have children. Well...some of that happened, but not the way I had envisioned.

I had the misfortune of being born during the latter half of World War II in January 1944, which meant that, a short 20 years later, I would be facing the draft and a possible tour of duty in Vietnam. Too young to be concerned about the Korean War, I hadn't really thought about life as a soldier until I graduated from high school in 1961. I was in a hurry to get started working, so I rushed through college, finishing my B.S. (not what you're thinking...) two years and ten months later. The Vietnam War (which was never a "declared" war by the U.S.) unofficially started as the Second Indochina War in 1954 and officially ended for the U.S. on April 30, 1975 and had the distinction of being one of the most unpopular "wars" in U.S. history.

The draft continued officially until January 27, 1973. Anyone of "draftable" age who had graduated from high school in 1961 was immediately classified "1-A," meaning "available for military service" and, of course, in immediate danger of being sent to Vietnam...*unless* that person was in college. Many of my friends were considering marriage at this time. But not me. As the Vietnam War dragged on, the rules changed, and by 1964 (when I graduated from college), college graduates were being snapped up...*unless* those graduates were married. The rest of my friends who weren't already married were looking for wives. But not me. It seemed that, at the tender age of 20, I was just getting started in life! Soon, however, because of Vietnam, the draft rule regarding marriage changed to...anyone who was married had to have children in order to escape the draft. My choices then became (1) get married and immediately start having children or (2) hope I would fail the pre-induction physical.

Now during all this time, I still wasn't too worried. My college major was in economics with a double minor in business administration and art, which, in reality, was about as worthless as a degree in philosophy without teaching credentials. But I still thought, because I had a college degree, surely I could get a job *somewhere*. What I didn't know was that, to fill the ranks of soldiers needed to fight (I'm not sure what...) in Southeast Asia, Uncle Sam was accepting virtually anybody who had a heartbeat and who didn't have rich, influential parents. (That part certainly ruled me out!) Back during World War I and World War II, it was a known fact that men (women weren't drafted, and very few, compared to men, volunteered) who had the following three conditions would flunk their physical: flat feet, hearing problems (more specifically, faulty eardrums), and bad eyes (more specifically, the need to wear glasses, aka "corrective lenses"). My father had worn glasses since the age of two due to amblyopia (lazy eye) and was significantly far-sighted, so he never had to serve during World War II or the Korean conflict. Well, I figured I would have no problems flunking said physical exam, because, although my eyes were fine, I had been totally deaf in my left ear since the age of 10. My cousin, Jamie, had failed his physical with a pinhole in his eardrum. And besides, I was so flat-footed as a child, I often entertained my young friends by showing them how my feet would suck the floor (we had "linoleum rugs" which were perfect for this marvelously entertaining activity) when I walked around bare-footed. (You can't make this stuff up.)

Although I was (and still am) a patriotic American, I had other fish to fry during this time, and I just couldn't picture myself as a soldier. With all of the "problems" I had, I honestly figured I was a shoo-OUT (as opposed to a shoo-IN) for Army life and a shoo-IN for serving my country in some other patriotic (civilian) way.

However, as I was to find out on the day of my pre-induction physical, the rules had changed, most likely, thanks to the Vietnam War. Apparently, flat feet no longer kept soldiers from walking or running, so I raced past that part with flying colors (no pun intended). And, oh yes, I found out that, so long as your eardrum was intact (no holes or tears in it), you apparently didn't have to hear at all. I also passed that test with flying colors, because although the cochlea in my left ear had been ravaged with measles at age 10 and left virtually useless in transmitting sound to my brain, my eardrums were left in perfect condition! Well, perfect enough for me to hear the doctor yell, "Next!" I flashed back, remembering how excited I was when my cousin, Jamie, had his physical and had come back bragging about how he had "beat the draft" by having a pin-point sized hole in his eardrum. He didn't even know about it until then, as he had never had a problem with his hearing (although, all through school his teachers complained about it). So…I managed to pass the pre-induction physical anyway, apparently because I had a heartbeat. This essentially meant that it would just be a matter of time before I was called for active duty!

The Alabama Army National Guard had been activated to guard the marchers during the Selma to Montgomery March, so I bit my nails until the march ended, and quickly (and "voluntarily") joined the Guard, shooting cannons (aka howitzers), if needed, and quelling campus and race riots.

All this time, I'm thinking *Oh, good, now I've settled this military service thing once and for all, and now I can get on with my life.* I was happy to be re-classified as "1-D," meaning "member of a Reserve component or student taking military training." Actually, I found out it wasn't going to be quite that easy. I did get on with my life by finding out that no one would hire me for that dream job as a manager of Sears (or any other job, for that matter). Although I no longer had the 1-A classification (meaning I could be shipped out overnight to basic training and subsequently to some war torn country protecting our freedoms), I had another unforeseen problem. It went something like this when I applied for a job:

Me: *Harrumph, hello, sir, I'm here to apply for this job.*

Prospective employer (excited to see a young, eager, handsome, intelligent, available college graduate in his office during war time): *Wonderful...what is your draft classification?* (hoping it wasn't 1-A).

Me (proudly): *Oh, I'm 1-D!* (figuring that will end the conversation I had had many times before in previous prospective employers' offices)

Prospective employer (suspiciously, but still somewhat excited): *Oh...? And when did you go to basic training?*

Me (dejectedly stammering, knowing the interview was probably about over): *Well, I haven't been yet...*

Prospective employer (brusquely interrupting before I could finish my sentence): *Call us when you get back!* (sounding agitated)

Me: (leaving, whining, with my tail between my legs)

Thus began two years of dead-end, senseless jobs just to pay the basic bills, and filling my resume with clutter that made it seem to future prospective employers that I was a drifting vagabond high school dropout with no purpose in life and certainly not worthy of employment.

In fact, I "celebrated" my two-year anniversary as a proud soldier in the Army National Guard completing Advanced Individual Training (AIT) at Ft. Sill, Oklahoma in August of 1967.

Ironically, and by some miracle, however, I had managed to snap up the job at the University of Alabama as a producer-director in the Department of Broadcast Services when the previous holder of the job had gotten drafted! So desperate for workers, they gambled on a minimally experienced, still wet-behind-the-ears faker (how I saw myself at the time), even promising me the job when I returned from basic training! I had been working there part-time while working on my Master's degree, so that fact gave me somewhat of an edge.

But now here's where the fun begins. First, I had to complete basic training. Let's just put it this way: If I could have been "discovered" first, there would have been no Sad Sack, Beetle Bailey, or Gomer Pyle. My military experiences would have made them look like General Patton.

My wife, Andrea, and I had been married about two or three months when, off to Ft. Campbell, Kentucky I went with a couple of friends from my home town (who had also joined the National Guard). The funny thing is, when we got to Ft. Campbell, we had to endure another physical exam (I guess to make sure we had made the flight OK and that we still all had heartbeats). This one was much more humiliating and included the brutal shaving of heads (I guess to check for, and get rid of cooties, aka a microscopic mite, the Sarcoptes scabiei var moninid, the dreaded "scabies"). Well, guess what? I passed the scabies part, but I flunked the heartbeat one! After being examined by a couple of other "doctors," I was immediately shipped out to the base hospital for a battery of tests, taking about three days to determine how bad my heart murmur was. Well, this was all news to me, because I had never had a problem with my heart before. A mixed blessing, I thought. I didn't want to have heart problems, but if it meant going home (even if they'd made a mistake in diagnosis), that was OK with me.

So at this point, I'm making plans to be joyously reunited with my family and getting back to work as a civilian. A couple of minutes later, it hit me. No hair! Mortification! How could I go back home without hair? Funny how your priorities can change within seconds.

After three days in the hospital, obsessively researching in my head where I might find a wig (the song, "You're So Vain" began running through my head), a burly drill sergeant interrupts my daydream. "Moody, get your gear! Let's go!" "Uh…am I goin' home," I sheepishly asked. "No, boy, yer in basic trainin'! Move it!"

Thus abruptly ended my short-lived fantasy about family reunification (and needless worry about finding a wig). And because my two buddies from back home had a three-day head start while I was in the hospital, I didn't see them until I got home. So much for the "Buddy System." Actually, I did run into one of them one day at the PX (Post Exchange, aka convenience store for soldiers) after we had both moved on to Ft. Sill. Oddly, we were both off duty at the same time, and in a spur of the moment discussion about fun things to do during off duty hours, we decided to rent some motorcycles and ride off into the desert sunset. I don't know how we pulled it off, but all went well until Horace's bike went belly up (meaning it broke down, not got wrecked…), and us in the middle of the desert with no cell phone! So, off I speed, back to the motorcycle place, leaving poor Horace on guard duty to keep his bike from being stolen and us having to pay for it.

Back at civilization (could have been militarization; I'm not sure…), Bubba tosses a few dirty wrenches and some rags into his saddlebag, and off we go! Back to the point of breakdown (double entendre there…). By this point in my life, I had logged a total of about 18 hours driving time over a period of two years on a Suzuki 50 at a top speed of, maybe, 55 miles an hour, and never on the back seat of a Harley without a helmet. So, it would be an understatement to say that, peering squinty-eyed over Bubba's shoulder, I was a little surprised to see (within about 15 seconds) the little hand on the speedometer bumping *90-plus miles per hour!* That's the last time I rode on the back of a Harley with anybody…and the last time I saw the Oklahoma desert until I flew over it (this time in an airplane) headed home!

The Rest of the Story...

After coming to the realization that I could possibly die during military service without it being related to combat, I figured it might be a good idea to detail an account of the rest of my Sad Sack Story regarding basic training, starting at the beginning, after my release from the hospital.

I'm not sure if raw recruits are always brought in on the weekend, but my first recollection that wasn't completely negative was after we had all unpacked our "gear" at the barracks and gathered outside for a friendly chat with the resident drill sergeants. I remember thinking, *Wow, these guys are really nice. This is not going to be bad at all!* They gently explained some of the rules, like for smokers how to "field strip" a cigarette so as to not "litter" the base with butts. Since I was (and am still not) a smoker, this didn't really apply to me, but I listened politely, still not believing how easy this was going to be. Next came the incredible disclosure that we would be allotted a full eight hours of sleep, as lights in the barracks would be turned off at 10:00 P.M. and on at 6:00 A.M.! Notice the sneaky term "allotted," not "allowed." The part about lights off and on, that part was true. What they didn't tell us was that there is *no way* anyone would ever complete all the stuff we had to do in the remaining 16 hours. This also didn't include guard duty (divided into "regular" and "fire") at two hours a pop in the middle of the night. It didn't take long to realize that the only time we could devote to "getting our stuff done" (cleaning our "area," polishing our boots, writing letters, serving on KP or "kitchen patrol," etc., etc., etc.) was when lights were out. And, by the way, you couldn't get caught doing any of this in the middle of the night by those "nice" drill sergeants, and you couldn't disturb others! So much for eight hours sleep.

One of the potential problems I had was discovered shortly after arriving at Ft. Campbell. We were told, in an ominously serious announcement, that having any kind of pornography on our person was strictly taboo. This would not have been a problem for me, except that, as newly-weds, my wife and I had decided it would be nice if I carried a picture of her with me at all times during basic training. So, the night before I shipped out, we borrowed my daddy's Polaroid camera. Need I say more?

After several days of "reminders" from the drill sergeants and the ringing in my (one and only good) ear of the original announcement about pornography, about the fifth night in, I sat bolt upright with my heart pounding and sweat wringing, with visions of movies past showing emaciated prisoners of war hanging from cinder block walls behind foreboding bars, I jumped up, guilt ridden and knowing that I was in the proverbial no-win situation. I knew what I had to do. I tore my wife's picture into tiny squares and flushed her down the latrine toilet!

Suddenly, all the guilt was gone, only to be replaced with consuming fear of what I would say when my wife popped the loaded question. I dreaded the phone call home, which I played over and over in my head probably a thousand times. I had hoped she would understand. But she was not going to let me get off that easy! It went exactly as I had suspected but hoped it wouldn't. In her sexiest, sweetest, most innocent, most playful voice, she loaded the gun. "Well, honey, have you looked at my picture?" Long pause. I feel sweat coming from every pore. My mouth opens, but my throat tightens. "Uh…well (should I lie or tell the truth…?), uh…no…I… She cuts me off, suspicion evident in her voice. "What! What do you mean? You haven't looked at my picture? Why not? Is there something wrong?" (Implied: Don't you love me? Oh, no, I knew it! You've found someone else? How could you! You cad!")

I had to interrupt her questions as I envisioned escaping one firing squad (the drill sergeants') only to be murdered by my own betrayal of my wife. I blurted, "I flushed it down the toilet!" Now believe me, if I had any illusions of this making the explanation any more palatable, I was sadly wrong. Let's just say, I no longer had to hold the phone up to my ear. The entire barracks heard the tirade. "What??!! You (sputtering…), you (more sputtering), wha…??!! (now breathless, not in a good way). This continued until Andrea finally found her voice and paused long enough for me to attempt a defense. Needless to say, it didn't work. By the time I hung up, I was sure that I would be served divorce papers before I got home.

Fortunately, I didn't, but I don't think Andrea ever got over it. And I sure do miss that picture…

It Can't Get Any Worse… Yeh, right!

As traumatic as the "pornography" incident was, I had other issues of a much different nature during my career as the Gomer Pyle of Ft. Campbell. Having never been a star athlete, I didn't relish the thought of months of forced "P.E." and the fear of being "recycled" if I didn't make it through. There were certain physical things we had to do that didn't really make sense until later on. For example, we had what they called a "horizontal ladder" at the entrance to the mess hall (cafeteria) which we were required to "swing" through with our hands before going in to eat. Usually, by the time we made it to noon, we didn't mind anything as long as we got some food. One day, though, I found out that things are not always as they seem. We were running, trudging, and walking back from bivouac (sort of a temporary camping, but without tents), and as we got close to the mess hall, the smell of (what I thought was) country fried steak filled the air. My steps became nimbler and brisker the closer I got, imagining how tasty that down-home meal was going to be! Making it through the horizontal ladder in record time, I was beside myself with anticipation. I was hoping I would get a big piece, 'cause this country boy was hungry!

The first bite caused me to gag, as I realized I had just bitten into my least favorite food of all time (with the exception of chitlins). *Liver!* The only consolation was that my appetite completely dissipated in seconds. From that day on, I was very careful when I smelled country fried steak in the mess hall. (We actually never had country fried steak.)

Even though I wasn't particularly happy to be in basic training, at some level, I was kinda glad I had been forced to do it. The way I figured it, most of my male friends from high school and college had "escaped" the obligation, and struggling secretly with low self-esteem myself, I reasoned, this is something I can say I was able to do that they didn't do. Maybe this would bring me up to par with the "jocks" I knew in civilian life, I thought.

Once I got settled into "Army life," however, I realized I had to compete with "jocks" in military life as well. It reminded me of the old commercial for Avis (the car rental company that wasn't quite as big as Hertz), which used to say, "When you're only No. 2, you try harder. Or else."

So that's what I did. I decided I was going to be the perfect soldier, even though I didn't want to be one at all. I just needed to get the job done. Well, that attitude got shot down the first "official" week of basic training. This particular morning, I'd been up and in the latrine (Army name for "bathroom") before anyone else, thinking I'd have a little quiet time before having to go out and practice war games. The fact was, I had probably been up all night on guard duty, which was a blessing, since I wasn't a morning person anyway. The next instant, I'm not only surrounded by confused, marauding recruits, it seemed that, almost as quickly as they had come, they were gone. And there I was with half my face shaved, when the command came loud and clear. "Fall in!" The expletive stuck in my throat as I surveyed the empty latrine and quickly gathered my belongings to hide away in my foot locker. Racing out the door, picking my brain, testing myself on the list of things I was supposed to do before formation (Army name for soldiers gathering in neat rows and standing at attention), I hoped I wouldn't have to do pushups for having a half-shaved face. Turns out, that was the least of my problems as a hush fell over the motley crowd and I snapped to attention. "Right Hace!"

We all learned early on that drill sergeants have a language all their own. Turning to the right, heels clicking, we eagerly waited for the next command. (Lesson on marching inserted here…) After snapping to attention (which actually means *paying* attention), soldiers are told to wait and to *not anticipate the command.* There are actually two commands within a command: the "preparatory command," followed by the "command of execution." The second one is the one you don't want to anticipate, because the sergeant (or whoever is leading the troops) can actually change his mind in mid command. (End of lesson...) Invariably, a few eager beavers would do exactly that right after the preparatory command "Forward!" and stumble forward (anticipating the command of execution "Harch!") and end up doing at least 20 pushups.

Anyway, back to the formation. Fortunately, no one anticipated the command. This was a good thing, because it never came. Instead, a thick hush fell over the group I was in, as sergeants circled the troops searching for violators of the smallest detail. Each poor soul prayed it wouldn't be him, but I wasn't sure it wouldn't be me (with half a beard).

As the silence slowly became deafening and nerves became frayed, I suddenly felt my head spin 180 degrees as Sarge slapped my helmet, almost knocking it off my head! I didn't have to wait long for an explanation, as he bellowed, "Git that helmet on straight, Trooper! And give me 20 (pushups)!" At that moment, it dawned on me. In my haste to get to formation on time, I had put my helmet on backwards! I would have been the laughing stock, except that no one is allowed to laugh at another recruit; otherwise, they'd end up "doing 20" along with the rest of us!

It wasn't too long after that humiliating snafu that another incident happened that was even worse. The military is replete with "rules and regulations," and I'm not just referring to the UCMJ (Uniform Code of Military Justice). I'm talking about those inane little things that separate boys from men...like not calling your weapon a "gun." That alone is worth about a full day of pushups. Consider then, what the punishment would be if you dropped the darn thing! Well, that is exactly what happened on this particular morning...again during formation. It had been a fairly rough night of restlessness, guard duty, etc., etc. I probably had gotten 15 minutes sleep, if any at all, the night before.

Yet, here we were, bright-eyed (not really) and bushy-tailed (probably), standing at attention, waiting for the command that would take us far away. (By the way, this was the day I learned something phenomenal. Did you know it is possible for a human being to go to sleep standing up? Yep! And I proved it! What I also learned that day is that, if you do fall asleep standing up, you don't always know what else you are doing.) I really thought I knew what was going on at the time. In fact, in my foggy mind, I was otherwise so alert, I actually heard someone's rifle hit the ground! *Impossible, I thought. Who would do something so stupid? Boy, is he gonna be in trouble!*

Well, I was right on that last count. I don't remember how many pushups I did, nor what other punishment I endured, nor when it ended. All I know is that I never dropped my gun, ever again!

Speaking of guns, the firing range was an important part of any basic training course. This was, of course, after several classes (and tests) on disassembling and reassembling the M-16 rifle as fast as possible, preferably blindfolded just in case it's dark somewhere or sometime and you can't actually see it. There were also hands-on courses on how to hold the precious instrument which might save your life, how to present it (the command, of course, being "Present Harms!"), and last but not least, how to shoot it. There was an interesting "attachment" to the rifle that I found quite unpleasant. It was called the bayonet. I remember as a child watching war movies, wondering how they made that "dagger" stick on the end of that gun. I learned how it was done during the class on how to "fix" (attach) the bayonet to the rifle and how to use it. We attached real bayonets only for show, but not for practicing. We used what was called a pugil stick instead. It looked like a huge Q-Tip, and the idea was to "stick" your enemy during practice, without injuring him. More colorful language accompanied the lessons. Commands like "Fhix Bhayonets!" and "Vertical Butt Stroke Sehrieees…Mhoove!" were drilled into our heads.

One memorable day, we were scheduled to make a trip (marching, of course) to the firing range for some old-fashioned shootin'. But first, I have to preface this story with a bit of information about one of the sergeants at the firing range. For identification purposes, I'll call him Sgt. Flack. (I remember only one of the sergeants from my basic training career specifically by name, a tough no-nonsense Polish guy named Jakubiak, who could do 50 *one-armed* pushups without breaking a sweat!) Anyway, I found out that the firing range guy was from Alabama, which I thought might give me a little break if he knew. So, I let it be known (or maybe he already knew), realizing almost immediately that this was a mistake. I don't think it was because Sgt. Flack was a black guy; I just think it was because he didn't want to be accused of showing partiality, but this guy tormented me from the minute he laid eyes on me, even pointing out "the guy from Alabama" every chance he got.

One particular day, I had forgotten to spit out my chewing gum (remember the "rules" mentioned earlier?). A few hundred of us were lined up, belly down, ready to shoot some evil targets (actually bullseyes about 18 inches in diameter) after the commands on the loud speaker. *Ready on the right?...Ready on the left?...Firing line is ready!... Commence Hiring!* The drill included firing at the target, then jumping up, racing down to "mark the target," then racing back to shoot again. The process was repeated until the target, basically, was pulverized.

I must have been the only one casually chewing gum when Sgt. Flack spied the infraction right after the first volley of shots was fired. He sneakily waited until I had run about halfway back (obviously so he could point me out to everybody), then shouted over the loud speaker, "Hey, y'all, look at that boy from Alabama! He's got sump'm in his mouth. Why, I think he's got some CHEWIN' GUM! And I bet he didn't even bring any for anybody else, did you, Trooper? (his favorite name for me) Well, Trooper, why don't you just take that chewin' gum out and stick it on yo' nose, so EVERYBODY can see it!"

It wasn't until the hour was over that I was allowed to remove the sticky mess from my nose. I don't think I chewed any more gum the rest of my time in basic training.

Another incident at the firing range had to do with lack of sleep and the rule about not lying down during the day, even during breaks. You were allowed to sit and actually lean back, but no further than propping on your elbows. That was the rule, and they were sticking to it! I knew about the rule, but I noticed some of my buddies taking a break, even lounging around, even almost lying down, but with their heads resting on their "steel pots." Helmets actually consisted of two parts. The helmet liner could be worn separately, but could also be inserted inside the "steel pot" for extra protection from flying bullets, debris or shrapnel. The steel pot also doubled as a wash bowl, cooking utensil, or whatever. It also could serve as a pillow to rest one's head, as I observed on the firing range on this particular day.

Sometimes during exercises at the firing range, I was excused from throwing the hand grenade (I'll explain later why I was throwing it in the first place), and this was one of those days. I apparently hadn't gotten much sleep the night before, and taking a lead from my comrades, decided to grab a quick snooze.

Sleep quickly overtook me, and seconds later, I was jolted awake by a swift kick to the bottom of my foot. "Get up, soldier!" *Thank God, it wasn't Sgt Flack*, I thought, else I'd be in real trouble!

My mind was still trying to comprehend where I was when Sarge (I don't remember this one by name) began barking orders. "You see that old truck down there in the woods?" The four or five of us responded in unison, "Yes, Drill Sergeant!" (We had all found out the hard way, the first day in basic training that even Southern boys address only officers as "Sir.") "Well," Sarge continued, "I think I saw a fly on the fender of that truck. Now git down there and see if it's still there! Move it!!" And off we ran, fully awake by this time. It must have been a hundred yards to that truck. I remember thinking, *Gee, those push ups really weren't that bad.* But that's OK, we reasoned, we'll just tell Sarge there's no fly there, and we will have learned our lesson about sleeping on the job.

Not so fast, thought Sarge. That would be much too easy. I don't remember how many trips we made to that truck, but after a half dozen times or so, we knew we'd been tricked. There was never a fly on that stupid truck! Sarge just wanted to see how long it would take for us to collapse. I used my steel pot many times after that, but never as a pillow, especially while at the firing range.

We had been told early on that there would be certain requirements we would have to meet, even "P.T." (physical training) tests we would have to pass. Otherwise, we would have to do it all over again. In other words, we would have to be "recycled." Even the "athletes" dreaded the thought, as most of my peers were also National Guardsmen and wanted only to get back to their families as soon as possible. The "acid test" was the final P.T. Test, which consisted of five "events." These were the same rigorous exercises we had been doing since Day One. They were, in no particular order, the low crawl; the run, dodge, and jump; the horizontal ladder; the mile run, and for me, the most dreaded, grenade throw.

I had had an issue with my right shoulder in elementary school. I think it was an injury of some sort that didn't heal correctly and which hadn't really caused much of a problem until now. Never having had to use my arm for anything very strenuous and never having played baseball requiring "throwing," I had no clue that I would have a problem lobbing the grenade. It soon became apparent to my drill sergeants that I just couldn't throw the darned thing. Their remedy, of course, was to *practice* (as in "practice makes perfect"). So, during my entire stint, while all the other soldiers would be taking the mandatory 10-minute break on the hour, I would be doggedly throwing the hand grenade. This, of course, only exacerbated the injury. Neither they, nor I, had any way of knowing that they were only making it worse. But, I was determined to persevere, thinking that anything would be better than being recycled. No way was that going to happen! So, I kept throwing break after break, day after day.

Finally, the day of reckoning came in the form of the P.T. Test, and we were allowed to choose in which order we wanted to participate in the events. I chose the grenade throw first and the mile run last. Each event was worth 100 points, and a total of 300 was required to complete the course (and to avoid recycling). I knew that, no matter how well I did on the other events, I would be starting out knowing that the highest possible score I could expect would be 400. This meant I had to score extremely well (I knew it wouldn't be 100) on three of the events, then figure how many minutes it would take me to score at least 300 total. Points on the mile run were calculated on the number of minutes/seconds above a minimum. In effect, it came down to how much time would be required of me to complete the mile run in order to avoid recycling. The pressure was on. I don't remember how I came up with the figure without a calculator. I just knew that I had to complete the mile run in *at least* eight minutes. My heart pounded as I prepared for the mile run. I kept repeating, *eight minutes or eight weeks, eight minutes or eight weeks, eight minutes or...*

With no watch or timer to measure my progress, at the word *Go!* I ran faster than I ever had in my life, and each time my foot pounded the ground, the words pounded in my brain, *eight minutes or eight weeks...eight minutes or eight weeks...*

Finishing the mile, I stood in line to get the verdict from the DS. "Moody! Seven minutes, forty seconds!" *Jubilation! Disbelief! Ecstacy! Joy beyond measure!* I couldn't describe it; I didn't know whether to faint, shout, or kiss Sarge! After running that mile, the prospect to moving on to Ft. Sill for AIT seemed like a piece of cake!

Finding Humor in the Army...

As much as I disliked military life for myself, I had learned to appreciate and respect the job our wonderful military does for America. I had several family members who served honorably. One uncle, who I never met, died during the Normandy Invasion, bravely assisting in the liberation of France in 1944, the year I was born.

I learned just a little of what it took to be a good American soldier shortly after I started basic training in early 1967. I had gotten sick with a cold, but I knew that I couldn't take too much time off, remembering what had happened when I first got to basic and was hospitalized after the examining doctors suspected I had a heart murmur. Anyway, this cold kept hanging on, and one brutally cold morning while running with the other recruits, I was having a hard time keeping up. I was sniffling, snorting, and gasping for breath when the drill sergeant races to my side to investigate what was wrong. "What's wrong with you, soldier?" he screamed. Hoping he would have pity on me, I pretended to be sicker than I was and whimpered, "I'm sick, Drill Sergeant!" "Get moving, soldier!" he shouted. I never complained again, thinking how silly I must have sounded and knowing the hardships my predecessors must have endured during real war. Even during night time exercises in mud, heat and cold, with no clean spot to even wipe one's mouth, all of that paled in comparison to the real thing, and I found myself thanking God that I had gotten off so easily.

I learned also that even drill sergeants have a sense of humor. One day, we had a class in "counterinsurgency" which dealt with the brutal techniques used by the Viet Cong in fighting their side of the Vietnam War. This was an important class, and we had been warned before every class to *not fall asleep*. We were told that, if we felt ourselves getting drowsy, we were allowed to go to the back of the classroom and stand, thus keeping us awake. Sometimes there would be half of the "students" standing in the back of the room!

Unbeknownst to us students, the teachers (drill sergeants) had cooked up a brilliant ploy to keep us awake. After the class was introduced (and many of us were getting drowsy, as expected), an unidentified soldier, rushed onto the stage and whispered something in the presenter's ear as he handed him a piece of paper.

Then the ominous announcement: (Dramatic clearing of throat) "OK, listen up! After class, the following named men, please report to the blah, blah, to prepare for deployment to Vietnam for active duty service (or something to that effect)!" And he actually named names of people in our class! Guys were crying, grabbing their throats, gasping, near fainting in disbelief. It was horrible! But amazingly, everybody started listening with rapt attention!

At the end of the class, the presenter disclosed that it was all a ruse, and had been concocted only to get the class to pay attention. The sergeants actually had to run for cover, the troops were so incensed! Some actually started to hyperventilate with relief! It was hilarious!

I learned also that the instructors, drill sergeants and officers could be compassionate as well. I must have been a "problem soldier" (the military version of a "problem child"), because one afternoon when I was off duty and walking into the barracks, one of my favorite drill sergeants (a dead ringer for Lewis Gossett) said that he wanted to talk to me. My first thought was *Oh, Lord, what have I done now!* But this time, there was something different about Sarge. He seemed softer, more human, as he started his little speech, which he had obviously thought about presenting just to me. "Moody," he started, "I know you think I pick on you and that it seems that I'm constantly riding you and making you *run* every time I see you." *(That part was absolutely true!)* He continued, "But I just want you to know that I take this job very seriously, and because I care about you, I have to know that, if there is ever a time that you are ever in combat and you are in danger, and you can't *run out of sight,* I would hold myself personally responsible if anything happened to you."

At that moment, anything negative I had ever thought about the military or drill sergeants or war or basic training, all left me. I was speechless and I don't mind admitting, I almost cried. But…I didn't want Sarge to perceive me as weak, so I gave him a hasty "thank you" and continued into the barracks.

He never mentioned it again, but I never forgot that day this nameless drill sergeant showed his soft side and changed my whole outlook on the reason for their toughness.

I "retired" from the National Guard in August of 1971, after serving six years of readiness, summer camps, monthly weekend drills, surprise alert drills, one actual activation to "guard" the University of Kentucky campus after Kent State, and taking with me an unwavering respect for the men and women of our armed forces. God Bless America!

CHAPTER TWELVE

THE CHICKEN FAMILY

I'VE NOTICED AS I've gotten older that I remember people, places, and things that younger people don't remember (mostly because they weren't alive at the time!). So, every now and then, a subject comes up that makes me think about how profoundly that part of my history affected me. A couple of people who crossed my path, directly and indirectly, really stand out: "Colonel" Harland Sanders and his nephew, Lee Cummings.

Not too long ago, I was having lunch with a couple of lady friends—actually, former high school classmates—back in the old home town. Somehow I launched into one of many stories from my past, which one of the ladies immediately began accusing me of making up. In defense, I told her, "No...you can't make this stuff up." She then asked me, "How do you know all these people?" to which I replied, "Well, for one thing, I married a Yankee." The utterance of the word "YANKEE" caused a hush to fall over the crowd at the Chicken Shack (the real name of the country eatery we had chosen for lunch), and I began my story.

I told them about finishing my undergraduate degree and then getting the job at the University of Alabama. I really enjoyed the work, but the pay wasn't that good. I had gotten married about that time, thus straining my budget even further, because my wife was a recent UA graduate and didn't have a job yet. So I was delighted when, during a three-day National Association of Educational Broadcasters' convention in Jacksonville, Florida, a man named Roger Koonce offered me a job at the University of Kentucky, making a whopping $9,000 a year—almost $50 a week more than I was making in Alabama!

A scant two weeks later, with all our belongings in a U-Haul truck, Andrea and I, along with our Siamese cat, Alfie, were headed north to Bluegrass Country and the University of Kentucky, and home of the Kentucky Wildcats, coached by the legendary Adolph Rupp (the Bear Bryant of college basketball). I think we spent that $9,000 the first week just moving and getting set up in our tiny house on St. Teresa Drive. Although we didn't know it at the time, our neighbors were relatives of the legendary "Colonel" Sanders. Although we knew about Colonel Harland Sanders and his Kentucky Fried Chicken, we had no way of knowing that we had moved in next door to the Chicken King's stepson, his wife, and their eight year old towheaded son!

It was an unfamiliar neighborhood, but friendly, and shortly after we settled in (with no boxes yet unpacked), we heard a knock at our front door. Assuming it was the local Jehovah's Witnesses congregation welcoming us to the neighborhood, we flung the door open, ready to announce, "No thanks, we gave at the office." Instead, to our amazement, there stood a rugged but pleasant-looking woman—I would say, a cross between Ma Kettle and Janet Reno, and before we could say "Howdy," our next door neighbor blurted out her invitation. "I know y'all been workin' hard to git moved in. Why don't y'all take a break and come over and have lunch with us?"

I looked at Andrea and she looked at me, and in unison, we both protested, "Oh, we wouldn't want to put you to any trouble" (hoping she wouldn't pay any attention to our protest). "Aw, it's awright, we got plinty." She told us her name and then began to tell us about her husband and their son. And, rather matter-of-factly, she added that her step father-in-law was none other than Colonel Harland Sanders! She further explained that her husband suffered from "shell-shock" (what we now call Post Traumatic Stress Disorder or PTSD) from World War II and wasn't "quite right" and that the poor kid just stayed out of sight. I don't remember their names, so I'll refer to them simply as the "Chicken Family."

Anyway, you can imagine what we pictured in our minds as Andrea and I made the trek next door: huge plates of juicy fried chicken, complete with trimmings in a fancy (but small) dining area, with perhaps a maid and a butler. WRONG!

Don't ask me how they managed to dig a basement out under that tiny house, but there it was! And that's not the strangest part. The entire basement (concrete floor and all), floor to ceiling was what looked like a fully-stocked grocery store! Apparently the Chicken Family liked the house, so the colonel had simply ordered it stocked with groceries to make it easier on Mr. and Mrs. Chicken and Chicken Little. And stranger still, the eagerly anticipated chicken lunch we expected turned out to be hot dogs and chips! (I told you…you can't make this stuff up.)

Throughout the year 1969-70, we often caught a glimpse of the colonel in his gold Cadillac with his picture on the side, visiting the Chicken Family. The colonel's wife would always be driving, because by this time, he was already in his late 70's, having started the Kentucky Fried Chicken franchise at age 65. I guess he figured it'd work out better that way, in case he ever needed to jump out and sign autographs. (I still don't know why we didn't get his autograph!)

An epilogue to this particular story is that, several years later, we confirmed that everything we had witnessed on St. Teresa Drive was true. But first, we had to get back to Alabama. There wasn't much to keep us in Kentucky, seeing as how the economy was driven by three primary enterprises: horse breeding (and racing), tobacco farming, and liquor distilling. Although Andrea liked horses and had grown up with them in the rolling hills of Wisconsin, neither of us knew anything about breeding them or betting/gambling on them. And we didn't smoke or drink, so we had little in common with anyone there other than my associates at the university. After a couple of years, I started applying for jobs back in Alabama, specifically Birmingham, as Andrea's parents lived there and had offered to help us get resettled should we decide to move back. We had moved to a new apartment complex (away from the Chicken Family neighborhood) due to the expense of keeping up a house, lawn, etc., and I eventually accepted a position with the Jefferson County (Alabama) School System in their media department. Moving plans were solidified, the apartment lease terminated, utitlites shut off, another U-Haul truck rented, and we were finally Alabamy-bound!

Unfortunately, upon arriving in Birmingham, I was told by Gerald Godfrey, who had offered me the position, that due to problems with desegregation, many of the communities within the Jefferson County System had decided to pull out of the county and form their own separate school systems. Thirty-three municipalities surround Birmingham, so with each withdrawal, the budget for the county grew smaller, and eventually the position I was to fill was eliminated.

Although this was devastating news, it led to a position as Program Director at an up-and-coming FM (Christian) radio station in Homewood, a Birmingham suburb. By 1984, I had accepted a position as Director of Station Operations (aka Station Manager) at the same radio station. And here's where the epilogue continues.

I was in the studio one day, deeply engrossed in the morning's programming and production activities and had just turned my back to the door. Suddenly, I felt a light tap on my shoulder and turned to face a portly, older gentleman standing over me. He held out his hand and offered me two "tickets." "Hello," he said, as though he already knew me, "I'm Lee Cummings. I'm opening a new restaurant in town (Lee's Fried Chicken), and with these two tickets, I'm inviting you to have lunch on me." And thus began "the rest of the story" of Colonel Sanders and the Chicken Family.

Mr. Cummings (he insisted I call him "Lee") told me how he had started his own chicken career with Colonel Sanders in 1952, traveling around with him and selling his famous recipe of "11 different herbs and spices" and chicken, pressure fried like nobody else's! The conversation didn't last nearly long enough (Lee was a very busy man!), but long enough to confirm the story of the colonel's stepson and his family who had indeed lived in Lexington, Kentucky during the time my wife and I resided there.

Although I never saw Lee again, I ate at his restaurant many times over the ensuing years and fondly remember my experiences with the entire "Chicken Family."

CHAPTER THIRTEEN

"HAPPY" DAYS WERE HERE AGAIN

DURING THE TIME we lived in Kentucky, Andrea and I met some amazing people. Some were absolutely unforgettable, but many would be unfamiliar to most folks under the age of 50 or 60. One of the most colorful was a man named Albert Benjamin "Happy" Chandler. Happy was a U.S Senator from Kentucky from 1939 to 1945 and was 44th and 49th governor of Kentucky from 1935 to 1939 and from 1955 to 1959. He also served as the second Commissioner of Baseball from 1945 to 1951, succeeding the first Commissioner, a man with the whimsical name, Kenesaw Mountain Landis. For those who might be interested in more information about Happy Chandler, I encourage you to Google his name and be prepared to be amazed. I had the privilege of meeting and actually visiting in the home of Happy Chandler in the fall of 1970, under circumstances that even my closest friends have difficulty believing. Truth be told, if my wife hadn't been with me to confirm it, I would have a hard time believing it myself.

It all started while I was working in the Broadcast Services

Department at the University of Kentucky in 1969 and 1970. Many students of history (and many people who lived through the era) would remember this being an exciting but troublesome time for America. To mention a couple of disturbing incidents, the Vietnam War was still raging, and the Democratic National Convention in 1968 yielded the Chicago Seven, a motley group of shaggy-haired far left communist sympathizers who were accused of inciting a riot in protest. Most such protests came to an abrupt halt when National Guardsmen opened fire on marauding students at Kent State University in Kent, Ohio on May 4, 1970, killing four and wounding nine others. I was a Guardsman at the time, and my unit in Lexington was activated in anticipation of trouble on the UK campus.

At about the same time, Andrea had become interested in the ministry of Dr. Carl McIntire, a Presbyterian minister in Collingswood, New Jersey, especially because of his conservative, pro-victory stance on the Vietnam War. After some corresponding back and forth, she was "appointed" chairman of the Kentucky March for Victory Committee. Dr. McIntire believed that the war was a "no-win" war, costing precious American lives as a result. He envisioned all 50 states organizing marches on their respective state capitals in support of total and unconditional victory in Vietnam. Andrea was to drum up support and publicity for the march, which was to take place on the same Saturday in every state in the Union. I was somewhat apprehensive about her accepting the "appointment" because of my being in the National Guard. Although I agreed with the idea in principle, I didn't want to be engaged in anything that would reflect negatively or politically on my military service. Also, Andrea hadn't really wanted the job (volunteer and unpaid, by the way), but apparently nobody else would do it, so…

OK, flashback to Alabama for a statement about my radical wife. Andrea had actually made a name for herself at the University of Alabama shortly before we moved to Kentucky. It seemed that, every time we opened a newspaper, some left wing radical group was burning an ROTC building somewhere in the country. Andrea had almost finished her degree in Broadcast and Film Communications at UA, and she had been bugging me to get her a part-time job at Broadcast Services. I was actually in charge of hiring student "crew," so against my better judgment, I hired her to operate camera, sound board, set up stage props, etc. By the way, I wouldn't advise this, because, with my wife, she would get offended if I treated her like an employee rather than my wife! I tried to explain to her that, as an employee, she had to be treated no differently than any other employee, but she had a hard time with that. I ended up having to "terminate" her employment. That wasn't very pleasant either.

She was still working there, however, when this next incident happened. To illustrate how passionate she was (and still is) about the conservative "cause" and all which that entails, there was an incident that took place one rather tense day when the radical element on campus had invited four extremists to speak. The list of speakers included William Kuntsler, lawyer for the infamous Chicago Seven, mentioned previously. Dr. Frank Rose was the president of the University of Alabama at the time, and a very popular one at that. In his wisdom, he cancelled the speeches of these idiot radicals who wanted only to foment violence and discord.

Shortly after Dr. Rose's announcement canceling the speeches, several students banded together in support of his decision. A good many of them were on the first floor in the Student Center getting petitions signed to let him know how much they appreciated him. Our studios were on the third floor of the Student Union Building, so on my way in to work, I had stopped by to sign the petition. Andrea was already at work, so when I walked in, I told her what was going on and asked her if she wanted to go down with me and sign the petition too. Of course, she jumped at the chance to show her support for Dr. Rose, as she was still a student.

There were no elevators in the Union Building, so we headed back down the winding circular staircase to the first floor. Andrea was ahead of me, and as we made our way to the first floor, we saw a "long-haired hippie freak" holding a crude hand-lettered sign aloft decrying the president's violation of their precious First Amendment rights! It turns out, that by the time we got down to the area where the petitions were being signed, apparently the leftist extremists had gotten wind and had decided to actually protest the people signing the petitions! And here's where it got interesting.

Andrea could be very sweet and beguiling when she wanted to be, so as she approached the sign holder, she feigned interest with, "Oh, may I see your sign?" Flattered that a cute coed would be interested in his cause, he quickly obliged, slowly turning toward her. She was still in the stairwell slightly above the poor guy as he turned the sign around. I knew Andrea could be a hot head, so I hoped she wasn't up to no good. No such luck. To my shock and horror, she gently lifted the sign from his hands and promptly tore it in half! You could hear the rumbling as the gathered crowd witnessed the violation of their civil rights! Fortunately, a nearby campus policeman came to our rescue. "Young lady, you can't do that!" he shouted as he pushed the hippie aside and grabbed Andrea by the arm to escort her out of harm's way.

Sputtering her own protest, but realizing she might get in worse trouble, she quickly calmed down as we made our way to the squad car. *So this is what it feels like to get arrested, is it?* All the while, Andrea is protesting verbally with her own speech about freedom of expression. *So, this is the thanks I get for supporting the president of the university, by getting arrested??* Although we weren't technically arrested, the officer did gently place Andrea in the back seat. It happened so fast, and I wasn't sure whether I was a "suspect" or not, so in my panic, I quickly circled around and jumped into the front seat with the officer! (It was months before Andrea forgave me for that one!)

It was a short drive to the campus police station where the tongue lashing began about how we couldn't be violating others' rights to peacefully assemble, blah, blah, blah. In the end, Andrea was ordered to go see the Dean of Women for another tongue lashing about civil rights, etc. It would be safe to say that we were both a little more careful the next time we saw a hippie with a sign.

OK, fast forward back to Kentucky. You're probably wondering where Happy Chandler fits into all this. So, it turns out that, unbeknownst to either my wife or me, Happy Chandler was serving on the Board of Trustees of the University of Kentucky. In fact, we didn't even know who he was until the fateful day the Department of Broadcast Services was covering one of the board meetings. It quickly became evident that the left-wing element was still alive and well at the University of Kentucky. The radicals were always looking for something to rally for or protest against. And such was the case on that day. Although I wasn't actually there to witness what happened, I quickly heard about it through the grapevine, in addition to reading about it later in the student newspaper.

The story goes that the board meeting had just adjourned, and the members were filing out. True to form, the radicals were out in force, swarming the hallways, shouting and chanting at no particular person and for no particular reason. (I'm not sure when they managed to attend classes.) Happy Chandler was making his way out of the conference room when he was approached by a young couple (apparently "boyfriend and girlfriend"), and the girl shouted to him at close range, "Why don't you do something about the war in Vietnam?!" (probably not her exact words) At which time, Happy gently pushed her aside and emphatically retorted, "Honey, I don't have a thing to do with that war over there." Well, apparently neither the push nor the answer suited the boyfriend, as he grabbed Happy's necktie and jerked him forward. Fearing that he was about to be assaulted, 73 year old Happy delivered a smart and swift blow to the poor boy's chin, knocking him down flat and out cold! As might be expected, the liberal student newspaper went nuts about the incident, and Happy Chandler became my (and Andrea's) hero from that day forward.

Eventually, the incident faded into insignificance on campus, but Andrea never forgot it. She had managed to arrange for me to speak (on her behalf, since she was terrified of speaking before a crowd of more than two) to the Veterans of Foreign Wars in Frankfort (Kentucky's capital) to try to elicit their support and participation in the March for Victory, which was fast approaching.

As we prepared to leave for the meeting that night, we realized that we would be driving right through the city of Versailles, coincidentally, where Happy Chandler lived. *Why don't we stop by his house and see if he'll speak at our rally?* A preposterous and wild idea, we thought, but hey, nothing ventured, nothing gained, we figured.

The presentation went well before the VFW, but we were eager to get on the road before it was too late to "stop by" Happy's place. We still thought it was an insane idea that would never come to fruition. Nevertheless, we decided to give it our best shot.

We stopped at the first convenience store still open, and fully expecting to be laughed out the door, asked the clerk, "Can you tell us how to get to Happy Chandler's house?" Even though we figured it was probably a lost cause, we also figured at least we'd find out where he lived. After all, Versailles was only about 7,000 in population. "Well, yeh," he started, "you just go…" And with that, a turn by turn detailed GPS description straight to Happy's front door!

By the time we drove up to the front of the house, it was already too dark to really determine if we were even at the right place. What we could see, however, was that this was a good sized house surrounded by a black, foreboding head-high wrought iron fence. We figured if it really was Happy's house, surely it would be flooded with lights and have armed guards keeping watch to prevent crazy thrill seekers from intruding on his privacy.

Still, we'd come this far, so it didn't make sense to turn back now. Miraculously, the unlocked gate swung open with our nervous push, and before we knew it, we were knocking on the front door. Seconds passed and Andrea and I began to imagine the consequences of our foolish actions. Surely, no one would answer. Surely, armed guards will appear at any moment to haul us away to the hoosegow. Surely, we should just quietly go away.

What seemed more like several minutes than probably less than half of one, a rattle was heard at the door! We fully expected a butler or maid preparing to tell us to scram. Instead, there stood the man we'd only seen pictures of on TV and in the newspaper, with about a four-day growth of beard, dressed in bedroom slippers, lounging pants and a T-shirt bulging with a tummy that would have put Santa Claus to shame!

A friendly voice boomed, "Hey, can I hep ya?"

Well, neither Andrea nor I was expecting this, and it had never occurred to us to have a greeting prepared *just in case we did meet Happy Chandler face-to-face.* You might say, it was the furthest thing from our minds. But here we were, in front of Happy Chandler with our pants down (metaphorically and figuratively speaking, of course), wishing we'd thought this whole thing out a little better.

I think I was the first to find my voice. "Well…uh…you see…we was, uh, we were just over in Frankfort…" I remember that was sort of the way it started and then I think I said something hurriedly, like how we wanted him to speak at our March for Victory rally. Expecting any second to find the door slammed in our faces, to our surprise, Happy grinned, "Well, y'all come on in. I was just watchin' Laramie (a popular Western themed TV show at the time). The bad guys are about to ride into town!" And with that, we were escorted into a modestly spacious, but cozy den where Happy's big black Labrador Retriever patiently awaited his master's return. We felt immediately right at home!

After the bad guys had been corralled and taken into custody, Happy turned his attention to his new found friends. "Now, what was it you said you was doin'?" Like he'd known us all his life. At that moment, I realized why he was so popular with "the people."

Thus ensued our unprepared presentation about the upcoming March for Victory in Frankfort and why we had "stopped by" to ask him to participate. While it appeared that he agreed with what we were doing, he told us how much he appreciated our efforts but said he didn't think it would be prudent for him to get involved as he was preparing for a third run as governor and just didn't think he'd have time. Andrea and I knew he was just being nice, so we didn't press him any further.

What happened next was totally unexpected. With a twinkle in his eye, Happy asked, "Y'all wanna see the rest of the house?" Still in shock that we had made it past the (nonexistent) armed guards, we certainly didn't want to turn down such a gracious but unbelievable offer!

It's funny how, without the ever-present camcorder or iPhone camera of today, we seem to be able to recall only certain weirdly particular details of an incident from decades past. The thing I remember most vividly was when Happy took us down into his basement, which extended the entire length of the house end to end. It was crammed with literally thousands of items personally given to and collected by Happy Chandler, including his picture with every U.S. president since Franklin Roosevelt, not to mention countless other dignitaries and politicians. Andrea and I had never seen anything like it! We had barely scratched the surface in viewing all the incredible items in his basement when Happy wistfully announced, "Yeh, when I die, all this is going to the University of Kentucky to put in their archives." He paused, as if to let what he had just said sink in. Then he continued, "This is one of my most prized possessions," as he walked to one of the smaller tables filled with memorabilia. "This is a Bible given to me by David Ben-Gurion." Matter of factly, he continued, "He autographed it for me. It's silver plated, and see that right there…those are emeralds on it." He slowly and carefully handed it to me for closer inspection. In school, I had never liked history, but when Barry Goldwater ran for president, I realized that I was more of a conservative after reading his book, The Conscience of a Conservative, and would probably have voted for him if I had been old enough. Since then, I had devoured newspapers, magazines and books dealing with politics and its history. I remembered that David Ben-Gurion was the primary national founder of the State of Israel and its first Prime Minister. And here I was, holding in my hands a Bible that he had held. I gently handed it to Andrea, and we relished the moment that seemed almost surreal.

Suddenly, it was time to continue the tour. Happy then took us back upstairs and into his bedroom, where he introduced us to his wife, Mildred, who was propped up in a larger than life king-sized poster bed, quietly reading a book. Amazingly, she greeted us as though our visit was an everyday occurrence!

Finally, Happy showed us all of his clothes in his closet, and was very pleased to show us his collection of shirts, some of which had never been taken out of the store wrapping! Andrea and I were indeed thunderstruck!

My estimate was that, by the time we walked back down the sidewalk and through that wrought iron gate, we must have spent 30 to 45 minutes with the one and only Happy Chandler. The saga, as I have related it, happened exactly that way. Even though I had my wife to corroborate my story, I'm still not sure any of our friends or my co-workers believed a word of it.

Happy Chandler died on June 15, 1991 at the age of 92 at his home in Versailles, Kentucky.

CHAPTER FOURTEEN

IN THE SWIM

I THINK IT'S interesting how important "appearances" are when we're younger. It's not so much what it is you wear; it's whether everybody else is wearing it, or whether others approve of what you're wearing that counts. The same is true with behaviors and skill sets.

For years, I often just didn't think I "measured up" to others. In "fashion," in abilities, in intellect, or whatever. In hindsight, though, I think I held my own in most areas. And I'm sure a survey of my friends from those days would validate me.

Still, there were certain things that bothered me. Like not living in a real house. Or a brick house (the true mark of upper-classedness, I thought). Not having a pair of Rock and Roll shoes (a popular style by American Gentleman back in the day).

I continued to struggle with esteem issues into adulthood (although I hid my insecurities well), but there was one thing that has bothered me, and still does, to this day. I never learned how to swim.

I know, I know, it doesn't seem like a big deal. But it's sort of like when people have plenty of money, they always tell other people that money isn't important. Well, if you don't have it, it is important! The same is true regarding the inability to swim.

The harsh reality of my shortcoming was illustrated in another horribly cringworthy experience in the summer of 1970. Andrea and I had just moved into a newer "yuppie-ish" apartment complex in Lexington, thinking that it was a better "fit" for us than the older "Chicken Family" neighborhood. We thought it would be more fun to be around people closer to our age.

The complex, being new, had lots of amenities to attract the younger crowd, including, of course, the proverbial swimming pool. I had determined that I wouldn't be intimidated by it, and that I wouldn't be bothered if Andrea wanted to occasionally take a swim without me. Since she wasn't working at the time, she could even work on her "tan" if she so desired. But, because of my shameful secret (of being a non-swimmer), I let her know in no uncertain terms that there was no way I would ever set foot in that pool. Right…

It wasn't long before the place was hopping with new, young tenants, and "the place to be," naturally, was the swimming pool. It seemed that most of them were married, confident professional people, and all the guys were handsome and muscular, and all the girls were beautiful and toned. And all of them were, of course, Olympic swimmers. I'm sure I'm exaggerating, but my perception made it all the more reason for me to stay away from that foreboding water hole.

Well, it didn't take long before Andrea started to harangue me to come out to the pool with her. Oh, and did I mention that my lily-whiteness would have blinded even wearers of the darkest Ray-Bans? Nevertheless, Andrea kept up her crusade to have me "join her by the pool." Oh, and did I mention that Andrea tended to be a little jealous when I was around other half-naked females, even though I assured her I wasn't looking?

Still, Andrea continued her onslaught to have me expose myself (and my little secret) to the world. And she eventually succeeded. One Saturday, in a fit of weakness, I let her talk me into doing the unthinkable: *"going swimming."*

After probably three or four hours of procrastination, me feigning leprosy, sudden weakness, blindness, paralysis, etc., etc., Andrea drug me out of the apartment, wearing my Hawaiian floweredy (never-used) swim trunks. "Oh, come on, it'll be fun; don't be such a fuddy-duddy," she goaded. "You can just stay on the shallow end." *A dead giveaway, I thought.* "You don't have to swim." *Really? Thanks a lot! Didn't I tell you?*

Soon, there we were. Standing beside the Atlantic Ocean. Waiting to walk the plank. Again, I'm thinking, *This is just not going to work.* The understatement of the year.

But, you know, I finally decided, *Come on, Moody, you're being silly. Go and have some fun. You'll enjoy it.* All lies! But it was already too late. So I had a plan. I would not let Andrea talk me into getting in the water. I'd just sit on the side of the pool. (All the chairs were taken. Darn!) I would nonchalantly dangle my feet in the water and no one would be the wiser. After a few minutes of skin-frying, I would excuse myself and leave Andrea to have fun on her own. It was foolproof. *Wrong!*

"Come on, Mike, get in!" *Oh, no, it's started! I have to stay strong!* My resolve lasted about 15 seconds, until Andrea started tugging at me. *The War of the Roses, Part Two!* "Come on, jump in!" *Splash!*

So far, this would have been bad enough. But, noooo, Andrea now proceeds to "teach me how to swim! *The humiliation! The mortification! My life was over!*

But it gets worse. "Just relax! You're not going to drown!" *Really? I've seen pictures. Don't you read the papers?* "You know, if you just relax, you'll float. You have to trust me. Here, just stretch out!" I had heard that "you'll float" lie before, and it made even less sense now…now that I was facing a watery grave.

It was not a pretty sight. After much kicking, sputtering, gasping and flailing, my feet somehow met concrete, and my torso torpedoed upward, my head clearing water and my mouth sucking in precious air! *Did I hear sniggering? Where was Andrea? Oh, God, please get me out of here!*

I heard Andrea reassuring me. "You're OK, you're OK. Let's try it again!" So, now I'm thinking, it's time to make a deal. Still struggling for breath, I assured Andrea that, really, I can do this myself. I remembered my past attempts at positive thinking, and I had seen other people swimming. It didn't look that hard. I figured I'd just mimic a few Mark Spitz moves, and maybe it would happen! Sure! That's the ticket! I convinced Andrea to back off and let me try. Scene II.

If no one had been looking or paying attention before I attempted this stunt, I certainly fixed that. I would have thought the mere thrashing would have prevented such a rapid descent. I did succeed in moving, but it wasn't horizontal. It was straight down!

When I again was able to get my head above water, I finally came to the conclusion the some people just aren't meant to swim. And I'm obviously one of them. I think, by this time, Andrea was getting the point. I could sort of tell by the way she was looking around and pretending she didn't know me. *Dead giveaway.* That was O.K. with me, though. I was through with her! I thought my embarrassment level had reached an all time high, but as I headed for the nearest ledge (on foot), I had one more river to cross. (Bad choice of words...)

I thought, O.K., I'm already the laughing stock, so why not just hang around and enjoy the scenery? I mean, who likes a coward, right? At least nobody could see how much I was sweating; I was already drenched anyway! So, reaching the edge of the pool (in the shallow end, of course), I did a watery pirouette, and grabbing the ledge behind me for support, I intended to spring backwards onto the ledge and take a seat.

True enough, I made it like a champion pole vaulter. Problem was, my trunks didn't! As soon as my derriere plopped down on the cool tile, I knew I was in trouble (again). *Overexposed!* I don't know which was more embarrassing, my miserable failure as a swimmer or my ineptness as a pole vaulter!

I quickly slid back into the water, and, carefully squatting so as to not submerge my nose, I pulled up the wayward swimming trunks, and sprinted (in slow motion) for the underwater stairs.

The nightmare was finally over, and Andrea never asked me to go swimming again. However, the PTSD is still a problem every time I take a drink of water.

CHAPTER FIFTEEN

Hitting the Road (And Other Things That Get in the Way)

It's amazing how many of my "adventures" have had to do with driving a car (or truck). Sometimes I would be driving, sometimes I would have a passenger, and sometimes I would be the passenger. There were a couple of times, the car I was driving actually caught on fire. One time was when I forgot to put the cap on after checking the oil, and the motor caught fire seven miles up the road. That one was totaled. The other time was just a fan belt that slung off and burned up. No problem there. But when it comes to hitting things with cars, I don't think most people really set out to do it intentionally. At least, I never did; somehow things just seem to get in the way.

I can think of many such incidents that happened to me. The following six very significant ones stand out in my memory.

The Mailbox

This particular incident stands out as totally unexpected and at the most inopportune time. It was in the spring of 1977, and I was preparing to move from Birmingham to Troy to manage a radio station there and to try my hand at running my own business on the side (an ice cream parlor, no less). It was a bold (or foolish) move, as I had never really had my own business, although I did have some experience growing up in that little Mom and Pop store. But, I had always wanted to follow in my parents' footsteps and see if I could be as good at it as they had been.

For the past two years, my little family and I had lived on a quiet street (Oak Street, of course) about 20 miles south of Birmingham in a little 'burb in Shelby County called Maylene. I had already turned in my notice at work, and we were going to be moving the next day. Most of the "little stuff" had been packed, and I was to pick up the U-Haul truck in the morning. Ashley, our four-year old daughter, had already been tucked in, and I had just finished taking a shower. After a grueling day of packing, I was looking forward to a little shut-eye myself. As I stepped out of the bathroom in my birthday suit, I saw a sudden flash of light outside Ashley's bedroom window.

I was headed for the clothes bin, dirty clothes in hand, intending to deposit them for one last wash before hitting the road. All of the bedrooms, including Ashley's, were on the second floor, so I wasn't necessarily in fear of totally exposing myself to the neighborhood. But the light startled me, as our home was in a rural area and not much traffic was common at that time of night (around 10 P.M.). Not wishing to be caught in my vulnerable state of undress, I instinctively hunkered down and ducked into Ashley's bedroom as I quickly pulled on a pair of boxers. The house was in a fairly new subdivision, and we liked the smart way the windows were built about a foot off the floor, providing ample light during the day. Unfortunately, without blinds, passersby had an untrammeled view inside the house, and of course we had already taken all of the window accessories down for the move. I scurried over to the window to see what caused the unusual flash of light outside and was shocked at what I saw.

I got to the window just in time to observe a car backing out of our driveway. *Just someone who had taken a wrong turn, I figured.* And I was about to turn away when the unbelievable happened. The driver of the car was clearly taking dead aim at our mailbox, and I watched in horror as the vehicle mowed it down!

Suddenly, Clark Kent became Superman, as I jumped into a pair of jeans, stepped into my favorite loafers and shouted to Andrea, "Call the police! I'm goin' after 'em!"

In seconds, I'm careening down our street, ignoring the stop sign at the end. Quickly glancing both ways, with no clue as to which way the culprits had gone, I fishtailed to the right and headed toward "town." Apparently, Andrea was successful in making contact with Andy and Barney, as we zoomed past each other at a combined speed of about 180!

It was obvious that Maylene's finest was ready for action, and the squad car made it back to the house before I could overtake it. Immediately, I realized there was no Andy, only Barney, who was already headed to the front door by the time I screeched to a halt in the driveway. "They…they… uh…knocked our mailbox down!" I sputtered as Barney whirled around. "Which way did they go?" he asked. "I don't know! I think they went toward town!" (A wild guess, as I had no idea where "they" went. I just knew I wanted those criminals apprehended and hung!)

Barney's obvious training was about to pay off. I couldn't help but notice that his hat must have been the wrong size, as it was resting comfortably on his already prominent ears, giving him an almost comical Yoda look. "Can you identify 'em?" he snapped. "Well…I don't know. I think…the car, maybe. A Chevrolet? It was kinda dark."

Barney is now reaching for the door of the squad car. "Get in," he snapped, "Let's go!" *This is not the way I pictured it, I thought.* "Who, me? I'm going with you?"

Exasperated, Barney repeats the command. "Let's go!" I hardly made it inside the car and slammed the door before the G-man laid rubber backing out of the driveway! I knew he was going to ask me "which way," so in my state of panic, I shouted for him to go left at the end of Oak Street.

We didn't make it very far "the other way" when suddenly headlights appeared up ahead! *Zoom!* "That's the car! That's it!" I screamed. And with another rubber-burning U-turn, the chase was on! *Siren blaring! Lights flashing!*

But it was too late. As fast as Barney was, the tail lights were out of sight before we could pick up enough speed. To be noted, I don't think seat belts had even been invented yet, so I was leaning forward, clutching the dashboard and peering into the darkness as we raced time, looking for justice!

With no other cars in sight and my adrenaline pumping full speed, I spied the Zippy Mart at the intersection coming up on our left. Suddenly, in the darkness behind the store, I could make out the Chevy's dim outline! "There it is! There's the car!" I heard myself trumpet. *Screech! Careen! Lurch forward! Left turn! Dust! Smoke! Gravel!*

Barney is out the door before the squad car comes to a complete stop. "Stay here!" he hollers, as he draws his weapon! It was about this time that I began to wonder if this was such a good idea. I mean, after all, it was just a mailbox. *We could be killed, I thought! Get hold of yourself, Moody. You've been watching too much TV.*

Squinting to get a better view, I could see two figures in the back seat of the Chevy. *Wait...they look like kids! These are supposed to be hardened criminals! What just happened?*

By this time, Barney had re-holstered his weapon, realizing the driver was nowhere in sight. As he sprints toward the front of the Zippy Mart, the apparent driver comes around the corner. Incredibly, he looked even younger than the two in the back seat!

I'll have to give Barney credit here. I didn't see his hands move, but somehow the handcuffs were on and the two of them were marching back toward the squad car. Then it dawned to me that both Barney and I were going to have a problem as I began to do the math. I suddenly realized that there were five total potential passengers, two total cars, and a total of one pair of handcuffs. Apparently, this was not "one-bullet Barney," but rather "one-handcuff Barney." I began looking for woods to run into.

But, no problem. Barney already had it figured out. Before I could utter, "Shazam!" I was wedged between two drunk teenage boys in the back seat of the squad car, and Barney's handcuffed captive in the front seat so he could "keep an eye on him."

Looking back on that night, I still have difficulty believing it happened as I've described it. But again, honestly, you can't make this stuff up.

So here's the rest of the story. After dropping me off at home, Barney headed back to the station (?) to "book 'em, Danno," and the truth came out. Apparently, it was graduation night at the local high school, and some of the graduates had gotten hold of some firewater, which, as we all know, tends to lower inhibitions, especially in teenagers. So, what better way to celebrate entering the real adult world and rewarding yourself for successfully completing high school than riding around the neighborhood knocking down mailboxes with your parents' car?

I got a phone call around 7:00 the next morning. The young boy introduced himself and informed me that he and his two friends would be over shortly to put up my mailbox. I found out later that the total mailbox re-installations in the neighborhood would reach a dozen or more. I just happened to be one of them.

Still later, I got a call from "the judge" assigned to the case, telling me that I would have to testify at the hearing in a couple of weeks regarding the charges, etc. I explained to him that, unfortunately, I had accepted a job three hours away and it just wouldn't be convenient for me to do that. Incredibly, the judge asked me what I thought he should do with "the boys."

I guess I must have thought quickly about my own child and my own foolish teenage years, and suddenly I softened toward the "hardened criminals" who had viciously knocked down my mailbox the night before. I told the judge that I thought the boys should somehow pay for what they had done. I emphasized that I didn't feel qualified to say exactly what their punishment should be, but I personally thought it might teach them a valuable lesson if he worked their butts off for the rest to the summer!

He must have taken my "advice." I never heard from the judge or those boys again. And that new mailbox looked really good when we sold the house.

The Mailbox Revisited

It wasn't until a few years later that I realized how those teenagers must have felt as the car's front end made impact with that mailbox. Because of the poverty I was dealing with after my divorce, I had to move back in with my parents in order to have time to "re-group" and decide how I would spend the rest of my life. Of course, that's putting it simply.

My parents had always told me that their home (where I grew up) would always be my home and that I would always be welcome there. I would never be expected to pay rent or "feel guilty" about coming back home. In fact, my mother, in particular, never demanded anything from me, especially during the hard times. Her goal in life was to do her part to make life as stress-free as possible for her family. And she never strayed from that goal.

Because of her selfless philosophy, I never took advantage of her generosity and goodness. Not ever wanting to be a burden on them, as soon as I pulled into the yard at my parents' house located behind the little Mom and Pop store they still ran, my first thought was: *When can I leave here and get on with my life?* I knew I was in limbo and that, for me, was an unnatural state. I loved my parents, but they had taught me to be proud and independent, and I didn't want to disappoint them.

They helped me in more ways than I could ever repay. Even when I would try over the ensuing years, they would refuse to let me, insisting that "we're family" and "you don't pay family back." Everything my mother did for me (and my sister) was a gift which she freely gave, and she would actually be offended if we ever tried to "pay her back."

My mother must have washed tens of thousands of dishes by hand, starting even as a young girl. Just before Mother's Day one year, my sister and I decided we had had enough and hinted to her that we wanted to get her an automatic dishwasher. Well, she let us know in no uncertain terms that she would have none of it, that she didn't need a dishwasher, and that it would be a waste of money.

Still, that didn't deter my sister and me, so we conspired behind her back to have the modern marvel secretly delivered and installed, so that she could not "send it back." And that's exactly what we did. It was a logistical challenge, because one of her favorite places was the kitchen, so we had to do some serious planning to keep her occupied while the mission was being accomplished. Although she "objected" when we finally presented the surprise to her, she eventually accepted it as inevitable, and we all benefited tremendously!

Although the preceding story may seem unrelated to what I'm about to report, I simply wanted to give equal time to both parents as I put both of their good deeds in perspective, "giving credit where credit is due." When it came to "the home," my mother was the boss; when it came to anything else, anything to do with maintenance outside the home, including cars and so on, Daddy was the man. Having lived in Crenshaw County nearly their whole lives, they had many "connections," and not only did this apply to friendships, it applied also to business. We never had strangers do anything around the house or the store. We personally knew everyone we did "business" with. And, I learned early on, you don't betray your friends.

So, that said, when I came back home, anytime I needed

maintenance on my car, or such as that, Daddy was quick to set it up for me. Just one less thing I'd have to worry about, I'm sure he thought. This was all very helpful when I decided to return to school (while living back at home) to work on my master's degree in counseling. School was 50 miles away from home, which meant an hour's commute time there and an hour back.

I suppose, as fate would have it, one of the times I was having my car serviced, I had to borrow Daddy's car, a nice late model Pontiac Bonneville. My classes were at night, usually from 6:00 to 10:00 P.M. I had never been a good "sleeper," and constantly had to battle falling asleep at the wheel, as this seemed to be the only thing that induced sleep for me! It must have been a particularly tiring day when I left for class. Already fatigued, I was looking for creative ways to stay awake, and decided to take the alternate ("scenic") route, as the four lanes tended to knock me out.

I was careening down a remote stretch on Highway 31, several miles from the I-65 interchange going into Montgomery. Fighting sleep, I could barely see the sign at a dark intersection indicating a less-traveled rural highway, Number 54.

And that's the last I remember until the increasing rumble of tires hitting loose gravel woke me just in time to see the mailbox I had hit fly over the windshield and hit the ground behind me. *Crap! What just happened? Did I just run over a mailbox?*

Incredibly, due to the speed of the car and the trajectory of the mailbox, there was virtually no damage to the Bonneville. Now fully awake—but a little too late to matter—I shook my head in disbelief as I tried to get my bearings. Apparently, the post holding the mailbox wasn't in very good shape anyway, and I saw only splinters as I got out of the car. The old house it belonged to was obviously still lived in, but after knocking on the door several times, I realized the occupants were not at home. I quickly scrawled a note with my phone number explaining what had happened and that, if they would allow me, I would repair the damage. I left the note on the door and hurried off to class.

I still hadn't heard from anyone by the next day, so I stopped at the hardware store and picked up materials for the repair, hoping I could catch someone at home when I got to the house. Having owned homes over the years, I had some experience as a handyman, including, fortunately, putting up mailboxes. So, with tools in hand, I headed back to Highway 31 to, hopefully, redeem myself.

The older, retired couple in the house were very nice and accepted my profuse apology, agreeing to let me put their mailbox back up. I convinced them that I knew what I was doing (although I wasn't sure myself) and began the two day job of repairing the damage. I set the post with cement, leaving it to dry overnight and returned the next day to secure the mailbox.

If I do say so myself, I did a pretty decent job, the completed project/mailbox actually looking better than the original decrepit one. Over the next several years, I had a chance to admire my handiwork every time I passed by the old house. I did fall asleep at the wheel a few times after that, but never as I approached Highway 54. As we used to say down home, "Good night! I hope you learned your lesson!"

Taking My "Deer" Sweet Time

One of the personal challenges I had after my divorce was to balance still being a father to my two daughters, classes, homework, work at The Triangle, and a semblance of a social life. Business at the time was pretty good at the store, which meant a steady stream of loyal customers, usually townspeople and families my folks and I had known all of our lives. It had been some time since I had lived there (actually about 25 years), however, and often I would meet people I didn't know at all.

I guess word got around that there was a new "eligible bachelor" in town, and soon I found myself "dating" again, albeit with trepidation. Call it vanity, or whatever, but I would often hint to my father that I needed his car (the Bonneville) to impress the ladies, as it was much newer and roomier than my tiny CRX. He was always happy to oblige, and in turn, I was always very careful to take care of his car and return it safely (especially since the mailbox mishap on Highway 31, noted above).

Ironically, through a friend of mine in Montgomery, I had met a young lady who worked in Montgomery but lived "down in the country" about a 20 minute drive from The Triangle. I found out that she commuted the hour's drive daily, so we eventually "connected" and got to know each other.

Jenny was an enigma of sorts, as she worked as an accountant/bookkeeper for a realtor's association and presented as the quintessential professional in that capacity. On the other hand, she was also basically a "country girl" and loved the rural life. She was a lover of horses and was as comfortable in jeans and boots as she was in a business suit. She was doing well "in life" and eventually planned to return to school to work on an accounting degree. However, her divorce had left her with two small children and dreams that seemed too far away. Her parents had helped her get a "cabin in the woods" not far from them, which allowed her to save money, keep expenses at a minimum and eventually realize her dream of finishing college.

I think one reason we "hit it off" was that I also had a rural background. The old saying, "You can take the boy out of the country, but you can't take the country out of the boy" definitely applied to me! But I also realized that I could never "make it" back on the farm. I loved to visit my "country" relatives and enjoyed the freedom of the great outdoors, but somehow, I couldn't see myself as an agri-businessman.

As a young boy, I had gone fishing and hunting, but I never was as good at it as I wanted to be. I even got a new "22 rifle" for Christmas one year, but being an animal lover, I couldn't bring myself to shoot anything with it! (I wouldn't let myself think about how we got hamburgers and fried chicken.) But I was aware that there was a phenomenon in the country called "deer season," which was that period of time allowed for legally shooting Bambi. It's still sometime between

November and February, I think, which, essentially, includes the coldest months of the year. I never knew if it was because of all the hunters shooting at deer, or just that deer like to roam around outside the woods during the cold weather, but it's not uncommon to see a lot of deer during this time. The problem being that cars and deer don't typically get along too well.

Although I didn't have to get up at the crack of dawn when I lived back at The Triangle, I still tried to get to bed at a decent hour. My classes were all at night, so naturally, I was up later than normal due to the hour long drive back from Montgomery. Jenny and I would usually get together on weekends when neither of us worked or had classes. In any case, neither of us were strangers to the "night life," but we still tried to be responsible, especially considering that both of her children were under the age of two. Consequently, we set midnight as our own "curfew," if you will.

I had just left Jenny's cabin one crisp November night (during deer season, remember?) and was anticipating the usual quiet drive home. Jenny's cabin was about a half mile into the woods at the end of a "dirt road," and I had turned onto the paved county road (known as the "Mt. Ida Road"), maintaining about 50 miles an hour on this rather "bright" moonlit night. It was times like these that made my hectic daytime schedule seem bearable, and life was good.

I was on the Mt. Ida Road, probably half way between Jenny's turn off and the main highway leading back into town, when I saw them over to my right. There were probably a dozen or more adult deer visible in the open pasture, slowly ambling toward the highway. Having seen the unpleasant results when, unexpectedly, deer meets motor vehicle, I instinctively let off the gas, intending to give the herd the right of way. Maybe it was the time of night, maybe the moon, maybe my fatigue, but it seemed that that herd and that Bonneville began to engage in their own surreal cat and mouse game. *I slowed down...the herd slowed down. I sped up...the herd sped up. Repeat...*

Determined to *not collide with Bambi*, I slowed to a crawl, and so did the herd. *O.K., I thought, shortly, I'm going to be in the middle of a herd of deer in the middle of the road. But I am not going to hit a deer!*

Still creeping, I watched the herd in slow motion cross in front of me. *One, two, three, fou...too many to count. Slow down. Too many... too close. Watch out!*

Miraculously, all the deer slowly galloped off the highway into the darkness of the woods to my left...*except* the last one. Out of the corner of my eye, I could see the glint in Bambi's eye, the moistness on her nose, the fog of her breath. Still moving ever so slowly, the Bonneville's grill is inches from Bambi's side. Seemingly oblivious of the car's presence until that moment, she suddenly stops, and at the precise moment that should have been impact, she slightly bends all four legs, springing straight up as the Bonneville (now barely moving) gently drives under her suspended body, nudging her legs, and laying her gently onto the hood of the car! Simultaneously, the car lurches to a complete stop, causing Bambi to slide effortlessly forward and off the hood, landing on all fours, and nimbly tiptoeing away with the rest of the herd!

I'm not sure how long I sat in the eerie glow, but I'm sure it was just long enough to close my gaping mouth and snap my mind back in gear as I contemplated what had just happened. To this day, I can honestly say, that was probably one of the strangest experiences I have ever had, and one that is totally impossible to explain or describe. Even decades later, it still seems unreal, and every time I hear an elderly person say, "Oh, dear," I'm tempted to respond, "You have no idea!"

David and Goliath

Although I favored a larger car when dating (get your mind out of the gutter; it's not for the reason you're thinking), I can't downplay the importance of the "tiny CRX" mentioned earlier. One thing that is significant to mention is that it was the last new car I ever bought. Made by Honda, the first time I heard about it was when Paul Harvey mentioned it on his radio program in early 1984 and noted that it would get an astounding 60 miles per gallon! It was new on the market, and I had just taken a job in Birmingham and needed something that would get good mileage due to my having to commute from Montgomery.

Another significant fact is that both of my daughters learned to drive in it. The manual transmission and its small size made it ideal for them, and I had always felt that, if you could drive a "stick," you could drive anything. And besides, it was actually fun, and a sharp looking little car at that.

But there were two dramatic incidents regarding the CRX that made an unforgettably indelible impression on me, making it impossible for me to appreciate any other car as much as this one. As I've stated often, I have never slept well, even after trying techniques, procedures, sleep studies, over the counter and prescription sleep aids, fad mattresses, and on and on. Nothing has ever helped to any appreciable degree, and I've pretty much learned to "live with it."

Interestingly, I don't seem to need as much sleep as I did when I was younger, and rarely "fall asleep at the wheel" as I used to. But there was one incident that literally "jolted" me into the importance of staying awake when driving. (I used to joke that I got my best sleep behind the wheel of a car, but unfortunately, it wouldn't last very long!)

The drive to Birmingham from Montgomery could be brutally boring, and during that era, I would try virtually anything to stay awake. Rolling the windows down in winter, turning the radio full blast, shaking my head violently, singing, screaming, rocking back and forth, and sometimes pulling over, if time permitted, for a short "power nap." All to no avail. Add to that, sometimes I would have tension headaches, or worse, the dreaded "cluster" headache. And sometimes, I would go to unconventional lengths to assuage the pain. Traditional OTC pills were worthless, but I did find something that helped. I never had a prescription for anxiolytics, but Andrea, occasionally took one, as needed, to "calm her nerves." And occasionally, she would have mercy on me and let me take one of hers for my headache.

Such was the case on that Thursday morning as I headed back

to Birmingham. My headache was kicking in, probably because I had gone to bed late and hadn't slept well the night before. So…this was a dilemma, because I was pretty sure a pill would take care of my headache, but it also tended to make me drowsy. A dangerous combination, I thought, but I figured I'd risk it because the pain was mounting. I just hoped I could stay awake.

The last thing I remember was seeing the 219 mile marker. The next thing I remember was being slung round and round, spinning out after leaving the road and finally coming to a stop in the median. I had just witnessed a miracle. Unfortunately, I had slept through most of it!

But now, here's the funny part. The radio station where I worked in Birmingham had a Honda repair shop that advertised with us, called Robe Mann. Because they were loyal advertisers and their shop was near the station, I would take my CRX in when it needed service. All the mechanics were great, and really friendly, amiable chaps. A few weeks or so after the spinout, I took the CRX in to get it serviced and was telling the guy about my near tragedy. He looked at me quizzically and asked about when did this happen, and where was I when it happened. I told him it was at the 219 mile marker several weeks ago. With a wide grin, he said, "Yeh, I saw that happen. I just happened to be passing by at the same time. I thought you were a goner!" I guess it just wasn't my time to go.

There was one other time that sleep overtook me, and again, it was on the interstate. This story is "out of sequence" but only to illustrate the immense power of sleep. It's interesting that two of only three cars I have ever had that were paid for are the very ones that seemed to be the most susceptible to the sleep monster. The CRX was one of them, and the other one was a sweet little 1995 manual transmission Ford Explorer, Sport model.

Later on, as my career as a licensed professional counselor progressed, I would occasionally get "contract" jobs to do evaluations on individuals for a number of reasons. One involved a sex offender evaluation on a teenage boy who was incarcerated in Opelika, Alabama, just east of Auburn.

The appointment had been set for 8:00 A.M., and my destination was about an hour away, so I was on the road by 6:30 just in case I got lost. Turns out, getting lost wasn't to be the problem. I was probably 20 miles from Opelika, when the Sandman decided to visit.

Here's the sequence of events: *Driving...alert...suspecting nothing...BAM!* My eyes flew open just in time to see the 18-wheeler I had sideswiped lumbering past me in the left lane. I have often wondered if I would have qualified for a diagnosis of narcolepsy back in those days, as I have no knowledge of "being sleepy," only awakening.

Apparently, I was dutifully traveling in the right lane and had dozed off, causing me to veer over into the left lane just as the big truck was passing me. I'm not sure the driver even knew what had happened. If he did, he didn't care to stop, and I didn't feel like chasing him down (this time...). I did pull over to survey the damage, which was quite extensive. The entire left side of the Explorer was scraped raw. The poor rearview mirror was hanging by a thread. If it hadn't been for the inconvenience, it would have been almost comical.

Apparently, the impact did something to the power window mechanism as well, because from then on, the window couldn't be raised. (Funny how, when something like this happens, the window never seems to get stuck "up." It's always down, leaving the window wide open.) Because the Explorer was paid for but not worth a lot of money, I didn't want to spend too much on repairs that weren't covered by insurance. I later made a cardboard template to fit the window and got some plexiglass at Home Depot, cut it to size and held it in place with Velcro. The only problem with this was when I went to the drive-thru at McDonald's, I had to open the door to get my order.

Anyway, getting back to the real story about the CRX (David) and its encounter with an 18-wheeler (Goliath). This time, it wasn't my fault. Honestly. This happened back before the spinout, about the time I hit the mailbox in the Bonneville. (It's a miracle I found any company that would insure me!) As noted earlier, I had a couple of alternate routes I would take when I was in graduate school. This route was the one that included I-65, the interstate that runs from Mobile, Alabama all the way to Chicago, Illinois. I was headed to class and had already been driving a good 45 minutes or so. I had just passed the exit to Highway 80 West, toward Selma. There was a light rain, but it was not a downpour, and manageable for traffic. I glanced in my rearview mirror to see if it was safe to pass the little slow red truck just ahead of me. I saw the 18-wheeler (later identified as a Ryder tractor pulling a Dollar General Store trailer) maybe a hundred yards or so back and figured I could make it with no problem. I switched on my left blinker and eased over into the lane to my left, making it around the little red truck without incident. This was the last intersection before the bypass where the traffic would obviously pick up, so I took a few seconds to breathe easy as I slowed back down to 50.

I'm estimating that I had been cruising for approximately half a minute when suddenly, *Bam!* The CRX shook violently and immediately pivoted 90 degrees to the left! Instinctively, my head jerked to the left and, to my horror, the 18-wheeler's grill on the other side of the window was no more than 10 to 12 inches from my face! My adrenaline level shot off the chart as I realized the giant machine was pushing me sideways down the interstate at 60 miles an hour! I was trapped on its front bumper with no way to escape and no power to control the CRX. I was literally at the truck's mercy and I was sure that, within seconds, it would be rolling over me. At times like these, I'm sure prayer becomes involuntary. I closed my eyes and waited for the inevitable.

What seemed like minutes, but was probably more like seconds, as soon as it began, it was over! Somehow, miraculously, the CRX was inexplicably flung free, but still spinning uncontrollably, it hit the median at full speed. The soft ground and slick grass were probably the only things that kept it from rolling over as it slid to a grinding and welcome halt. The truck zoomed past without missing a beat, and in spite of the spinning, the CRX had come to a stop facing in the same direction as it started! I watched helplessly as the rain and darkness swallowed the 18-wheeler, and it sped out of sight.

Suddenly, fear turned to rage, and to my amazement, I realized I had slammed my left foot down on the clutch, and the engine was still humming! Irrationality took over as I rammed the car into first gear and let out the clutch. The little beast started to whine with a mighty roar as the tires fought for traction on the wet grass. In seconds, the car lurched forward as the tires hit asphalt, and the chase was on! Increasing my speed, I hoped the CRX wouldn't fly apart as I leaned forward, squinting into the darkness. *What's that? Do I see lights? Yes! Dollar General!*

The accelerator is now through the floor as I zoom past the cab, frantically blinking the headlights and veering in front of the truck. I could hear the air brakes hiss behind me, as I pumped my right foot on the pedal. I rolled the window down and motioned for the driver to pull over. Total distance from impact to touchdown? I had no idea, but I knew I had succeeded in accomplishing the impossible! I had made it before we hit the "bypass traffic," which was a miracle in itself!

With both vehicles still steaming in the cool mist, I jumped out... expecting, I wasn't sure what. I was still lightheaded from the adrenaline drain, but whatever happened, I just wanted to let that driver know he couldn't "push me around" and get away with it!

I was actually surprised when he didn't protest my flagging him down. I don't think he meant to hit me, but incredibly, though, he denied any knowledge of the mishap and insisted that he didn't see me until, he said, "you did a 360 in front of me!" I could tell by his body language that he knew he wasn't fooling me with such an insane lie.

Of course, this was way before cell phones were a twinkle in Steve Jobs's eye, but I knew I had to somehow call the police. Fortunately, I could see the sleazy motel down the embankment from where we had stopped, so I told Bubba I was going to use their phone to call the police. He seemed to be just a hard working stiff trying to make an honest living, so I figured I could take him at this word when he said he would wait. I was sure he didn't want to have a "hit and run" on his record.

It didn't take long for the police to arrive (they were probably out and about anyway, what with all the rain). And sure enough, the officer determined that it was the trucker's fault by the damage and paint transfers on both vehicles. I wouldn't say we parted friends, but at least we weren't enemies. I didn't want to cause any trouble, but after all, I didn't ask for the accident. Soon, with insurance information in hand, we went our separate ways.

At the time the accident happened, the CRX already had right at 199,000 miles on the odometer. Fortunately, it wasn't "totaled" and I was rather attached to the little guy, so I opted to have it repaired rather than selling it for scrap. Although the settlement didn't cover anything except the obvious repairs, I decided to spend some of my own money and have the whole car repainted. I had always wanted a car with a sun roof, so to top it off (no pun intended), I decided to have one installed while it was in the shop. Oh, and while I'm at it, why not have the motor rebuilt?

The Overhaulin' crew would have been proud of me when I picked it up. It had been transformed from the standard factory navy blue and grey to a shiny jet black, with a smokin' hot sun roof and a motor that purred like a kitten. "Snazzy" wouldn't describe it, and I couldn't have been happier!

Eventually, though, after another 80,000 miles, I came to realize that it was just a matter of time before the CRX would become more and more of a liability. The young man who bought it was somewhat of a handyman and promised to take good care of it. I held back the tears until he drove it away, never to be seen again.

I know God saved my life that rainy night, and I know He's not offended when every time I hear the story of David and Goliath, I think of the last new car I ever bought and all the memories that went with it.

Like a scared Rabbit...

Although this story is not about hitting or getting hit, the story about my "little Volkswagen Cabriolet Rabbit diesel" begged to be included in this chapter. I did have a small "fender bender" in this car, but that part of the Rabbit's story is not very interesting. The Friday afternoon I left the radio station in Birmingham headed home to Montgomery for the weekend was not unlike any other commute I had made many times over the four and a half years I worked at WDJC in the 1980's. That is, until I stopped for "gas" at the Chevron in Vestavia before getting on the interstate. This Chevron was convenient, as it was near the exit/entrance in Vestavia where Highway 31 crosses I-65. And most importantly, they had diesel fuel.

Prior to this car, I had never owned a diesel automobile, so I had to get used to searching for a "filling station" that sold diesel. I had stopped at this particular station many times, so I was familiar with the configuration of the pumps, where the diesel pump was, etc. My point in stressing this is to state unequivocally that there is no way I would have made the "mistake" I was later accused of.

I usually tried to leave a little early on Fridays, since the time I had to spend with my family was precious, seeing as how I was able to come home only on Wednesday nights and on weekends. I had just filled up, gotten my receipt and pulled out onto Highway 31, taking the entrance ramp to I-65 South. I estimate that I had gone less than a half mile when suddenly the Rabbit died! No warning. No sputtering. Nothing. It. Just. Died.

Fortunately, nothing on the Rabbit was "power," and I was in the far right lane, so I was able to coast to the edge of the highway and "park" away from the dangerous speeding traffic. I've never known the first thing about cars, so I knew it would be fruitless to lift the hood. Although it was still fairly early, I didn't want to waste valuable time. I certainly didn't want to be walking on an interstate in Friday evening rush hour! I needed to take care of business while it was still daylight.

Waiting for a break in traffic, I hastily crossed the interstate and started the trek back to the Chevron, where I hoped I could get some help. If you're wondering why I didn't use my cell phone, well, there weren't any at that time. I was instinctively keeping my eye on traffic in both directions, and had walked probably halfway back to the exit when I noticed an older model Dodge just ahead with the hood up on the southbound side. There appeared to be a young man in his 30's looking under the hood. As I continued to walk back toward the exit, the young man began frantically waving to me! This seemed rather strange, and my initial reaction was to look away and ignore him. However, as I got closer I could hear him shouting! I guess it just seemed so bizarre that I stopped and peered in his direction, wondering what he expected me to do.

Incredibly, it looked like he was motioning for me to cross the interstate to where he was! Maybe it was divine intervention, or maybe sheer curiosity, but for some odd reason, I found myself running back across the highway, dodging traffic, simply to find out *what the heck...?*

I don't remember either one of us introducing ourselves, but "Bubba" started the conversation. "Hey, where ya headed?" Now I'm thinking, *Wha...I just risked my life running across the interstate, and this guy is asking me where I'm headed??*

"Well...uh...my car broke down," I stammered.

"I know, I saw you up ahead there git outta yer car," he replied. Apparently, I had passed him just before the Rabbit died and had pulled over, not realizing he was there until I saw him on my way back on foot. Immediately, I thought, *I wonder if this guy is mad at me for not stopping...and now he's going to rob me??* I started looking over my shoulder for a break in traffic, although he didn't really look dangerous. I was in pretty good shape, so I figured I could probably outrun him anyway.

"Did you run outta gas?" he asked. I figured if he was going to rob me, he probably wouldn't be asking me questions. I didn't see a gun or anything, and I'm starting to be amused by the whole thing. Still, I knew I didn't have time to waste.

"Uh, no, it just quit. I don't know what's wrong with it. I just filled it up so I know it's got gas." (I said gas, because I wasn't sure he knew what diesel was.)

Bubba then asked where I was going. I explained that I worked in Birmingham but lived in Montgomery, and I just needed to get my car back down there to find out what was wrong with it. All this time, I'm wondering why I'm even having this conversation with some stranger on the interstate who's obviously got the same problem I have.

What happened next shook me to my core, and I'll have to say, restored my faith in people. "Well, ain't that sump'm. I live in Montgomery too! I can gitcha down there!"

Still, I'm wondering if this is a con game, so I counter with, "But what about your car? I thought you were having car trouble too."

"Naw, it's awright. I's jist checkin' it, cause it was makin' this funny noise. I think it's OK though; it's been doin' it a while." He continued, "What I's gone say was, I got this rope in my trunk—it's a new one too. I can pull you down there!"

You can imagine my skepticism at this point, but I thought, *Well… if he's willing…*

However, although I was really eager to get home, I still wasn't sure this was a good idea. In fact, it seemed outlandish to say the least.

I heard myself ask, "Do you think it would work?"

With more confidence than I had, Bubba replied, "Well, yeh, I've done it before…a lot of times." Again, I thought to myself, *Yeh, I'll just bet you have!*

One last minor detail had to be addressed, and Bubba exuberantly explained how it was going to work. "All you gotta do is git in yo' car and steer it; jist keep the rope tight and don't run into the back uv me! Les go!"

I can still picture the scene, as we pulled out into (by this time) rush hour Birmingham traffic, headed home! And I still can't believe we actually made it. I'm guessing it was about two hours later when we pulled in to Powell's Automotive in Montgomery, ending probably the longest prayer I ever prayed! Although Bubba didn't want any money, I paid him for his trouble (and for his kindness) and I never saw or heard from my Good Samaritan again.

The good people at Powell's Automotive had been repairing my vehicles since I had moved to Montgomery. "Pearl" was the matriarch, diagnostician, and bookkeeper, while her husband led the team of expert mechanics, so I knew they would figure it out. Since it was late Friday night, and I had no "after hours" phone numbers, I simply left it and called Pearl first thing Monday morning to let her know what had happened. I trusted her and her team explicitly, but I was worried about the cost.

I received the call from Pearl before noon with what I thought would surely be bad news. "Mr. Moody," she began in her thick Southern drawl, "your car is ready. We just pumped 12 gallons of regular gas out of your diesel Rabbit." After I recovered from the shock, I asked her what the cost would be, and unhesitatingly, she replied, "Oh, I'm not gonna charge you for that."

And now...the rest of the story. I had used that same pump countless times over several months, and had never had any problems. For some reason, I remember exactly where I had placed my hand *on the diesel pump* as I was pumping it, so I am positive that I was not the responsible party. Despite my insistence that I did not "accidentally" pump regular gas out of the wrong tank, the manager denied any wrongdoing on Chevron's part. The only conclusion that makes any sense at all is that, somehow, someone was responsible for the wrong fuel (regular gas) being put into the wrong tank (the diesel tank).

My parents had sold "Standard Oil" (later Chevron) gas since buying The Triangle in 1947 (I still have the plaque from "Standard Oil Kentucky," presented to "Triangle Service Station") until we closed it after their deaths. I was actually a trainee with the Chevron Company in Birmingham in the early 1970's for a short time. But after the Rabbit incident, I've always been a little trepidatious when shopping at the Chevron station!

Boston... But...

Now, back to the Explorer. Upon graduation, both of my daughters decided to move far away. Crystal ended up in Phoenix, Arizona with my granddaughter, MaKayla, and Ashley moved to Boston. Ashley was a wonderful "auntie" and, although in a distant area of the country, was very close to MaKayla as she was growing up. We kept the "friendly skies" busy and would often fly MaKayla out to visit "Daybo" (the name she had given me), and we would then fly together to see Auntie Ashley.

MaKayla was nine years old in the summer of 2007 when she came for her annual visit to Daybo's. I had gotten tickets to fly to Boston the day after she arrived in Montgomery. It was sometimes difficult to make connections from Montgomery, so we usually would drive to Atlanta, then fly on to Boston. Our flight out of Atlanta was to depart around 7:00 P.M. Eastern time. It's almost a three hour drive, and we lose an hour, so we left Montgomery at 1:00 P.M. Central time, hoping to get to the airport a couple of hours before the flight.

Light rain was forecast, but we didn't see this as a problem. I do, however, need to point out a couple of other facts about the Explorer. By this time, it's already over 12 years old, and, well, you know, things wear out. Such was the case with the driver's side seat belt. And, please, no judgment here. You have to understand that I didn't grow up with seat belts, and I still struggle with whether cars really are any safer with them. So, when the latch started to malfunction shortly after I purchased it, I just never got it fixed. About this time, there had been this push going on to enforce the seatbelt laws though, and I certainly didn't want to get a ticket. ("Click it or ticket" the warnings on the billboards would read.) MaKayla was brought up in the seat belt era and never failed to tease me when we would go anywhere in the car, "Daybo...what do I have on that you don't...?" And I would obediently snap my seatbelt in place.

Still, I just didn't want to spend the money on something I wasn't sure was worth it anyway. So…I discovered that an expertly fashioned coat hanger would do the job of making it look as though the belt was fastened, thus preventing detection by law enforcement. It turned out this probably wasn't the smartest thing I ever did.

It was about 5:00 P.M. Eastern time as we approached the outskirts of Atlanta, and traffic was starting to pick up exiting the metro area. It had started to rain, but not heavily, and we were inbound, so traffic was moving fairly swiftly for us. Depending on the area, there are sometimes four to six lanes or more in either direction, and I was in the far right lane, traveling at about 50 to 55 miles an hour.

Feeling good about the time we had made, I wasn't in any particular hurry and was casually scanning the traffic patterns when I noticed a pickup truck across the median in the outbound lane start to fishtail on the wet pavement. Smug in my ability to handle any kind of driving situation, even in Atlanta traffic, I thought to myself, *"Boy, I sure am glad that's not me!"*

No sooner had the thought occurred to me than the Explorer started to weave back and forth! Within seconds, the SUV was thrashing from side to side, as I shouted to my granddaughter, "Hold on, MaKayla!" Of course, she had safely buckled herself in, so we both braced for the inevitable.

By now, the Explorer was on its own, violently lurching out of control. Certain that we were going to roll over, I prayed that MaKayla would be OK. The front end of the Explorer bounced off the guardrail and headed back into the traffic approaching from behind us. Back to the guardrail, once, twice, three times! *Both airbags deploy! Pow! Pow!*

Finally, the Explorer scrapes the guardrail one last time, screeching to a halt against the metal barrier. Breathing a sigh of relief, I turn to MaKayla. From behind the balloon, I hear her say, "I'm OK!" *Thank God! That was all I wanted to know!*

Pushing the air bags aside to assess the situation, I again turn toward MaKayla. "Daybo, you're hurt!" she screams, a pained expression on her face as she slaps her hand over her mouth. "No, I'm fine," I assure her.

As the reality of the situation sets in, MaKayla begins to cry, pointing in my direction. "Your…your…face…!" With the ebbing of adrenaline, I feel a stinging in my left eye, and I realize my vision is blurring. I quickly reach for the rear view mirror, but it's now gone. Surveying the inside of the car, I can barely detect the mirror dangling off the dash. I reach for it anyway. Although the frame is destroyed, the mirror itself is still intact. I suddenly realized why I couldn't see. Somehow, my left eye had sustained an injury, and immediately had formed a blood clot around it, causing it to completely close. *No wonder I can't see, I thought! I can't see…my eye…!*

Nevertheless, I assured MaKayla it was OK, that it looked worse than it was. (I wasn't sure, but I didn't want her to panic.) I began looking for my cell phone (the old "flip phone" Nokia), which had somehow disappeared in the melee. I told her to stay in the car, that I would see if I could flag down a motorist for assistance.

As I stepped out of the car into a steady downpour, I heard the splash as the Nokia fell out of the floorboard and into a convenient mud puddle! I quickly scooped it up and was attempting to dry it off when I saw flashing lights behind me and to my left.

I really believe that God has a sense of humor, and He had just proven it! He plopped my cell phone into the mud, then sent an ambulance to rescue us! Within seconds, two EMT's were at my side, reassuring me that we would be OK. They explained that they had just left after assisting at the scene of another accident. *Incredible timing! Thank You, Jesus!*

MaKayla was checked for injuries (she had none), but the precautionary brace was placed around her neck. Despite her protests, she was loaded onto a stretcher, and in the back we go! In no time, MaKayla and I were on the way to a local hospital, leaving the Explorer to fend for itself.

On the way, I borrowed a cell phone from one of the attendants to call a dear friend of mine who lived within five miles of where the accident happened. Alex had lived in Newnan for several years, and owned his own crown molding business in Atlanta. He was one of my best friends in high school, and we had kept in touch; fortunately I had his number in my pocket, along with my other important "black book" numbers.

The doctors at the hospital had determined that there was no damage to my eye, only heavy bruising from some sort of impact. I later discovered that, before the airbag deployed, the coat hanger gave way, sending the seat belt in a circular trajectory, first hitting the rear-view mirror, knocking it off the windshield, then striking my left eye. Mystery solved.

As a best friend should do, Alex had left immediately after I called and actually got to the hospital about the same time we did. He selflessly transported us to his home, where he and his wife, Jackie, fixed dinner for us and helped us contact the airport to reschedule our flight for the next morning. After a restful night, we had breakfast, and Alex drove us to the airport and offered to help me take care of the Explorer when we got back from Boston.

The towing company had picked up the Explorer in the meantime, and it was patiently waiting for us when we got back to Atlanta. However, when the owner of the salvage yard told me how much it would cost to fix—or to tow back to Montgomery, I decided that, even with insurance, it would probably be cheaper to just leave it there. And that's exactly what I did.

I've flown to *Boston* many times since then...*but* I no longer fly out of Atlanta.

CHAPTER SIXTEEN

THE GOVERNOR'S NIGHT OUT (WITH C'NELIA)

MOST PEOPLE I know haven't met a lot of famous people...and neither have I. However, in a previous chapter, I did share the story of my crossing paths with Kentucky Governor Happy Chandler. I've had other path crossing with many other wonderful people, and I would never place them on a lower par than the few "famous" people I have met. The former are countless in number. The latter are few, and most of those were unexpected (as was my meeting Happy Chandler). And so it was with George and Cornelia Wallace.

The first time I came face to face with Alabama Governor George Corley Wallace was on May 29, 1964 when he handed me my diploma upon graduation from Troy State College. Needless to say, I never got a chance to speak with him, but I was pleased to say that I had "met" him. I, officially, but this time very unexpectedly, met him almost seven and a half years later on October 24, 1971.

Andrea and I had just moved back to Alabama from Lexington, Kentucky in July 1971. As I noted earlier, the job I had hoped to start with the Jefferson County Board of Education a couple of months earlier had not worked out due to reasons beyond my control. I had been fortunate enough to get a night job "flipping burgers" (actually roast beef sandwiches) at Arby's in the Birmingham suburb of Vestavia Hills. Andrea's parents lived there and had been gracious enough to help us get settled in until I could find a "real" job.

I was nearing the end of my shift and was tasked with closing the store at 11:00 P.M. It was a Sunday night and business had been slow, and I was the only one working at the time. In fact, there were no customers, so I thought I'd start "straightening up" and be ready to hit the road home when my time was up. But, wouldn't you know, one more car was about to show up.

I saw the headlights as the big black luxury car turned into the parking lot. *Oh, great, I thought I'd get out of here early tonight,* I fumed. I regrouped in my mind, checking to make sure I had everything in place to make a couple more sandwiches.

The car seemed to be moving awfully slow, and I silently gritted my teeth, hoping that whoever it was would move faster once they got out of the car. I didn't want to appear rude, so I looked away, pretending to be busy.

When my customers entered, I greeted them almost before looking up. Suddenly, I felt flushed when, in an instant, I recognized my honored guests. In front of me stood the Governor of Alabama, George Corley Wallace and his lovely bride, Cornelia. George had been inaugurated for his second term as governor on January 18th, having married Cornelia exactly two weeks earlier on January 4th.

Just like ordinary folks, George ordered an Arby's Roast Beef sandwich and Cornelia asked for a vanilla shake. The gentleman with them, whom I assumed was their chauffeur/bodyguard, didn't order. Back in the day, when Arby's was a relatively new chain of stores, there were no tables in the restaurant. Instead, customers came in and ordered take out, or could elect to sit on a bench on the front wall facing the counter. The Wallaces seemed to be quite comfortable on the bench

(George served as a Circuit Judge back in the early 50's, so…) as I quickly prepared their order to "eat in."

The reason I remembered the date exactly was because October 24, 1971 was the day "Red" China (aka Communist China; aka the People's Republic of China) was officially admitted to the United Nations. I had never been fond of history, but Andrea and I had joined the John Birch Society when we lived in Kentucky and had learned a lot about the evolution of China. The Birch Society billed itself as an "educational army," which it definitely was, but it was also very conservative. Anyway, I have my own version of what happened and don't claim to be a history buff, but this is what I know. Apparently the "Republic of China" was a charter member of the United Nations when it was founded in 1945. But the subsequent civil war resulted in the establishment of the People's Republic of China on the mainland, prompting the original (non-communist) followers to flee to the island of Taiwan. Both governments believed they were the "official" China, and each side refused to accept "dual representation." Since the U.S. was opposed to communism, we sided with Taiwan, and therefore, the UN recognized only the government on Taiwan as the real deal. Much happened in the ensuing years, but then Richard Nixon decided to play ping pong with Red China, somehow rendering them more credible. Finally the United Nations General Assembly passed Resolution 2758, thereby recognizing the People's Republic of China as "the only legitimate representative of China to the United Nations," and expelling the representatives of Taiwan, headed by Chiang Kai-shek.

Now back to Arby's. I had followed George Wallace's career even during the two years we spent in Kentucky and knew him to be a staunch anti-communist and therefore very conservative. So I thought I'd ask him what he thought about the vote at the UN that day.

"So, Governor Wallace, what did you think about Red China being admitted to the UN today?" I asked, sounding quite intelligent and knowledgeable, if I do say so myself. I had heard that the governor had hearing problems and in fact had to wear hearing aids. He knew I was addressing him, but he couldn't quite make it out, so he asked his driver, "What did he say?"

The driver then repeated my question verbatim, and suddenly it was like a switch was turned on! Apparently he had been in Birmingham all day, and hadn't had an opportunity to express how he felt about the situation with China, but must have heard the vote was pending. The governor jumped up and began making a political speech about the evil United Nations, preaching to an audience of three right there in Arby's!

"Well, I'll tell you what I think! I think they oughta take the United Nations and throw it in the East River!" he shouted, flailing his arms and pacing back and forth, alternately balling his fist and pointing his finger skyward.

The speech lasted long enough for me to realize I had hit a nerve with the governor! Of course, nobody, including myself, got a word in edgewise once he got started. Somehow my guests managed to finish off their order, and when they finally left, I kicked myself for not getting their autographs. I guess I was too excited to think about it, or maybe I didn't think it would be appropriate. I mean, after all, how do you ask for somebody's autograph after he's just told you he wants to throw the United Nations into the East River? It seemed a little anticlimactic. All I have to say about it was when George announced for president again (for the third time) in 1972, he had definitely earned my vote!

You might think that's a great place to end this story. But, no, it picked up again on August 12, 1987. I was working at WDJC-FM, in Homewood (a suburb of Birmingham), having worked there in the 1970's, and returning in 1984 as Director of Station Operations. During my tenure there in the 80's, I was still living in Montgomery because my wife had a job teaching school there, and both of our children were in school there as well. I had found a place to stay in Homewood during the week , so I would drive up on Monday morning and come home on weekends.

Upon my return to work on the preceding Monday, I had read that Cornelia Wallace was in UAB (University of Alabama in Birmingham) Hospital. I thought about the opportunity for a couple of days, and on Wednesday, I decided to visit her.

I waited until rush hour traffic had thinned out and headed downtown. When I walked into the hospital, I figured that my chances of seeing a former First Lady of Alabama were not that good. So, with nothing to lose but a little time, I told the lady at the front desk I was there to visit Cornelia Wallace (she had kept the Wallace name after she and George signed papers for the divorce on their 7th anniversary, January 4, 1978). To my surprise she told me what room Cornelia was in and how to get there!

On the ride up in the elevator, I still had doubts that I would be able to see her, and I felt rather apprehensive as I approached the door to her room. Surely, I would be stopped by hospital staff, or perhaps a caretaker assigned to the First Lady.

A pleasant female voice resounded cheerfully after my knock, "Come in!" Still not believing my good fortune, I pushed the door open slowly, and there she was. Although it had been almost 16 years since that night in Arby's, and I knew Cornelia had been through a lot, I was somewhat taken aback by her appearance. (I suddenly flashed back to the image of Cornelia shielding her husband after Arthur Bremer's bullet smashed into the governor's body on May 15, 1972. Cornelia was only 33 years old at the time.) The former elegance had faded, and time had taken its toll on her, but her gracious and kind spirit was still evident. "Hello, come on in," she greeted me, as though I were an old friend.

Our conversation almost immediately took on a personal touch as she began asking about me and my family! Some 30 to 45 minutes later, I could tell Cornelia was getting tired, and I didn't want to "wear out my welcome," but when I told her I had to go, she seemed disappointed. I got the idea that she hadn't had many visitors, so I asked about the stack of books on the table beside her bed. I couldn't help but notice that the picture adorning the covers was of a much younger and beautiful First Lady. I quickly scanned the name above the picture: "C'NELIA" and at the bottom, which read, "An Intimate Self-Portrait…Cornelia Wallace," identifying it as her autobiography.

"Yes, I wrote this about my life and the experiences I've had. That picture on the back was taken right after George was shot in Laurel, MD when he was campaigning for president," she lamented, her eyes immediately becoming misty. It sort of choked me up too, and suddenly, I was at a loss for words. I think I stammered something like, "You were really brave to do that; it must have been horrible…"

Before we knew it, several more minutes had passed, with Cornelia recounting the event that changed everybody's life that day, then adding more intimate details of their life after George's paralysis. Although I could tell she wanted to tell me more, instead, she reached for a pen and offered to give me a signed copy of her book! I started to protest, but she insisted, so we reached a compromise. I agreed to accept the book, but only if she would accept a monetary gift from me that she could donate to her favorite charity. She agreed and wrote on the inside (in green ink to match the outside title) these heartfelt words: To my friends Mike and Andrea Moody, With all my good wishes for many years of happiness and "Joy" together—May all your problems be "small ones." She signed it "Yours in Christ, Cornelia Wallace 8/12/87."

Incredibly, Cornelia paid me a visit at WDJC when she was released from the hospital. She stayed a good part of the day, and unfortunately the day ended too soon, with me attending to my duties, but wanting to continue the trip down memory lane we had started just days earlier.

When I read of Cornelia's passing on January 8, 2009, I was deeply saddened, as much as if I had lost a dear friend. And I was once again reminded of a poem another friend had given me, which read in part,

It seems wherever I go
People come into my life or go out of it
Touching me where I can feel
Then leaving me only a memory
Like the gossamer fairy tales of children –
Leaving me,
And I wasn't finished knowing them…

CHAPTER SEVENTEEN

MOVING ON AND STARTING OVER

IT GOES WITHOUT saying that, no matter how it happens, divorce is not a pleasant experience. In whatever situation I find myself, I've always tried to take responsibility for my own actions and not blame others. That applies all the more to the failure of my marriages.

Suffice it to say (and I'm sure it's an understatement) that there were some significant changes in both of our lives, when Andrea and I divorced. I've had to be discreet in reporting certain events during that time *as I remember them*. My reporting of events may not necessarily be as they actually happened. I often use a "disclaimer" to protect myself, lest others believe my reporting such personal history that includes them is being represented as absolute fact.

Sharlie wasn't really what I had expected. But, then again, I'm not really sure what I was expecting. The best way I can describe Sharlie (short for "Charlotte") is that she seemed full of life. She was the friend of a friend who had previously "fixed me up" with another friend of hers some time back. Although that relationship hadn't worked out (I was the one who actually bowed out), I decided I had learned all there was to know about relationships (yeh, right!) and was ready to give it another go.

Sharlie was working at a local doctor's office, and my friend, Dawn (who also worked there) had arranged for us to have lunch. I was a little nervous (an understatement…) when I walked into the doctor's office and asked to see Sharlie. I guess she had been warned that I was there to pick her up, as she briskly walked out, and before I could tell her my name, she thrust her hand out and loudly proclaimed, "Hi, I'm Sharlie!"

They say you never get a second chance to make a good first impression. No second chance needed with Sharlie. She did all the right things, and within minutes, I was under her spell. Destination: Martin's, a local eatery not far from Sharlie's office.

Normally, I would be cautious about self-disclosure on a first date, but with Sharlie, it didn't feel like a first date. I was 48 years old and with far too many heartaches behind me. Still, before I realized it, I was reaching into my wallet to share my "personal philosophy statement" with her. This little paragraph was something I had written at probably the lowest point in my life. A mere five sentences, it summed up how I felt about what I thought I had learned about myself once I stopped blaming others for my own shortcomings.

Something must have struck a chord, as I saw Sharlie's eyes glisten with tears. The next several seconds, we communicated without speaking, and I suddenly felt closer to Sharlie than I had felt with anyone in a very long time.

Our next date was dinner at a remote out-of-the-way country café called Red's Little Schoolhouse, which was actually converted from a genuine, ancient one room schoolhouse from years gone by. Although Sharlie's home town was Mobile, Alabama, she fancied herself a country girl, and, in fact, had lived on a small farm she and her previous husband of 24 years had bought in rural Elmore County.

I wanted to surprise her, and I thought Red's would be the perfect place to get to know Sharlie better. She later told me she had started to get a little worried after about 40 minutes of driving down a dark country road with an almost total stranger! To make matters worse, there had apparently been a "gully-washing" thunderstorm the day before that had washed out a bridge just a few miles from our destination. We had to take a detour which took us an additional 20 to 25 minutes. Since I wasn't that familiar with the area myself, I didn't tell her then, but I was starting to get a little worried too!

We finally made it, and after the initial setback, the night was fabulous. We had gotten there a little late, and most of the customers had left, leaving us with the place almost all to ourselves. Lost in our discovery of each other, we didn't know how late it was until they brought out the mop bucket. We took the hint and reluctantly headed home, agreeing to see each other again very soon.

And thus began a deep relationship, full of new discoveries, new adventures, and plans for the future we both had dared not hope for. My parents had been married 53 years, their marriage cut short only due to the passing of both within eight months of each other. I had always wanted to live to see my own Golden Wedding anniversary, and after only a few weeks, I started to believe that Sharlie would be the one to help me fulfill my dream.

Life was good as we shared our dreams for the future and, after several months, started planning our wedding. I had been single for almost six years, and I felt I had learned enough to get it right this time. Having spent most of her married life being a devoted wife and mother, Sharlie had always wanted to travel but never seemed to find the time. I enjoyed going on short trips, but "traveling" wasn't really something I relished. I didn't mind being somewhere new; I just didn't like taking the time to get there! During our "engagement," we took many trips on weekends, rushing to get back to start the work week on Monday. We would sometimes take a couple of extra days here and there to travel to faraway places like the Grand Canyon, which for many years, both of us had wanted to see.

It's probably not a positive thing that I have always thought of myself as a "hopeless romantic," as I tend to have difficulty with the reality of serious matters...like marriage. Once Sharlie and I had decided to make it official, I thought it would be fun to officially propose to her in a way that she would never forget. I enlisted my children to help me with the scheme.

I would invite Sharlie over for breakfast. The plan was to tell her that we would have all the trimmings, including grits, eggs, bacon, sausage, pancakes, toast and jelly, coffee, orange juice, the works. I knew she wouldn't be able to resist, because she liked that kind of Southern "country" breakfast. I had figured out how to use my Dremel to meticulously cut the end off of one of the eggs just big enough to drop in the fake diamond engagement ring. Then I would place the end back on and plaster it back together with white putty to match the eggshell, thus sealing the ring inside the egg. The final product looked great, and the repair job was almost undetectable.

On the designated day, Sharlie was to "help" prepare the eggs while my daughter, Ashley recorded the festivities with a camcorder that I had "inherited" from my Dad.

All seemed to be going as planned until I handed Sharlie the third egg (the "loaded" one) to crack. Apparently, with all of the goings-on, Sharlie became momentarily distracted and looked away as she plopped the egg's contents (including the ring) into the bowl for scrambling. *Flop, slush.* Ashley, the videographer, immediately realized that the ring had sunk to the bottom of the bowl, undetected by the bride-to-be! At which point, I stepped in to save the day and, peering into the bowl, exclaimed, "Oh...wait... what was that?" Sharlie was oblivious and wondered why I was asking such a stupid question. "What was what?" she asked, reaching for the next egg. It was obvious that the plan had failed, but continuing the charade, I reached into the bowl, swishing my finger around, trying to fish out the missing ring, so the "surprise" breakfast wouldn't be a total loss.

With Sharlie still having no clue, I triumphantly retrieved and held aloft the egg-drenched ring. "What…is…this…?" I queried, trying to sound incredulous. Slowly, it dawned on Sharlie that "something" had just happened, although she was not sure what. It was sort of like, you know, one of those times when you've just told a joke and nobody gets it, and you have to explain it? Somehow, it just doesn't have the same impact. But at least we recorded it, and we could get a big laugh out of it anyway, right? Well…not exactly. To top it all off, when we attempted to play the video back, Ashley realized she hadn't pressed the record button! So much for well-laid plans.

Anyway, back to the more serious matter of the marriage itself. Sharlie had managed to save some money from her divorce and had bought her own house in a new development within walking distance of mine. After setting the date for the wedding, we started rearranging our lives to accommodate the merger of our families. Although Sharlie loved her new house, I convinced her to sell it and move into mine. I reasoned that her house would be easier to sell and probably also bring more money. In retrospect, this was probably not in Sharlie's best interest, but the good news is that her house sold almost immediately, and at a nice profit. With this nest egg, plus funds from her divorce settlement, and a small retirement she got from her former employer, things were looking good for her.

However, things were not boding that well for me in the finance department. Unlike Sharlie, I had the opposite experience with my divorce and had emerged from it all alone, depressed and deep in debt. One reason for this was because I didn't have a lawyer to represent me in the divorce, and had agreed to let Andrea have everything just to "settle" and be done with it. Plus, I had agreed to not only child support but alimony as well. I didn't know that I was not "required" to pay alimony, but I did know that there was no way I would not provide for my children. Much of this was simply guilt I felt over the divorce in the first place. Every attorney I saw had told me that the provisions of the original divorce decree were "written in stone" and couldn't be changed, even to the custody of my children.

I had seen a half dozen lawyers before I found one who assured me that I could get custody. I was told, however, that it would cost me dearly. And the attorney wasn't referring to money. My children would have to testify against their own mother, I was told, to prove that she was unfit and in order for me to convince a judge that I was the "better" parent.

I was very disturbed at having to do it this way. I'm sure I wasn't too different than most people in divorce situations; I just wanted primary custody so that my children could live with me and not just have "visitation." Because of the provisions in the divorce, I had been paying out everything I was earning in salary to keep up with child support, alimony, and my own living expenses (and they were legion). I had had to move back in with my parents in Luverne, so I felt it was really important for me to move back to Montgomery to be near my children. Even though I knew it would be hard for my parents, I had asked them to help me with a down payment on a house in Montgomery.

Fortunately, our respective lawyers reached an agreement the night before our court date, at which our children were going to be asked to take the stand against their mother. The terms were horrendously unfavorable for me financially, but the only thing that mattered was that I would gain custody, and the children would not have to testify. In addition, I had to agree to pay Andrea a lump sum of $10,000-plus in alimony, as well as release her from any future child support payments to me. By this time, I had a "steady job," having finished my master's degree, and somehow, I managed to borrow enough money to comply with the final divorce decree.

My older daughter, Ashley, was already working and "finding her way" by the time Sharlie and I decided to get married. But, unfortunately for my younger daughter, Crystal, who was in the middle of her teen years, I spent a lot of time away from her and, frankly, was not there for her many times when she needed me. This became a bone of contention in my relationship with Sharlie, because she couldn't understand why I would be so preoccupied with Crystal at times. Her two daughters were older and on their own, so they didn't need to be "looked after" as much as Crystal did.

So, this was the "excess baggage" I would be carrying into my second marriage. Sharlie seemed to understand initially, but she would often insist that we take "trips" to various places when possible. There was one thing I had always wanted to experience (it was on my "bucket list" before the term became part of the vernacular), and that was to go hang gliding. I had told Sharlie this on more than one occasion, and at one point in our courtship, while I was at work, Sharlie sent me a fax that totally convinced me she was "the one." It was a picture of someone hang gliding over a beautiful mountainous ravine. Below it, she had written, "I will if you will." We eventually went twice to Tennessee, jumping off a 2200 foot cliff the first time, and several months later, being cut loose from a tether being pulled by a boat, then hang gliding down into the river. The view was fantastic and the thrill indescribable!

Sharlie had a similar item on her bucket list, which was to go up in a hot-air balloon. We had actually done this once and were immediately hooked on the fun! So, in preparation for our marriage, we started looking around for someone to take us up on our wedding day. Since most of the "rentable" balloons were equipped to carry only four people, we had the idea to have the ceremony in the balloon as we soared over the countryside! It would be perfect, we figured, with the two of us, the "pilot" of the balloon, and the preacher to administer the vows! A marriage literally "made in heaven."

So, with approximately 40 special guests, friends and relatives invited, on that cold day in January 1994, Sharlie and I headed for the launch site. We had researched enough to know that conditions had to be just right for liftoff. One hard and fast rule, of course, was that the weather had to cooperate.

As we neared the open field, most of our guests had already arrived, and we could see the balloon beginning to inflate! With hearts pounding and excitement mounting, we drove closer, only to realize that the ominous clouds that had earlier been evident, were now becoming a threat...and a dangerous one, at that.

Although we had a "Plan B" in place, we had hoped we wouldn't have to resort to it. As the wait grew longer, it became obvious that our dream wedding was not to be. We salvaged the day by forming a caravan back to my house and having the ceremony in our living room. This worked out fine, because we had arranged to go back there anyway after the actual wedding in the balloon.

Although neither of us wanted to admit it, both Sharlie and I had started to sense tension between us in the weeks prior to the actual date, but we chalked it up to normal pre-marriage jitters. Just before the preacher started his recitation, Sharlie asked me if I was sure I wanted to go through with it. (I think this was her way of saying that she was having second thoughts as well.) Of course, I reassured her that I had every intention of marrying her, and that we would live happily ever after.

We divorced less than five years later.

I could write another book about what went wrong, but it would be simply an exercise in Monday morning quarterbacking. The short version would include a couple of pertinent points, however.

For one thing, Sharlie had gotten past the raising of children, and the adjustment to having a dependent child at home was just too hard for her to handle. This was extremely difficult for her and proved to be a major factor in our separation. I felt torn between having to choose either her or my children.

Also, I believe we both had a problem communicating with each other. Sharlie and I both had read a book during our engagement called The Five Love Languages, a sort of self-help book on relationships. I had determined that my love language was "Words of Affirmation." Essentially, according to author Gary Chapman, a person (let's say, the husband) who tends to speak in his own love language (words of affirmation) feels loved when the other person (the wife) "affirms" her love by letting her husband know verbally, in a myriad of ways, how great he is. In other words, if someone compliments me, tells me I look great, or that I'm doing a good job, or that I'm appreciated for doing something for my partner, *I feel loved.*

Sharlie's love language was "Quality Time." Theoretically, she felt loved if I took time to go on trips with her, or spend more time with her at other times. And I felt loved if she told me how great I was. But, in reality, I was always making excuses for not taking time to be with her because I was constantly working, trying to keep my head above water. I had even told her that I would be OK with her taking trips without me, since I couldn't afford to "pay my way." But each time, she would offer to pay expenses because it wasn't as much about the trip as it was spending time with me.

Conversely, when I complimented her (which was easy to do because she was a beautiful woman), it didn't seem genuine. By this time she had started working for an office of plastic surgeons, who had done some excellent work on her (not that she needed it, in my opinion), and she was constantly being told how beautiful she was and what a gorgeous figure she had. So, being told repeatedly by her husband just didn't seem to have an impact. She just wanted me to spend time with her so she could feel loved. In a strange sort of way, it reminded me of O. Henry's short story "The Gift of the Magi."

Many other elements came into play, such as the wreck Sharlie had shortly after we got married. And then there was the criminal who tricked us into spending several thousand dollars (of Sharlie's money) to add an extra bedroom onto my house and then "took the money and ran." It was only after our divorce that we finally brought him to justice, but clearly it took its toll on our marriage. I still don't have all of the answers regarding the failure of our marriage, but I have tried to accept responsibility for my part in it. I only hoped that we didn't hurt each other too badly and that we learned something that left us having more positive memories than negative ones.

I really enjoyed the hang gliding.

CHAPTER EIGHTEEN

LIFE IN A FAIRY TALE

AFTER EARNING MY master's degree in counseling and human development at the ripe old age of 47, I didn't realize how much I didn't know. I had made it through two marriages and subsequent divorces, several jobs, far too many dead end relationships, and now I was going to be a counselor and help other people with their problems?

Nevertheless, I thought I had all the tools I needed to get started in my new career. Without listing my entire Curriculum Vitae, I think it would be safe to say that I did have to change jobs a few times to finally settle on something that fit for me. In addition to a full time job, I would sometimes also work part-time jobs at night and/or weekends. One of those part time jobs was with the Pre-Trial Diversion Program under the auspice of the Montgomery County District Attorney's office.

The idea behind the program was, in a sense, two-fold. First, it was to deal with first-time felony offenders in a legal sense. And secondly, it was to give those law-breakers a "break" by allowing them to participate in group therapy, to learn about themselves and their behavior, and if completed fully, to have the offense stricken from their records. The program has been highly successful, with a very low recidivism rate.

I had already done several "groups," to include substance abuse, domestic violence, and sexual offending. I had also worked full time as a counselor at Kilby Correctional Facility, and when I accepted the position with Pre-Trial, I was working as a guidance counselor at an elementary school in Pike County. A fellow counselor and friend of mine had put in a good word for me, and I already knew Pat, the director of the program, from graduate school. So, I figured this would be an opportunity for me to broaden my experience.

As the weeks went by, I learned a lot of new techniques in dealing with people from all walks of life. A typical group consisted of around 15 to 20 men and women sitting in a circle, with normally a male and a female "co-facilitator" who kept the members of the group on track. One night, Pat introduced the group I was co-facilitating to a new idea. The group participants were asked to write their own "fairy tale" in order to gain understanding of how their past may have somehow influenced their errant (and in this case, criminal) behavior. The facilitators were encouraged to also write their own fairy tale to share with the group. The idea was to (1) get experience from the offender's perspective and (2) to give the facilitator/counselor an opportunity to deal with their own personal issues.

At first, I was skeptical that this was just another Freudian "touchy-feely" ploy to get the group to "open up." Nevertheless, I thought it couldn't hurt, and maybe it would help me with some of my own "inner child" issues.

The assignment was to be completed by the next week's session to be presented to the group. I had always justified my procrastination tendencies by telling myself (and others) that I work really well under pressure. In keeping with this affliction, I had put off getting the assignment done until the last day. It was a Thursday afternoon with the group coming up that night as I forced myself to sit down and seriously think about my "fairy tale." Although I knew basically what a fairy tale was, just to gain insight, I had looked up the definition to get going on the project. The definition I was most comfortable with was "…a story in which improbable events lead to a happy ending." I could live with this, but I thought, *how could I make it apply to my own life?*

I began to analyze the elements of a fairy tale and realized that the ones I had read as a child and read to my children consisted of both truth and fiction. Then I thought of it from my own personal view, and because it is a fairy tale and my life was still in transition, I could leave it "open-ended" and go back and change it any time I wanted to.

Suddenly, I found myself in time warp mode as my mind flashed back to stories I had heard over the years, experiences I had had, and dreams I had hoped for. Thirty minutes later, I was holding in my hand what I called…

THE DRAGON SLAYER
A fairy tale by Mike Moody

Once upon a time long ago, there was a beautiful young peasant girl who lived on a small farm outside a little village far, far away. The beautiful young girl's days were spent cleaning the little cottage, doing chores, taking care of her elderly father, and preparing meals for her two younger brothers who worked the land and provided food for the family. The young girl's mother had always told her that her mission in life was to take care of the men in her life, and never to question why.

As the years passed, the young girl grew into a beautiful woman. She dreamed of someday having a cottage of her own, with children, and enough food to eat. One day, a dashing, handsome, young prince came from a nearby country and asked her to go away with him. They would start a new life together, he told her, and they would live happily ever after. Although she was not particularly unhappy, this sounded really good to the beautiful young woman, and the handsome prince was very persuasive and charming. She'd never known anyone like him before, and he seemed to really care about her. Finally, she bid farewell to her family and set out with the handsome prince to start a new life as a princess.

As time went by, however, the young woman learned that her handsome prince had entered into an agreement with the evil king in exchange for their good life. The prince had agreed that, for as long as he lived, he would be forced to fight and, if possible, slay as many dragons as the king saw fit to send his way. The land was full of vicious dragons, and the prince never knew when he would be called away to fight them. At first, there would be a dragon only once in a while, and the prince was able to spend time with his beautiful princess and their little family, which now consisted of two children—a boy and a girl. In time, the princess came to realize that times were never as good as she had been promised, but this didn't really bother her because, for her, times had always been hard. Still, the dragons were beginning to come more and more often, so the handsome prince was beginning to spend less and less time with his little family.

Sometimes he'd be gone all day, sometimes all night, fighting the dragons. Sometimes he wouldn't come home at all. One night, the handsome prince was attacked by a vicious dragon and almost killed. When the prince's little boy was told what had happened to his father, he was very upset, and couldn't understand why his father had to spend all his time fighting dragons. And it never occurred to him that his father would ever be injured in such a way. That's when he decided he would have to learn to be a dragon slayer too, to protect his mother and sister, and now his father from the evil dragons. He vowed then and there that no dragons would ever hurt his family again.

It took many years for the little boy's father to recover from his injuries. In fact, the boy found out later that the dragon had given his father a terrible disease that could eventually kill him. But even worse, before death came, the disease would turn his father into a dragon himself. The boy knew that, if he were not careful, it could spread through the whole family, making dragons out of them all. Fearing he might eventually have to fight his own father, he left home, never to return, and grew up spending most of his time fighting and slaying dragons as his father had.

Much later, the boy, now grown had become a prince himself; he received word that an extremely vicious and ruthless dragon had slain his beloved mother, and in grief, his father had fallen on his sword and taken his own life. Although the young man had devoted a good portion of his life to fighting and slaying dragons himself, he was not a very good dragon slayer. And, even though he had once met a damsel in distress, and rescued her from a dragon and taken her to be his princess, dragons were coming around more and more often. As time went by, they seemed to be bigger and stronger, and the man was becoming weak and discouraged with his failure to slay the many and varied dragons that came his way. So, in desperation, he sent his damsel and children away, and continued his lifelong quest of dragon slaying, as it was all he really knew how to do.

Consumed with his quest, and nearly defeated, one day after an arduous and hard-fought battle, the smoke began to clear, and he saw something he'd never seen before. He had rescued many other damsels in distress, and saved them from dragons, but in the clearing in the forest, he saw the most beautiful woman he had ever seen. Why, if he didn't know better, he'd have thought she was a dragon slayer too. But that's impossible, he thought, women are to be rescued, not be dragon slayers themselves. Somehow though, this woman was different:

eyes that looked into his soul, eyes like fire, yet warm; her hair, flowing and soft. Her fragrance was sweet, yet full of spice. Her lips were like a cool welcome rain after a hard day of dragon slaying.

As their eyes met, they both knew that somehow their quest was over. No more lonely nights slaying dragons, and coming home to an empty castle. Together, they would be no match for the evil vicious dragons. Because now, facing them together, there are no dragons....and no need for dragon slayers.

The End

I leave it to the reader to not only "interpret" this fairy tale, but to write his or her own, if only for therapeutic purposes. You might be surprised what you discover.

CHAPTER NINETEEN

JANICE'S LESSON
("THE GIRL FROM GRENADA")

THEY SAY THERE'S nothing like a relaxing cruise to a faraway place to refresh and regroup, to "recover," if you will, from life's stresses and pressures.

I'd heard of these mysterious journeys on huge ships, and had even seen the 1997 blockbuster "Titanic," starring Leonardo DiCaprio and Kate Winslet, making the idea of taking a cruise on such a vessel even more appealing. I found out later, on a trip to North Carolina, that George Vanderbilt, creator of the Biltmore Estate in Asheville had been booked with his family on Titanic's maiden voyage in 1912. However, just a week before Titanic set sail, the Vanderbilts altered their plans, taking another ship, Olympic, instead. George and his wife, Edith and their daughter, Cornelia, had spent the winter in Paris and were eager to get back to Biltmore. Mrs. Vanderbilt explained the change to Mrs. Emily Skeel in a letter on November 21, 1912: "For no reason whatsoever we decided to sail on the Olympic & had only 18 hours to get ready in. We were homesick, & simply felt we must get home,

& changed our ship, as I say, at the Eleventh hour!" The Vanderbilts reached New York on April 10, traveling by train to Biltmore, and soon learned the shocking news that Titanic had struck an iceberg, sinking within three hours and taking the lives of more than 1,500 people.

It might have made me a little more reticent to take the cruise if I had known these details beforehand. I had been in a relationship with Reba since meeting her at the Probate Office while purchasing a tag for my motorcycle. We had later taken several day trips and weekend trips on my "Yamaharley," something neither of us had ever done. So, when Reba got a call from her sister, Emily, telling her about a cruise we might be interested in, we got excited. Emily needed some CEU's to maintain her RN license, and Carnival Cruise Lines was offering them on a five-day cruise to Cozumel, Mexico. Emily could get a better deal if she could get another couple to accompany her and her husband, Jeff, so we were the logical draftees. And, besides, it sounded like a good deal (around $400, plus a few extras and whatever you wanted to spend for gifts and souvenirs). "Sail" date was Thursday, April 29, 2010, returning to the port of Mobile on Monday, May 2nd.

However, after booking the cruise, Reba began to have second thoughts. Could she really take the time? She had been her parents' "caretaker" for many years, and they had grown more and more dependent on her the past few years. Understandably, she just wasn't sure she could risk leaving them alone at that time. Her decision came at virtually the last minute. It just wasn't meant to be. Of course, I was disappointed, as I hadn't had any appreciable time off from my job as a licensed professional counselor in over five years, so Reba encouraged me to go anyway. At least I could keep Emily and Jeff company, and it would be fun to just enjoy doing something new. I was determined to make the best of it.

As soon as we set sail, I spent most of my time early on finding my way around the ship. The dining room(s) were my first discoveries, and then, the bedroom (which was actually a small box with a porthole!). On the advice of friends and family, I had been prepared to take my camera and "get lots of pictures." Being totally on my own most of the time, I decided, just for fun, I'd see how many other passengers I could have my picture made with. I'd never been much of a casino gambler, so that was out. And having had a short bout with skin cancer, I wasn't too keen on getting a lot of sun. Plus, my alcoholic father had turned me totally against alcohol of any kind, so I wasn't going to do any drinking. This cut my options down substantially on a cruise ship, so I figured this would be something harmless I could do—and stay out of trouble at the same time. Thus began my quest for "pictures." By the third day or so (including the foray to downtown Cozumel), I had found several willing passengers—actually mostly ladies—to help me with my "photo-quest."

It seems that everybody on a cruise ship is really friendly, probably because most of them are uninhibited due to alcohol, and knowing they most likely won't see the people they meet ever again.

On one of my forays, I stumbled into one of the many "watering holes" on the ship called Cleopatra's Lounge. And that's where I caught Janice's eye. She was seated at the bar and had obviously been drinking adult beverages. She was quite attractive, and I surmised, the classic picture of a cruise ship sophisticate. I soon found out that she was a true Southern Belle from Grenada, Mississippi. I'd never really been a shy person (especially after my "first kiss" in high school!), but as I approached Janice, I felt suddenly uneasy, probably because I had become comfortable with Reba, and hadn't really talked to "another woman" in quite some time. I desperately hoped my (redneck) "roots" wouldn't show as I groped for words. I mean, honestly, I just wanted to get a picture anyway. It wasn't like I was trying to hit on her, I thought.

Sensing my awkwardness, Janice's eyes again met mine as I stammered, "I...I wondered if...if you could...uh...help me." (Not how I pictured it sounding.) My fears were allayed by Janice's friendly—dare I say—sultry response.

"Why, sure, Honey, what is it?"

"Well, you see, I, uh, I have this, uh, bet with the people at work that I could have my picture made with 20 beautiful women...so, can you...I mean, would you...let me...if I could get somebody to take my picture with you?" (That wasn't how I pictured it, either!) I was sure she picked up on the clumsiness, but I was just hoping she wouldn't think I was some sort of pervert!

"Well, sure, where do you want to do it?" I felt her alcohol-induced unsteadiness as she grabbed my arm for support.

"What about right here?" I asked.

"I think this is so cute! Let's do it up here!" Janice headed for one of the "stages" in Cleopatra's, with me in tow, as she hailed her friend, Rita, on the way. "Hey, Rita, this guy wants to take his picture with me. Come 'ere and take our picture!"

Suddenly we were on display, flashbulbs flashing. Before it was over, Janice had talked two other attractive ladies into having their pictures made with me too—and several at that—complete with hugs and squeezes, cheek to cheek! In no time, the assignment was completed. Now on her own quest, Janice seated me at the bar and began her story.

Janice and her husband had been married 27 years—well over half of her life—but, tragically, dreaded colon cancer had snuffed out Steve's life three years ago. Although smiling with her lips as she took another drink, her misty eyes betrayed her. "I don't care if I live or not," she blurted. Then silence, while her words, like a sedative, took effect. "I can't picture my life without him..."

So, here she was, a lonely beautiful woman, in a room full of people engaged in contrived merriment fueled by atmosphere and Demon Rum, sharing her misery with a total stranger. For the next several minutes, Janice conducted her own "therapy," leading me through her life as she had once known it. As the drinks continued to take their toll, Janice directed her attention to the stranger who simply wanted to have his picture made with her. "So...what about you?"

Not wanting our therapy session to end so abruptly, I pressed Janice for more details about herself, and where she would like to go from here. Still sparkling with tears, her eyes again met mine. I suddenly felt a good warmness as Janice's misty but deep gaze transformed counselor into counselee. She slowly took my hand and murmured, "I just want to be happy. Thank you for listening. I'm glad we met. Can we be friends?"

"I'd like that. Maybe we could…" Janice's lips were soft and sweet as her gossamer kiss cut my sentence short. It was totally unexpected, and for a couple of seconds, I wasn't sure if it had really happened. It was only Janice's firm grip on my arm that kept me from falling off my stool!

"I'd like that too," she purred.

The next morning, I discovered her email address in my pocket, and only the memory of "the girl from Grenada."

Although I did email her, just to thank her for sharing her story with me, I never saw or heard from Janice again after her acknowledgment of my email. But she did teach me a valuable lesson. I worded it this way: "Never miss a chance at having your life changed by a stranger with a story to tell."

CHAPTER TWENTY

CELEBRATING "STEWARDESS-SHIP"

It appeared to be one of those routine flights to visit my daughter in Boston on a warm August morning. For some reason, I had chosen to fly out of Birmingham instead of Montgomery, probably because of the timing of flights. And, no, this is not going to be another one of those edge-of-your-seat airline stories where the hero saves the lives of 280 passengers and makes the Today Show the next morning. This one might not be as exciting or suspenseful, but I think it is much more meaningful.

Anyone who has flown much over the years has seen tremendous changes in ticketing, boarding procedures, airline amenities, and even passengers themselves. And whether we realize it or not, we "look" for things and worry about things when we go to the airport. For example, no matter how many times I've flown, I still can't remember the rule about nail clippers (size, blade sharpness, chrome, lead or zinc material, or whether it has a file attached). So, on this particular trip, I decided to simply live dangerously and not worry about *anything*. Or at least focus on more important issues, such as whether I had used enough of the after shave spray to finally make it under the 1.75 ounces to get through the check point without having to spend the night in jail, charged with suspected terrorism. While running the risk of being labeled xenophobic or racist or paranoid, I have often wondered why, for the safety of all flyers (except terrorists), we don't "profile" at airports.

First of all, let me state unequivocally that I believe in as much freedom as possible for every person. But that applies only at airports where I might run into somebody who wants to attack, or worse, murder me. Let's say, for example, that I am a frequent flyer (and I would probably be considered so). And let's assume further that, periodically, a dog will come into the airport and savagely attack unsuspecting passengers. And let's go even further and assume that this has happened countless times. Let's say that these attacks are never done by cats or elephants or zebras, or any other animal on earth. Just dogs.

Now, here's my question. Wouldn't it make sense to figure out some way to restrict dogs in airports, or at least require they be muzzled or placed in cages before entering the facility? Of course, it would make perfect sense to do that. But "authorities" at the airport keep telling us that there is no way to distinguish dogs from humans. I disagree. With modern technology, we can do amazing things.

By now, you've probably figured out that the point I'm trying to make is not about dogs. It is, however, about a particular "breed" of human being who, 99% of the time, is the breed that likes to shoot and blow up other breeds of people in the name of their "god." It's more than likely not going to be a Caucasian Granny in a wheelchair.

You see, I'm the vice-mayor of "Realville." Some who read this will know where (or what) Realville is (and why I'm the vice-mayor and not the mayor). A very prominent talk radio talker has been bragging for some time about being the mayor of Realville, meaning, simply put, he doesn't care about "political correctness" and just tells it like it is. In other words, if it is "real" or actual, he tells it that way. To cite an example, if someone is "weight-challenged" (the politically correct term), he refers to that person as fat. It's real, it is what it is, albeit tactless and brutal. (Incidentally, this said talk show talker/host is very weight-challenged.) Since I live in Realville, you should know that you can focus on *what* I am going to say rather than *how* I'm saying it.

But, I digress. So, without really worrying, I did, as always, do my own version of politically incorrect profiling by looking for things, like whether there were any darker-skinned, turban-wearing, bearded men between the ages of 17 and 34 boarding my flight (the "profile" description of 99.99% of the known murdering terrorists in the past 50 years). Or whether the plane is departing on time. Or whether there are any attractive females who might, by some miracle, be sitting beside me. (Scratch that last one. That has never happened in my years of flying, and I've come to realize that, for me, the odds are better for winning the Power Ball than sitting next to a "looker" on an airplane.)

All seemed to be going well, except that the stated boarding time of 9:45 A.M. actually started around 10:07, which meant that passengers would have to board at lightning speed, and the plane would have to burn rubber in order to depart at the stated time of 10:15. (We finally left the ground around 10:37 without burning rubber.)

Digressing back to boarding, the first thing I noticed was that the large hoodie that's over the ramp leading to the door of the plane didn't quite make it to the door, leaving an untrammeled view of the airplane cockpit. And, to my amazement, there were two teenagers sitting in there! Now, I know I'm getting old(er), and *everybody* I see these days looks younger, but trust me, these guys couldn't have been a day over 15! Anyway, I comforted myself by rationalizing that the real pilots must have let their sons come to work with them for father-son day at the airlines.

The next "essential" thing I began looking for was my seat number (it was supposed to be "2A") on the overhead bin above the designated seat. Apparently, the Mexican cleaning crew in their zeal must have scrubbed the numbers off, but I overlooked this (no pun intended) and relied on my keen eyesight and finely-honed mathematical skills to count the rows. I was sure I had counted right (*wrong!*), and I knew that "2A" meant 2nd row, window (A) seat. And besides, I knew I had to be in the right place, because there was no attractive female in what I thought was "2B," only a fat smelly guy. After the awkward excuse-me-but-I-think-I'm-going-to-have-to-disturb-you apology, seat unbuckling, struggling to stand up and move into the aisle (this guy was really *fat...*), I took my seat in what I thought was "2A" (it was actually "3A"). After realizing that I didn't know how to turn off my new iPhone 6 Plus (and the prospect again of spending the night in jail on a separate, unrelated charge of not turning off all electronic devices), I set about finding somewhere to put my elbows (and pretending to turn my phone off). After a few moments of struggling (but not as much as the fat guy), I'm leaning over to put my bag under the seat, when I hear a pleasant (breathy, female) voice sweetly proclaim, "Sir, I think you're in my seat." *Lo and behold! It was the attractive girl I'd been looking for!*

Now the process repeats itself, only this time in reverse. The Oh-I'm-sorry-I-didn't-mean-to-take-your-seat-I-guess-I-read-the-numbers-wrong. (*What numbers?*) The struggling to unbuckle and stand up. Add the gathering of items already tucked under the seat and the disdain I felt for the fat smelly guy who would now be sitting next to Miss America.

The good news: Miss America offered to sit in the seat that was supposed to be mine in the first place (the real "2A"). The bad news: I still didn't get to sit next to Miss America. The worst news: I still had to sit next to the fat smelly guy. The even worst news: The fat smelly guy was now mad at me for cheating (albeit inadvertently) him out of sitting next to Miss America.

Now, back to the real purpose in reporting this saga. Over the years, we've seen the characteristics of what used to be called stewardesses change dramatically. In the old days, they were all young and pretty (like Miss America), and female, and of slight build—aka not fat—and acted like they liked their jobs, and treated passengers like they (the passengers) paid their salaries. Not any more. Now most of them (not all) are the opposite of the aforementioned, and are now called flight attendants.

Today, however, my faith in stewardesses was restored in more ways than one. Our lone stewardess on Flight 3942 was very dark (and I don't mean like a comedy). I mean, this girl was *Black*, with a capital B, and not what you would call attractive by Hollywood's standards. But she was, nonetheless, beautiful to behold. And, did I mention... very fat? I didn't get this young lady's name, but she was obviously from Zimbabwe or Uganda and hadn't been in the United States long enough to totally master the English language (not uncommon these days). But she was undoubtedly the friendliest, happiest, and most appreciative of having her job than any stewardess I have ever had the pleasure of attending to me on an airplane. She must have announced at least a dozen times how happy/delighted/thrilled, etc. she was to have us on her airplane. And she said it like she meant it! And like we were paying her salary, and she was working for us! She was so excited that, at one point, she ran out of words to describe it and proudly announced, in her broken English, that she was "incredible" to have us aboard! Before we departed the airport in Birmingham, she made an announcement that the captain had asked her to let us know that someone in rows 1 through 4 would be (*more broken English*), which was met with a collective "Huh?" and puzzled looks from everyone in rows 1 through 4! At which time, Miss Congeniality raced down the aisle (barely squeezing by), apparently to try to find out from the captain what she had just announced.

We never did find out, and she never came back and clarified, but it didn't really matter. We all (including even those past row 4) just felt good that this wonderfully cheerful flight attendant loved her job so much, she couldn't help but make us feel welcome. It's been a long time since I've had that feeling before and after a six-hour airplane flight.

Oh, and by the way, the teenagers *were* piloting the plane.

CHAPTER TWENTY-ONE

A JOB OR A CAREER?

You name a job, and I've probably had it. My first memory at age three was watching workmen sawing and hammering in the back yard, readying the old Triangle for us to live in. Back in the day, it was unheard of for customers at a "gas station" to pump their own petrol. Incredibly, I remember being so small I had to reach up to unscrew the gas cap to pump their gas! The store was in a sort of rural area, and a few short years later, I talked our neighbor across the road into letting me do some yard work for her. I worked literally all day cutting grass, raking, clipping hedges, and cleaning up Miss Alma's yard. I'll never forget the exhilaration I felt when she handed me a check for $6.00, made out to me! That was my first paycheck, and of course, I cashed it at The Triangle.

There was always "work" to do at The Triangle, so my sister and I had become no strangers to working. Jean was two years older and was glad to "show me the ropes." Later, as a young teenager, I asked my mother about getting a "real" job. She gently reminded me, "But, Mike, you've got a job right here." As true as that was, I told her that

I understood that, but I wanted a job where I could make my own money. She then further reminded me, "Well, you know, anytime you need money, you can just get it out of the cash register." An incredible arrangement looking back on it, but for me, it just didn't seem like I was really "earning" it. I knew that, whether I did any work or not, I could go into the cash register any time I wanted to. Because my parents trusted my sister and me, we never violated them by "stealing" out of the register. We always told them when we took any money out.

I guess, because of my "simple" upbringing, I believed that, when someone told you something, they meant what they said. This was so ingrained in me that, even though I had earned a degree in economics and studied about social security and income taxes, it didn't dawn on me that I wouldn't get a check for $60 after my first week selling shoes at Sears in 1964. That was what the assistant manager, Mr. Munday, had told me the weekly salary would be, so I took him at his word. Aghast that my check was $10 short, I immediately paid a visit to the payroll department. The lady who cut the checks doubled over with laughter to the delight of the other employees within earshot. "Boy, haven't you ever heard of the income tax and social security?" she chortled. Not wanting to appear imbecilic, I covered by lamely whimpering, "Uh…oh, yeh…I forgot."

You would have thought I had learned to not take people literally when they make statements about anything to do with business. A few months earlier, a "representative/recruiter" from Sears had spoken to the seniors in my college economics class and had told us that Sears started their manager trainees out at $110 a week.

I had difficulty not raising my hand on the spot and asking when could I start, because this was an astronomical figure for a little ol' country boy like me. The Sears store on Court Street in Montgomery was brand new, and they were looking for quality graduates. That's me, I thought. They gotta hire me!

I found out later that the guy wasn't really looking to hire anybody that day (or ever). That's just something big companies do, I discovered, just to spread the word about how good their company is. On the day of the interview, Mr. Munday (remember him?) was very brusque and not nearly as nice and accommodating as Mr. Recruiter and preached to me about how he had started his career at Sears mopping floors in the paint department. The best he could offer me was selling shoes on commission (what's that?) at a draw of $60 per week. The last three words were all I understood about what he said. I accepted the job that day, and the rest is history. The "commission" was 6% on men's shoes and 8% on women's and children's shoes. I was competing with two full-time salesmen, plus two part-time ladies and a part-time teenager. The most expensive pair of men's shoes (or boots) at the time were $19.98 (a gold mine in sales). I couldn't figure out why I couldn't ever make more than $60 a week. Then, I started doing the math (which I, admittedly, wasn't very good at) and realized that it was impossible! Here was my reasoning. Let's make it simple and just say it was possible for me (an inexperienced novice) to sell 50 gold mines a week, roughly 10 a day, or a little over one an hour. This would probably mean that NONE of the other part-time and full-time sales people sold anything that week (highly unlikely). They'd have to be literally backing trucks up to the warehouse door and unloading shoes all day long for the entire department to make a living! I quit four months later after buying that red convertible with payments of $88.35, or roughly the commission on roughly 75 gold mines a month. You get the idea.

A friend and former roommate of mine in college had graduated a year ahead of me and had gotten a job with the F. W. Woolworth Company. Not as prestigious as Sears, but the salary was $100 a week (straight salary), so upon application, I was accepted into the "manager trainee" program at their Springdale Plaza store in Mobile. Too far away for comfort, but I had to pay for my car, so I loaded up the Chevelle and headed south.

Unlike the shoe salesman job, I found out that manager trainees at Woolworth's are more like slaves and to "get the feel for what everybody does," they are expected to do whatever the manager tells them to do. In the short time I worked there, I found that it was really good experience, because—to put it mildly—the jobs were varied, ranging from janitor (of course) to cashier (been there, done that), horticulturist, and hamster breeder, to name a few.

I made quite a name for myself as a hamster breeder, in fact, because every time I would feed the little boogers, I'd pull out the ones that looked "fat," suspecting they might be pregnant females. I had been told that, if born in "mixed company," the litter would be eaten by the rest of the herd, no questions asked. The size of the litters ranged from 6 to 12, so it didn't take long for the population to explode, meaning eventually more sales of hamsters at a clear profit. I guess I was the only one who had thought of doing that. It probably helped that I spent a lot of time on my grandparents' farms as a boy.

It would be years in the work force before I eventually "found my niche" and eventually settled on counseling as my profession. Before that discipline, however, I spent 20 plus years in broadcasting, starting part-time in radio while working on my master's degree in Broadcast and Film Communications at the University of Alabama. I landed my first radio job as a disc jockey with the help of a fellow classmate who had a great voice and was already working at WJRD-AM (back when nobody thought FM would make it) in downtown Tuscaloosa. It wasn't much, but it got my foot in the door, so I was glad to get it. It was a Sunday morning shift, signing on the air at 5:30 A.M., spinning a few records, playing pre-recorded sermons by local preachers, and "going to the network" (CBS) for news on the hour.

My first day on the job, I was to meet my friend, Don, a little early, so he could show me how to "run the (audio) board." I was so excited about the job, I don't think I slept any the night before. I got to the studio around 5:00, figuring Don would already be there waiting for me. As the clock ticked the minutes off, I became more and more nervous. I had "worked" at the campus radio station, WABP, but everybody knew that nobody listened, as it was just for training broadcasting students. On a clear day, you could actually pick up the signal down in the parking lot below the Student Union Building!

Anyway, 5:15 came and went, then 5:20, 5:25. Still no Don. Panic started to take over as I paced the sidewalk in front of the studio. 5:30! Sign on time! The street was as quiet as you would expect for downtown at that time of morning, but my head was exploding. Logic told me that I had lost my first job in radio before I even started it.

It was close to 6:00 A.M. (well, actually about 10 minutes 'til) when Don came lumbering down the street. I charged him as soon as he stepped out of the car. "I thought we had to sign on at 5:30! It's almost six o'clock!" I croaked.

"Aw, don't worry about it. Nobody's listening anyway," he assured me. *What? Seriously? Then why did you tell me to be here at 5:30?* At that point, I don't know if I felt more rage or relief! In any case, I made it through my first day as a D.J. and felt pretty good about it, actually. By noon, when my shift ended, I felt like I had worked a full day, and by Sears shoe salesman standards, I probably had! I didn't care what Don said about the audience. I always signed on at 5:30 sharp from that day forward.

This job led to a night shift Monday through Friday from 9:00 'til midnight at WACT, a newfangled FM country music station, the listeners of which were questionable as well, because most people back then had radios that received only AM. I did manage to garner somewhat of a following though, and the same listeners would call me every night. I was a celebrity!

Years later, while working at WDJC-FM in Birmingham, I met a man named Tom Owen, who had made a name for himself as a muscle builder and "strongman." He would often do stunts, like letting 18-wheelers run over him to raise money for an orphanage he had started in nearby Wilsonville called The King's Ranch.

Tom came by the station one day and asked if I'd like to go with him to the Birmingham Airport. He had made a deal with Red Baron Pizza to do a stunt to raise money for the ranch. They would pay him to do the stunt, and it would be great publicity for both the ranch and for Red Barron Pizza. I figured he'd let another truck run over him, and I'd seen him do that one, so I was about to decline his offer when he explained what the stunt was. He was going to attempt to hold a Cessna back using only his teeth!

Well, of course I couldn't turn that down, so away we went. If I hadn't seen it with my own eyes, I wouldn't have believed it. I was so stunned watching the stunt that I didn't even ask him how he did it. I'm sure he must have practiced it, but he made me think he just casually decided to do it. To reward me for accompanying him, one of the pilots took me up in a genuine Red Baron Pizza open cockpit bi-plane. And I have pictures to prove it!

This led to an incredible stunt of my own—something I had always wanted to do. (Don't ask me why.) During my time at WDJC, the owner of the chain of Christian stations decided we needed more coverage, so he contracted to put up a new tower, a hundred feet taller than the old one. I decided it would be a great time to fulfill my fantasy of climbing the tower!

It was fascinating to watch the workers perform their magic. First, they had to start building the new tower right next to the old one, using it as their base. After laying the foundation and adding the first section with a crane, they would gingerly climb the old tower, then swing over to the top of the new section, bolt it in place, then repeat until the new one was completed. To help them along, the crew had a makeshift "elevator" rigged with a couple of wheels and pulleys, the bottom to which they attached a crude "sling" to sit in as the worker went up and down for supplies. The worker would hold on to a (very heavy) steel "wrecking ball" to keep the cable taut. It worked like an "open air" elevator!

I thought it would be great to take the ride up to the top so I could take some pictures for my scrapbook. This way, it would be a lot easier than actually "climbing" the tower. I somehow made a "deal" with the crew to take me up in the sling. I almost fainted when they agreed to do it!

It was a cold, cloudy and windy winter day, but the excitement kept me warm. And I have the pictures to prove that one too!

Obviously, I've stopped taking such risks as I've gotten older, and I can't include all of the foolishness I engaged in before I wised up (nor would I want to). One thing I can say without reservation, and that is that I take my job as a Licensed Professional Counselor very seriously. People share their lives with me, and they place their trust in me.

One of the most sacred rules in counseling is that of confidentiality. A person who comes into my office must feel they are safe in disclosing whatever they have to in order to "get better," knowing that it won't make the local (or national) news.

I could write volumes of "case studies" about the interesting people who have graced my doorway in my short 27 years as an LPC. But I won't do that, because their secrets are safe with me. My work has been with children and adults (the youngest not quite two, and the oldest 84) from all walks of life, all races and ethnicities. I've worked for a salary, but also as a contractor, in private practice and in public "service," in a state youth facility and a state prison. My work has included sessions with married couples, as well as singles and single couples. I have been privileged to learn about more issues than I even knew existed before I discovered this wonderfully rewarding career. There have been "normal" people with complex problems, complex people with normal problems, and all in between. Addicts, sex offenders, domestic violence perpetrators and victims. All of them struggling with life. And, I'm not too proud to admit that I've even seen a few therapists for counseling myself.

As serious as this work has been, there have been interesting and amusing incidents that beg to be reported. So, with great care, I have decided to share some of the most memorable ones.

My First Counseling Session

Because of my father's alcoholism, I decided early on in my master's program that I would probably be an addictions counselor because I thought maybe I could help others who were struggling with addiction or who had family members who were. But then, when my marriage ended, I decided I needed to know more about that discipline as well. I had always been interested in why people committed crimes, so I thought I might go into forensics. (I did eventually work in the prison system for almost nine years.)

Nonetheless, I was required to do an internship before graduation, so I chose the Chemical Addictions Program (CAP). The entire semester I had to do therapy a couple of times a week with someone chosen as representative of the problem. As expected, I was very anxious as I prepared for my first "client." Although I had done well in my classes (actually ending up with a 4.0 GPA), I had no idea what I was doing. It seemed like a good idea to just get to know the person first, try to identify the problem (i.e. find out why that person had turned to drugs or alcohol), and then work toward a solution. I had studied "solution-focused" therapy and it made sense, so I felt I was as prepared as I was ever going to be when I heard the knock on my door. All I knew about my client was that she was a young woman (I'll call her Susan) with a cocaine addiction, so I immediately set about getting to know her and to find out how she ended up in drug rehab.

After finding out about her family, specifically her mother and father, and her childhood (Freud would have been pleased), we got down to business. Surprisingly, Susan was open and candid about her life, and I remember thinking how well it seemed to be going.

"So, tell me, Susan, how did you end up here?" I asked, trying to sound like a seasoned professional.

"Well, you know, I was doing well, had a good job, making good money, then I started using cocaine. It wasn't a lot at first, but somehow it got out of hand," she confessed.

I pressed her for more information. "What do you mean?" I asked.

"Like I said, I had a good job, and I only worked five days a week, but it got so bad…my addiction, I mean, and I was using so much that

I had to start working six and seven days a week. In fact, I was working all the time, just to support my habit."

Susan seemed to be getting upset, so I attempted to ease the tension and paused before asking her, "So, what kind of work were you doing?" I was expecting her answer to include some kind of menial work, probably paying minimum wage, so her response shocked me.

"Oh," she replied matter-of-factly and almost with pride, "I'm a shoplifter."

It was then I realized what a sheltered life I had led. I tried to not show my disbelief (one of the rules in counseling), and I guess I was successful, because she spent the rest of the session explaining "the rest of the story."

If there were two things I learned that day, they were to never assume you are prepared, and to always expect the unexpected. And those lessons served me well over the next 27 years.

Common Sense Logic

Shortly after finishing my degree, I was shopping around for employment and accidentally found that a former classmate, Judie, had gotten a job with the Council on Substance Abuse, an information and referral agency which helped addicts determine treatment options for alcohol and drug abuse. I was applying for a job there, and she saw me in the office. We chatted for a short time, and she told me she would put a good word in for me with the Executive Director.

I started my new job within two weeks. Part of my duties included "manning the phone" in the wee hours, and it was about 2 o'clock in the morning when the ring jolted me awake.

"The Council. May I help you?" was our standard greeting. The caller identified himself only as "Al."

"Uh, yeh, I need to go into treatment," he stated simply. He went on to tell me that he had already been in treatment *nine times* and that he was very discouraged. I asked him what he thought would be different this time and why he thought he had failed the nine times previously.

"Well," he explained, "I have three things that are holding me back. First, I'm a black person, and I feel like that's a strike against me. And, second, I'm handicapped. I'm in a wheelchair; I can't walk, and I'll never be able to."

By this time, I'm beginning to wonder what I can say that might help poor Al. I couldn't imagine what he would say next. "And the third thing is the worst. I'm…uh… I'm a homosexual, and I don't think I should be. I think that's the main reason I drink so much."

I was struggling to find something in my fund of knowledge about addiction that might address Al's specific issue, but I had no idea what to say. We didn't study this one in the textbooks, I thought. Quickly, I began to take inventory. A common sense answer seemed to be the only thing that would fit. The first two reasons Al gave me for drinking could not be changed, so they weren't "negotiable." The third reason might be something we could talk about, I told him.

"It seems to me that, if you genuinely want to stop drinking and, if the reason you feel you drink too much is that you are a homosexual, you don't have but two choices." I paused. "What do you think they are?" I asked.

I knew Al had gotten the point, but I could tell he wasn't comfortable with either option. So, I filled in the blanks for him. "You can either stop being a homosexual, or change how you feel about being a homosexual," I said.

We didn't talk much after that. I guess there wasn't much left to say. I simply passed along to Al what I knew to be fact. I didn't judge him, nor did I try to "change" him. I knew that, as a counselor, I had to put my own beliefs and prejudices aside and let him make his own decision. After all, his decision would affect him, not me.

I don't know whatever happened to Al. I never heard from him again.

The Alzheimer's Workshop

Alzheimer's disease is classified as a neurocognitive disorder in the Diagnostic and Statistical Manual of Mental Disorders and features acquired cognitive decline in such areas as memory, attention, language, learning, and perception. It affects an estimated 5.7 million Americans of all ages and is a very serious condition for which there is no cure. I have to stress this, because I don't want this story about a humorous experience I once had to be perceived in any way as disrespectful to those who have had to deal with this devastating malady.

I became specifically interested in Alzheimer's as a counselor because I have worked with several families who have been affected. In fact, I had a maternal great aunt who was diagnosed when I was in college. So, several years ago, when I heard about an Alzheimer's Workshop at a large church in Dothan, I decided to go and find out more about it. When I arrived, I was surprised to see the parking lot filled with cars. I assumed that the workshop was for counselors only, but realized when I went inside that the room was packed with probably 300 people, mostly nurses and mostly females. The reason this is important to know will become clear as I relate the story.

When the workshop started, the announcement was made that, because the majority of attendees were females, the organizers had arranged for the men's room to be used by the ladies. To ensure there were no "accidents," a sentry would be posted outside the men's room when the ladies were using it. It sounded like a foolproof plan. As long as the sentry did his job…

Anyway, all was going well, and the workshop was informative and actually even entertaining at times. The presenter had personal experience with her grandmother, who had been diagnosed with Alzheimer's several years earlier. Cheryl was a registered nurse with a whimsical personality and was full of comical and enlightening stories of how she and her family had learned to manage Grandma, by keeping it as light as possible during times of stress. Her experience had shown her that, in order to maintain her own sanity, she had to find the laughable element and learn to enjoy just being with Grandma in spite of the frustration of caring for her and her special needs.

One thing that stood out for me was when Cheryl told about how, sometimes, men with Alzheimer's would look for places to go to the bathroom (in inappropriate places). She noted that, if their eyesight was poor, they would often mistake flat, white surfaces for urinals, places like window sills or counter tops or even ashtrays. Of course, I wasn't as old as I am now, but I guess the story stuck with me, because I thought, if I ever have an issue with Alzheimer's, I would want to tell my caretakers to watch out for that specific behavior.

I thought nothing more of that particular story until later at bathroom break. Mother Nature had been calling me, and I tried to get out into the hallway before the swarm of ladies commandeered the men's room. As swift as I was, the area was teeming with nurses as I approached my destination. Success! No sentry was posted, and I quickly pushed open the door.

I hardly had time to step inside when three women whirled around to face me, embarrassment and shock showing on their faces! A cringe-worthy moment for all of us, I'm sure, as I immediately bowed my head and made a hasty exit backwards out the door. But only to be visually drilled by several more ladies waiting in line and the male sentry grabbing me by the arm. "Sir, you can't go in there!" he shouted. (A little late for that warning, don't you think?) Still steaming with sweat, I tried to defend my faux pas by explaining that I didn't see him. (I'm sure he wasn't there 10 seconds earlier!) I guess this softened him up, because he asked me, "May I help you?"

By this time, the hallway was thick with bodies, most of whom had witnessed my mortifying blunder. And being somewhat of a class clown, I thought I'd lighten the mood by referring back to the story about men with Alzheimer's looking for flat surfaces to go to the bathroom. I spied a nearby water fountain, and with a confident jerk of my head, proclaimed, "No, I'll just use the water fountain."

Although well-intended, not the best choice of jokes I thought, as a hush fell over the throng and all eyes fell on me. And no one was smiling. I still thought I could redeem myself, and I frantically attempted to explain. "Oh, no, it's O.K., I'm with the Alzheimer's Workshop!" I had no way of knowing that there were several other workshops being held in the building that had nothing to do with Alzheimer's. As the crowd began to murmur and slowly turn away, it dawned on me that I had just succeeded in planting my foot deeper in my mouth. I immediately realized the look on their faces as pity. They thought I actually had Alzheimer's! You just can't make this stuff up.

Impressing the Inmates

There are some dates you just can't forget. Like birthdays of significant others. Anniversaries. Graduation Day. Things like that. But I remember the day I started working at Kilby Prison. It was March 2, 1992. I had been working at the State Youth Facility called Mt. Meigs, just around the corner, counseling teenage drug addicts, when a former classmate called and told me about a job at the "big house." I checked the ad in the paper and called the number. I think my age (I was pushing 50) and my gender were pluses, because the guy hired me sight unseen and on the spot! He even wanted me to start the next day, but I told him I didn't think it would be professional for me to not turn in two weeks' notice. I believe he respected me for doing that.

March 2nd was on a Monday, and I had never seen the inside of a prison before, except for Mt. Meigs. It didn't seem like that counted because the youngest "prisoner" I had worked with there was only eight years old. And the accommodations were more like concrete dorms without bars. Shortly before I had started to work there, they had actually put up a big fence with razor wire at the top, because several months earlier, a teenager had walked out of the facility and killed a local nearby resident. It wasn't surprising, because the "guard shack" was often not manned, and when it was, the guard usually just waved you through if he recognized the car. They had gotten a little more cautious after the killing. Even after they put up the fence, there was an incident when one of the inmates made a drug deal (go figure...) with one of the guards to let the young boy drive his car out of the gate in exchange for some marijuana.

I wasn't prepared for the security measures at Kilby, but I should have known, because it was, after all, a maximum security prison. Any male convicted in the state of Alabama had to go through there for processing, and their crimes were all felonies, ranging from petty theft to sexual offenses to murder. Some of the inmates became "trusties" if they proved worthy. These also became known as "permanent party." As prisons go, it wasn't that bad, other than overcrowded, so an inmate was considered kind of special if he got to stay there.

That first day, I counted seven gates that opened and closed electronically before I made it to my office in the bowels of the prison. I actually liked the location, because my door looked directly out the back door of the prison where all of the inmates came through for processing. It made it convenient for me, as a counselor, because the "mental ones" didn't have far to walk to get to my office. And believe me, it was a steady stream.

There was never a dull day, and my learning never stopped. I actually met some people who I believe were innocent and wrongly convicted. These were exceptions, however, and to be fair, I have known people in the "free world," as the inmates called it, who never got locked up, but should have.

It was ritual for the mental health staff to do "rounds" daily. There would be a group of us, including usually a psychiatrist, a psychologist, a couple of counselors and a couple of guards (who liked to be called "officers"). The lower functioning mental health inmates were housed on "C" block upstairs. If they made it off "C" block and proved they could behave themselves, they were moved downstairs to "D" block, then later, if appropriate, they transferred to "general population." Each block contained 25 individual cells.

Then there was the dreaded P-1, which was reserved for suicidal, self-mutilating, or floridly psychotic inmates. A counselor had to be careful in there, because a resident's favorite pastime on P-1 was spitting and using urine and feces in inappropriate ways, to include tossing on anyone who passed their cell. Although this didn't happen often, you never knew when it was going to.

So, back to my first day. I was making rounds with the other staff, pad and pencil in hand, strolling down "C" block, and pretending I wasn't nervous. We were about half way down the block, and I guess I was getting eager to finish up, so I decided to walk ahead and get the jump on my notes. (I didn't know this wasn't allowed.) Although it was quite noisy, some inmates were actually snoozing in their bunks. And such was the case with "John." I had a roster, so I knew the name of the prisoner in each cell.

I must have made some sort of noise, because, in a flash, John threw the covers back, jumped up and raced over to the bars toward me! *Wow, I thought, this guy is really eager to see me.* I had no time to prepare for what happened next.

I saw John's face about a foot from mine as he grabbed the bars, and with a mighty heave, spit solidly in my face. *Splat! What the...?* I instinctively staggered back, blinking in disbelief. I had glasses on, so they took the brunt of the assault, and it was over almost as quickly as it had started. Attempting to focus my eyes, I realized John was nowhere in sight! In a split second, he had done an about face and flung himself back in bed! Apparently, the "officers" heard the ruckus, rushed over and pulled me away from John's cell. *A little late, I thought...I wondered what I had gotten myself into.*

"Mr. Moody! You can't do that!" one of them yelled. "That's John! He's crazy as a loon!" And thus was my first encounter with an actively psychotic paranoid schizophrenic. John was a huge black guy and his size and persona alone were intimidating enough. He meant no harm, I was told; that's just what he does.

The end of the story actually turned out O.K. The mental health department was eventually allowed to "force medicate" psychotic inmates, in spite of groups like the ACLU and the Southern Poverty Law Center who were more concerned about inmates' civil rights than safety of the staff.

After successful treatment of John's schizophrenia, he and I actually got along really well. He was crazy about dill pickles and, every now and then, I would secretly sneak some in for him. He was eventually released and returned to his home in Birmingham.

Limits and Boundaries

In working with children—and having raised two of my own—I've discovered that an important tenet is knowing how to set boundaries. Most of the parents I've worked with are good parents, and many of them are hard working "single moms" who have little time to do anything but provide the bare necessities of life. One of the most rewarding counseling experiences I ever had involved a little boy I will call Larnell, and his sweet mother, Bernita, whom he called "Bee Bee."

When a new patient shows up on my schedule, I usually scan the file for basic information to see if anything out of the ordinary stands out. With Larnell, I noticed that he was not quite two years old. Not surprisingly, Mom's presenting complaint was his behavior, precisely his uncontrollable "meltdowns."

Over time, I had learned how to take personal experiences and use them as "teaching moments," especially with children. Some years ago, I had visited the Grand Canyon, which I have since described as "the biggest hole in the ground I've ever seen." I have also used it to illustrate how important limits and boundaries are.

I had heard about the Grand Canyon my whole life and thought that, because it was so talked about and well publicized, surely I was the only person who had never actually seen it. On the day of my visit, one of the things that struck me was how diligent the Park Service had been in providing necessary "boundaries" for the safety of tourists. I have pointed out many times since then that, although the various fences and guard rails sometimes obstruct the gorgeous vista, they are necessary to keep viewers from falling into the abyss. In fact, I stress, because those boundaries are there, we actually feel safer.

The same is true when it comes to children. And once parents overcome their children's "objections," those children later come to appreciate the boundaries we set for them.

This is where Larnell and his mother were having difficulty. Because of Bernita's gentle nature, she usually let Larnell have his way with whatever he wanted to do. I had been seeing them weekly for the past month when Bernita brought Larnell in and told me about his recent birthday party. The party was a big deal, because Larnell was turning two. He was Bernita's only child and the rest of the extended family doted on him, "spoiling him rotten," as the saying goes. Bernita had gone to Walmart to get a large specially-made sheet cake for the celebration. She had judiciously placed Larnell inside the shopping cart as she paid for the cake, but because of its size, the only place for it was on the precarious front edge of the cart. Apparently Larnell objected to some minor detail about the cake and, in a fit of rage, promptly shoved it off the cart, upside down on the floor!

As Mom was relating the story, I noticed Larnell sitting sullenly, with his arms folded across his chest. He was a bright little boy, and even at his age, I knew he understood what was being reported. I asked her what happened next. "Well, the lady at the bakery rushed over and told me not to worry, that they would make another one," she said. Out of the corner of my eye, I could see Larnell getting more uncomfortable.

Assuming that Mom had taken further action with Larnell, I asked her the obvious question. "So, what was Larnell's punishment for that? Did you still have the party?" Sheepishly, she replied that they had indeed had the party and that all of the relatives had come to celebrate with Larnell.

I probed further to see if Bernita had meted out any consequences for Larnell. "But, surely, you didn't let him have any cake, did you?"

Incredibly, Bernita told me that she couldn't bear to see everybody else eating cake, laughing and having fun, and Larnell not having any, so she let him eat all he wanted! After all, it *was* his birthday, she said, somewhat defensively. By this time, Larnell was almost gleeful, realizing that, once again, he had shown everyone he was in charge.

I explained to Mom what I thought would have worked better, from a discipline standpoint. I was glad to see that she agreed, but Larnell was having none of it. I could tell he was getting "antsy" and had started trying to climb onto his mother's lap.

It was time to take action, I thought, so I told Mom I thought I should have a "come to Jesus meeting" with Larnell…alone, without her in the room. I think she realized that the way she had been handling her little angel had not been working and that it was finally time to set some limits and boundaries with Larnell.

The first step was to get her out of the room so I could show Larnell how boundaries worked in real life. And, of course, to try to get it across to him that grownups are in charge, not children.

As soon as I told Mom it was time for her to leave, it was like a switch was flipped in Larnell. I could see the alarm in his eyes as he began to scream at the top of his lungs. As Mom got up to leave, Larnell clamped on to her leg and held on for dear life! This was obviously something new for Larnell, and he was not going down without a fight!

They say that the first word a child learns is "NO" and Larnell had learned that one well. "No! No! Noooo!" he began to scream, kicking in protest and shaking his head violently for added emphasis.

For obvious reasons, I rarely touch my patients, but I realized that there was no way Larnell was going to turn loose of his savior if I didn't physically pull him off her leg. All in now, Bernita was trying to help, but even with her size (she was a large woman), she was unable to break his death grip. Still, I was determined to follow through with my "teaching moment" on boundaries.

After what seemed like a lifetime of pulling and tugging, kicking and screaming, Mom finally made her exit without Larnell, leaving him alone with me to continue our lesson. For the next 20 minutes or so, Larnell cried, screamed, rocked, stomped and chanted at the top of his lungs, *"I want Bee Bee! I want Bee Bee! I want Bee Bee!*

It was a classic battle of the wills. I had drawn the line in the sand, and I knew I had to win, for Bernita's sake and for Larnell's. Larnell pulled out all the stops, using all the tricks he had used since birth, vacillating between whimpering, screaming, raging, and any other manipulative ploy he could come up with. It was not a pretty sight. Tears were flowing, snot was flying, and the incessant *"I want Bee Bee! I want Bee Bee! I want Bee Bee!"*

I knew this was hard for Mom, and I expected any minute that she would fly into the room and rescue her little boy, never to be seen by me again. But, to her credit, she stayed out of it. I was hoping that this would be a turning point for everyone!

During the melee, I decided that I would settle for 60 seconds of silence on Larnell's part as a condition for Mom coming back in. As the raging meltdown dragged on, I shortened the condition to 5 to 10 seconds, with me alternately and calmly making my own declaration between his "I want Bee Bee" demands. "When you get quiet, your mother can come back in. When you get quiet your mother can come back in." The entire office was in an uproar; nobody was getting any work done as Larnell and I took center stage. Several people warily peeped in to inquire if everything was O.K. and to see if I needed any help. I flashed back to my first day at Kilby Prison and thought how trivial being spit in the face by a 200 pound schizophrenic seemed. I seriously wondered if I was doing the right thing. But I knew I was in too deep to back out.

After about 25 minutes of counseling hell, the tide began to turn in the adult's favor. Larnell calmed for five seconds! Just long enough for me to make a deal with him. Kleenex tissues littered the room, as I had made several unsuccessful attempts at nose-wiping, only to endure more incessant screaming, thrashing and crying.

Still sniffling and jerking from over-exertion, poor Larnell listened, wide-eyed, to my proposal. "Now that you're quiet, your mother can come back in. Do you understand?" *No response.* Hoping for the best and assuming Larnell did understand, I continued. I still had to demonstrate that the adult tells the child what will happen, not the other way around. "When your mother comes in, you will not move. You will wait for your mother to come over and get you. You will not go to her. She will come to you. Do you understand?" Larnell weakly nodded his head. And he remained quiet as I slowly went to open the door.

Mom was eagerly waiting, and stepped inside my office. Then, all hell broke loose, as Larnell bolted toward his mother, screaming and crying at the top of his lungs, as if we had wasted the last 25 minutes.

I sprang into action just as quickly, however, and re-established the boundaries I had just set with Larnell. "Whoa, buddy, that's not what we agreed on! Mom, you'll have to leave!" I emphatically declared.

I suppose I was under the illusion that it couldn't get worse. But with Mom's second exit, it did. Thus ensued 10 to 15 more minutes of battle, with Larnell attempting to regain control. This time, I let him finish the tirade on his own. Somehow, I think he knew it was over, and he slowly and quietly began to calm himself.

I calmly repeated the conditions of our "agreement," and asked Larnell if he was ready to see his mother. He slowly nodded and remained quiet as I got up to let Mom know he was O.K.

As she entered the room, I told her how proud I was of her for being strong and how well Larnell had done. I told her that Larnell was waiting for her, and suggested she reward him with a big hug and tell him how much she loved him. Incredibly, Larnell remained still and quiet as Bernita followed my instructions. This time, Mom was the one crying, and suddenly I noticed the room seemed misty. Blinking back my own tears, we wound up this very exhausting session. I found a place on my schedule the next week for Larnell and his mother to come back for a follow up, but I didn't really expect her to keep the appointment.

A week later, the intercom buzzed at the designated time, indicating that Larnell and his mother were waiting to see me. I had barely opened my office door and stepped outside, when I saw Larnell headed toward me, followed closely by Bernita. He raced over to me, and with the scene from the previous week still reminiscent in my mind, Larnell clamped onto my leg, holding on tightly for several seconds!

Suddenly I remembered why I had gotten into counseling. It's benefits like Larnell that make it worth the struggle.

CHAPTER TWENTY-TWO

A Good Doctor is Hard to Find

IT'S INEVITABLE. NO matter what it is, sooner or later things wear out. And it's no different with the human body. If you're like me, you remember as a child seeing "old people" and thinking they must be 200 years old, because, from our perspective, they looked it! You may also remember that some never did seem to grow any older. (They were usually movie stars who got a little help from their plastic surgeons.)

I have to admit that I don't know what "average" is anymore, especially when it comes to health, energy levels, aches and pains, or number of surgical procedures in one's lifetime. I thought I'd had more than my share until I had a man in my office recently tell me he'd had 53! (He had some kind of flesh-eating bacteria that required surgery every time it attacked.) It made my 21 procedures seem paltry. I asked my sister recently, and she told me that she has had only three, and she's two years older than me! I always hated it when, as a youngster, I would hear the "old folks" make comments like, "Uh, did I tell you about my gall bladder…" The next thing you know, we've gotten their complete medical history, which nobody was really interested in.

Now, I'm not one to be overly positive or negative, especially when it comes to personal health; I'm just a realist. But since such a discussion can be really dull (and wouldn't make for very interesting "book material"), I decided I'd just pick a few of the funniest or strangest or weirdest health issues I've experienced over the years, and put 'em in this chapter.

I don't know if it's just me, or if back yards, garages and patios really are more dangerous in the summertime. Things just seem to "happen." Like the early sunny morning I went on a mission to fix my computer desk. My daughter, Crystal, and granddaughter, MaKayla, were visiting from Arizona, so I thought, with their help, it might be a good time to get some projects done.

When I look at doing projects, I'm always looking for ways to save money. I don't mean like when you put your spare change in a piggy bank. I mean the kind when you don't have to spend money because you figured out a way to fix something without having to buy something new.

I had already saved a lot of money by picking up some used pieces of wood and making a sort of desk for my man cave. I hadn't intended to use it for a computer; it just sort of evolved into that. The problem was the carpet. The computer made the front of the desk a little top heavy so that it tilted forward on the soft carpet, making it unsteady when I would peck away on the keyboard. I was pretty sure the legs were all the right length, as I'd paid a lot of attention to detail when I built it. And, it was fairly good sized and heavy, so I didn't want to have to move it around too much to fix it. I figured I could slip a crowbar under the front legs and prize it up (that's Southern for "pry") and put some washers under the legs to tip it back and steady it up.

So, I headed out to the garage to rummage through my stash of super-sized washers. I filled my pocket with enough to do the job and grabbed the crowbar on my way out. What should have been about a 30-minute job, max, turned out to be almost three hours. The morning was about shot by this time, and my frustration level was through the roof. And I find that, when I get in a hurry, I tend to make careless mistakes.

I'm usually fairly organized, and most of my tools have their own special place. "A place for everything and everything in its place" is my motto. The crowbar's "special place" was on a hook on a large peg board along with other similar tools. It was already getting quite warm, and I was dressed for the season, with shorts and flip-flops. In retrospect, not a good idea when you're handling heavy equipment, like crowbars. I think crowbars come in different shapes and sizes, and mine was sort of shaped like a long question mark, with a hook on one end and kind of flat and straight and sharp on the other end, perfect for jacking up computer desks.

I had put most of the other "stuff" away, and was attempting (notice I said "attempting") to hang the crowbar on the pegboard. There is no way I could have choreographed what happened next. I researched "terminal velocity" and found that it is "the constant speed that a free falling object eventually reaches when the resistance of the medium through which it is falling prevents further acceleration." In other words, if something drops, it only goes so fast before the drag force equals the force of gravity, and it doesn't get any faster. This little science lesson is important in explaining how fast the sharp end of the crowbar was falling when it hit my right big toe. I just know that it was going fast enough to split the toenail and hurt like hades!

My screams summoned Crystal and MaKayla as I hobbled to the patio, holding my bleeding right foot. Since it was the beginning of the summer and most (notice I said "most") flying, stinging insects were not yet out in force. I plopped down in a dust-covered lawn chair, hoping for relief from the pain, only to hear a familiar buzzing under the chair. *Wasps!*

I apparently disturbed their little nest when I sat down, and the attack was on! Suddenly the pain in my toe took second place as I raced for the laundry room to get the wasp spray.

I had downed a couple of attackers in mid-air and was feeling pretty victorious when one brute took a kamikaze dive and, smelling blood, buried a stinger in the same toe the crowbar had hit seconds earlier! I've said it before, and I'll say it again; you can't make this stuff up!

This story segues nicely into what was probably the most disastrous summer of my life. It actually started in May of 2017. I'm not going to try to cover everything that happened that summer; just making mention of a couple of things, then highlighting the most profound parts.

Without going into graphic detail, let's just say that I began to notice that certain "colors" weren't the color they were supposed to be. So, after going through four doctors shrugging their shoulders and giving me the name of a symptom (hematuria), not a diagnosis, I finally found one who gave me a diagnosis. All I heard was the word "cancer." I got a second opinion (actually from the sixth doctor), who performed surgery a couple of months later to remove what the doctor described as a malignant, very aggressive, insidious cancer in my left ureter. After the procedure, he informed me that he thinks he "got it all," but there is no treatment, per se, for this type of cancer. I just have to go back and get "re-checked" every three months to be sure it hasn't come back. I agreed that this was a good plan, since I had been declared "cancer free" in 2004 after removal of a tumor as a result of Non-Hodgkins Lymphoma.

About the same time, I started having pain in my left heel (?) for which I managed to get more shoulder shrugs from doctors, and three or four names of some foot malady nobody had ever heard of or didn't care to treat. Oh, I almost forgot…one of the doctors who tried to give me a bona fide diagnosis on the foot thing had also performed surgery on my left hand after an inexplicable and painful "knot" wouldn't go away. If you have a history of cancer like I have, any "knot" is cause for concern. He explained that it was an anomaly that is common in white men of European descent. (Again, I'm not making this up.) Oh, and I also forgot to mention that, about the same time, I was in my garage (of course) when an unwelcome visitor surprised me. I know we grow cockroaches big in the Deep South, but this one was the granddaddy (or maybe the mother) of all cockroaches. I later named it "Brutus." As anyone knows who has ever had cockroaches infest their personal space, the best treatment is to squash 'em with a heavy foot.

Remember I told you about my left heel and my right big toe? Well, I didn't think about them when I began my hot pursuit of "Brutus." I thought I had him cornered when our game of run, dodge and jump turned into a tap dance. Due to the aforementioned injuries and defects, it didn't take long for me to lose my footing, which was about to hurl me to the concrete floor. I would probably have broken my arm if the wall hadn't stopped my sideways Irish Jig. In an effort to stop the fall, I hit the wall backwards, which happened to be at the precise spot I had hung my aluminum step ladder. *Crash! Clatter! Clang!*

The cockroach was never seen again, and the good news is, I didn't fall down. I found out what the bad news was a month later when I was with the doctor, following up on the knot he had cut out of my left hand. I just casually mentioned would he please check out my shoulder, which by this time looked like a Pablo Picasso portrait of Dora Maar. It had turned just about every color of the rainbow and was still producing a lot of pain, but I thought maybe it was just badly bruised.

The X-ray told the story. "Mike, your collar bone is broken," the doctor said. "How did you do that?" After explaining the tap dancing story to him (which didn't really impress him), he told me that, unfortunately, there is no treatment for a broken collar bone, except to put your arm in a sling, and maybe a little ice on it. O.K., the good news is that it was my left shoulder, so what's a little more incapacitation on that side, right?

I could go on all day, but I'll end this historical foray into my now battered and bruised body, by relating what happened on MaKayla's 17th birthday. It seems that she had disappeared the day before I flew out to Phoenix to celebrate with her and her mother. The following will be the "short version," of the story.

MaKayla had been seeing "this boy," and had been sowing some typical teenage wild oats, so we were hoping that she was just trying to show us how "grownup" she was by staying out all night with him. After much searching, worrying and hand-wringing, Crystal and I decided to fervently pray before going to bed and resume our search the next morning. Surely she would turn up; after all, it was her birthday.

The next morning, after a couple of hours of driving around the neighborhood where we thought she might be, and still no MaKayla, Crystal got a call from her school. She was there and seemed to be O.K., but we might want to come and check on her, the teacher told us.

It's been said that your mental state can affect your physical condition and vice versa. I must have had this in mind as Crystal and I concluded our meeting with school officials, with poor MaKayla, still in a semi-catatonic state, listening in. I attributed the uneasiness in my lower back on my previous "back issues" which included surgery in January 2005 to insert "hardware" to keep the vertebrae in line. However, as the pain worsened, I had excused myself to take a bathroom break.

Discoloration of bodily fluids is disconcerting, even for people who don't have a history of cancer. Those who do have such a history tend to react with paranoia, but I decided to remain rational, although my instincts told me to panic.

I will spare the sordid details and skip to the "scene" late that afternoon when the decision was made to admit MaKayla to the hospital for observation. The three of us were at their apartment on the second floor, and the key would not open the door! Crystal told me that there had been a problem with the lock and that sometimes the mechanism would malfunction, requiring a maintenance person to bring a ladder and climb onto the deck and enter through the only other entrance to the apartment. This presented another problem, because it was after 5:00 P.M. and no one was in the apartment complex office.

Approximately an hour and a half later, "maintenance" showed up and opened the door, and we were back on schedule. Except that my pain had now become almost unbearable. The plan was for Crystal to stay at the apartment to make arrangements for MaKayla's hospitalization, and since drugs were suspected, Child Protective Services had sent a couple of attendants to drive MaKayla to the hospital. They were very kind and agreed to drop me off at my hotel on the way.

To complicate matters, the attendants weren't familiar with the area where my hotel was. What should have been a 15 minute drive turned into a 45 minute nightmare of wrong turns and dead ends, even with "help" from their GPS. I was almost delirious from pain by this time, and, at one point, I had to have the driver stop the van to let me throw up by the side of the road. I finally decided that I too should go to the hospital.

I dialed 911 and gave the operator the address of my hotel, and incredibly they arrived about the same time we did. Leaving MaKayla with two total strangers and me in an ambulance on the way to the ER was not the way I had envisioned spending my granddaughter's birthday!

Because of the "opioid epidemic," I wasn't allowed to have anything for pain, and I can't describe how horrific it was. As morbid as it sounds, at one point, I would have welcomed death. Crystal had arrived (I don't remember when) to provide background for the doctors on my medical history.

Later that night (actually morning), I was diagnosed with renal lithiasis/nephrolithiasis (kidney stones). The doctor said there were five to be exact, three in my kidney, one still in my ureter, and one which I had undoubtedly passed the previous afternoon (which explained all the blood!). At 70 years of age, I had never had any history of kidney stones, so the diagnosis was somewhat of a shock. It was also a relief, knowing that it didn't have anything to do with dreaded cancer. Laprascopic surgery the next morning blasted the stones into oblivion, leaving only a stent to be removed a week later.

I really liked the doctor who performed the surgery and removed the stent. He was a jovial middle-aged chap with some sort of "foreign accent" which added to his mystique. Immediately upon removal, he jumped back as if surprised and loudly proclaimed, "Oh, no, you've just had a green Martian baby!" I wanted to tell him that the delivery wasn't too bad, but the labor pains were brutal!

CHAPTER TWENTY-THREE

THE END OF THE ROAD

MY LOVE AFFAIR with motorcycles goes back to my early teens. I've told the story many times about how my friend, Sammy, got a "motorbike" to ride to school, and I immediately coveted it. I was 13, going on 14, and from Day One, I knew I had to have one, but had to put the dream to rest after months (years?) of begging my mother if I could have one and being rejected at every turn with the best excuse a parent could come up with: "I'm afraid you'll get hurt." Truth be told, I probably would have, but it still didn't quench my thirst for that motorized (bicycle) marvel I didn't have to pedal! My mother remained steadfast over the years in her opposition to me having one despite all the advertising that finally made them respectable. Most people back then associated a motorcycle of any kind, shape or size with the stereotypical "Hell's Angels." (Refer back to Chapter Eight.) Honda came out with the Honda 50 (CC) even before they started making cars. Their advertising centered around the fact that it got "90 miles per gallon on gas, single or double!" The theme topped it off in their catchy jingle, "You meet the nicest people on a Honda."

A scant eight or nine years later, when I landed my first real, meaningful, full-time job, I began to think about fulfilling my dream of owning a motorcycle. I was closer to making that dream come true than I had ever been!

And then...along came Andrea, a cute (barely) five-foot blond from Wisconsin who preferred horses to motorcycles. Somehow, before I knew it, I had asked her to marry me. *What was I thinking?* It certainly wasn't what I had worked for all my life, which was to own my very own motorized...er...motorcycle. After setting the date two or three times and (me) getting cold feet, and (she) deciding we should seal the commitment with an engagement ring, we were off to the discount jewelry store. I could see that motorcycle sputtering out of sight before my very eyes.

Andrea must have noticed how crestfallen I looked after walking out of the store with a $279.00 rock and the contract to pay $15.00 a month, plus interest until old age or paid in full, whichever came first. She suddenly softened and said, "That's OK, Mike, I know that's a lot of money. We could use that money for a lot of things we need worse." Just as suddenly, that motorcycle turns around and comes roaring back in my mind! If it's possible to feel shame and elation at the same time, I did it as we walked back into that store and voided the contract. I knew where I was going the next day, and it wasn't to another jewelry store. I heard someone say once, "I'd rather beg for forgiveness than ask for permission." (After all, we weren't married yet, right?)

So, the next day, as soon as I could get off work, I headed first to the Honda dealer because of my past indoctrination through advertising. But for some reason, I couldn't settle on the Honda. It likely cost too much, or the terms weren't right, I don't really remember. I ended up going over to the Suzuki place and got the same model, the exciting Suzuki 50! Hard to believe, but the price was around $279.00, exactly what I was going to pay for Andrea's engagement ring. Guilt started to set in. With taxes and tag, it cost me over two weeks salary, which of course I paid on the installment plan.

I was living in a one room apartment (well, actually three rooms, if you counted the kitchen and bathroom) upstairs, several blocks from campus, where I worked. The rent almost broke me at $50 a month, but I figured I could cut back on something in order to make the payments on the bike. I was still making payments on that red convertible. Life couldn't have been better!

I had a problem the day of purchase though. I tried to pretend I knew something about bikes, so the guy (I'll call him Bubba) wouldn't rip me off, but I had no idea what I was looking for. All I knew was the one I was checking out looked a lot like the Honda 50 I had dreamed about for years, and I couldn't wait to get my butt on it!

So, after some inane questions and conversation in general about riding (which I'm sure the guy knew I was faking), the deal was closed. It didn't dawn on me until I was handed the keys that I didn't have any way to get it home. And I really hadn't thought about where I would keep it. I began to think about how easy it would be for somebody to steal it.

I don't remember outright lying, but I needed answers from Bubba. I sort of nonchalantly asked about the gears. "So, is it the same as most bikes…uh…you know… the gears?" Bubba took the bait. "Oh, yeh, it's up for reverse, and four down." I had no idea what he had just said, but I faked it. "Oh, yeh, right, I…uh…kinda thought so…"

By this time, I'm considering backing out of the deal, realizing how stupid I must've sounded. Then I pictured myself riding into the sunset like my old friend, Sammy, with my hair flying in the breeze, and suddenly my courage was bolstered. (Back then, there wasn't a helmet law; hence the hair-flying reference.)

With my ignorance still showing, I asked Bubba a big favor. "Well, do you think you could drive it home for me, and let me follow you in my car? I can bring you back." It was almost dark, and time was a'wastin'. Bubba agreed to my terms, and in a flash, we were on the road, my anticipation building.

Now the next problem. There was no way I was going to go to bed without firing up that chariot and takin' 'er for a test run. (I know, my redneck roots start to show when I get excited...) Anyway, fortunately, there was an alley behind my apartment, so I pushed the Suzuki around back, tested the seat, did a run-through of the gears as best I could (having zero experience riding, except on a bicycle), and fired up the engine! I hoped nobody would decide to drive through the alley or surely I'd be run over. Also, I knew I'd be "choking it down" a few times before I got the hang of it, and I didn't want to endure the embarrassment. After a few times doing just that, I felt like Evil Knievel!

The hardest part was pushing the darn thing up the stairs that night, because there was no way I was going to leave it outside for somebody to steal! I still can't believe how it all played out so perfectly.

But I still had to "fess up" and tell Andrea what I had done. And that's exactly what I did the next day. I knew I couldn't put it off forever, so I decided to sweeten the deal by agreeing to let her parents buy her a horse after we got married. Did you know you can actually outrun a horse on a Suzuki 50? It was only one of many "races" we enjoyed until be both decided a couple of years later that it was time to grow up. What sweet memories!

By the time my mother passed away on February 13, 1992, I had owned five motorcycles, none of which she knew about, because I knew she would worry about me riding. I think it's the only secret I ever kept from my mother. I was fortunate I never got seriously hurt riding motorcycles, even though I owned an additional four until throwing in the towel finally in 2017. It had gotten to be scarier than it was fun, and I knew the time had come to close that chapter. However, I would be remiss if I didn't recount a few of those "scary" highlights from years past.

I think the first time it really hit me how dangerous motorcycles could be was one night when Andrea was riding double with me. We had ridden downtown to see the sights, of which there were always plenty in a university town like Tuscaloosa. By now I had become fairly proficient at riding, but I was always a little skittish and unsteady having Andrea on the back, knowing I was responsible for her safety as well.

Although I had been riding for several months, I still wasn't experienced enough to know the rule about approaching railroad tracks. The Rule: WHEN RIDING A MOTORCYCLE, ALWAYS CROSS RAILROAD TRACKS PERPENDICULARLY! Fortunately, this particular night, we weren't going that fast due to the speed limit downtown. I did actually slow down below the limit as we approached, but because it was nighttime, I didn't realize that I was about to cross the tracks at probably a 45 degree angle.

Just before the tire struck the rail itself, it bounced down into the "groove" in the pavement, jerking the wheel violently to the left. Just as suddenly, the right handlebar was nearly forced out of my grip. In my panic, I instinctively pulled back on it, causing me to rev the engine and thrust the bike careening forward with the tire still imbedded in the rut. Anyone who has ever driven a motorcycle knows that the right handlebar controls the throttle (and the front brake), and the left handlebar contains the clutch. With both feet on the pavement trying to keep from tipping over, I had no way of applying the rear brake (which is controlled by the right foot). So for a few harrowing seconds (which seemed like much longer), it was touch and go as we wobbled parallel to the track before I finally was able to stop the bike with my dancing feet!

Another scary, near disaster happened some time later when I "traded up" and got a nice 175cc Honda Scrambler. It was a great bike, which had tough, "knobby" tires and could be driven on road or off. Andrea was a good sport, and although she liked riding horses much more than motorcycles, she rarely turned me down when I asked her to hop on the back. We had decided one late fall afternoon to try the Scrambler out in the woods. After a short drive into the country, we found a seldom traveled dirt road and slowly turned off, looking for a break in the trees to try out those "knobbies."

We knew it would be a little more, shall we say, treacherous in the woods, but, the bike was light and Andrea weighed a little over a hundred pounds, so I felt confident that we'd be OK. It wasn't long before we spied the perfect incline to tackle, so we pulled up to the base of the hill and adjusted our helmets, reassuring each other that this was going to be fun and something we had never done before. (We were still young, foolish, and maybe stupid, and I guess it never occurred to us that this might actually be dangerous.)

With one last check of our vital signs (on the bike), I revved the engine and let out the clutch. I could feel Andrea's arms tighten around my stomach as we roared up Mt. Everest! It was a little wobbly to begin with, but with each revolution of the knobbies, our confidence grew. I'm estimating that it took less than 30 seconds to reach the top, and with euphoria setting in and our eyes on the goal, we could see the sky though the trees!

Suddenly, the unthinkable happened. Just before the front tire reached the crest of the hill, the engine began to sputter! The momentum at the start had taken us most of the way, but we found out the hard way, that a 175 Scrambler is not designed to pull a hill at that angle with a driver *and* a passenger.

The engine died! I had always told Andrea, "Don't ever put your feet down. That's my job. You'll have to trust me that I can drive the bike and you just enjoy the ride." But this was a different situation entirely.

My feet were now attempting to dig into the spongy autumn leaves, but it was too late! Over my right shoulder, I hear myself shout to Andrea, "Jump! JUMP! I'm gonna try to take it down!" By the time the words left my mouth, we were already picking up speed back down the hill as gravity did what it does best! We were hurtling backwards, and out of the corner of my eye, I could see Andrea preparing to launch! She made it! Smartly, she laid out flat to slow her descent, while I struggled to save the bike. I tried to remember how many trees we had passed, and suddenly they appeared much thicker and closer together than I remembered going up.

It was obvious that I was going to have to abandon the bike and save myself. With both feet still trying to find footing, I shoved the bike sideways, attempting to separate myself from it as we both picked up speed. But, at this point, I'm also fighting gravity, and I can see the bike flying off to my left as I tap dance backward, arms flailing! My eyes blur as I blindly make my descent backward.

There is no way I could stop, unless God sent a miracle. Which He did, in the form of a good-sized pine tree. *BAM! UGH!* The blow knocked the air out of my lungs; I felt my head spinning. And then another miracle! I hit that tree at the perfect angle, and incredibly, taking a much needed deep breath, I realized I was still standing up!

I still wasn't sure if I was going to pass out, and as I shook my head, my eyes focused on Andrea as she stumbled to her feet. *We were alive! Thank You, Jesus!* It was truly a day of miracles. Because the autumn leaves had cushioned the bike's fall and partial descent, we were able to roll it back down the hill, fire it back up, and although a wee bit shaky, we made it home in two pieces, never to ride off road again!

As I recalled that harrowing experience, my mind flashed back to a (sort of) similar incident—the only time I ever rode a horse in earnest. Andrea had invited me to go with her and her parents to Syracuse, New York to visit her Uncle Clyde and Aunt Dorothy. Even before we left, Andrea was planning to rent some horses to ride when we got there. Early on in our relationship, she had asked me if I liked horses. Not wanting to offend her with the truth, I sidestepped the question by declaring, "Oh, I like ALL animals." Truth be known, I hated horses, and still to this day, believe them to be one of the stupidest animals on God's green earth. Andrea, of course, disagreed with me, finding them to be virtually next to humans in intelligence and loving devotion.

Anyway, soon (I think it was the same day we arrived in Syracuse) we were watching the stable keeper saddle up two of his finest steeds. The rent was $30 an hour per horse. My math had never been good, but I figured that, for $60, I could find something much more fun to do. So, I started making deals. We could rent one horse for $30, and

Andrea could ride alone for an hour (my preferred offer). Andrea didn't like that deal, so I compromised on two horses for a half hour.

The guy had asked Andrea which horses we wanted to ride. (I didn't care, of course, I just wanted to get it over with.) Andrea told the guy that I hadn't ridden very much (that was a stretch), so I should get the horse that was "gentle" (meaning she would get the more "spirited" one).

Well, just my luck, wouldn't you know, the guy somehow got the horses mixed up, and I got the "spirited" one. I didn't know, because to me, all horses were alike—mean and stupid. It was decided that I would go first, and Andrea would catch up with me, since she was an accomplished rider and loved riding fast horses. And since she had the spirited horse (or so we thought), this shouldn't be a problem.

I will give horses credit for one thing. I think they know when you don't like them or are afraid of them. And in their own sadistic, sick way, they can't wait to buck you off. Well, no sooner had I gotten my left foot in the stirrup and had thrown myself into the saddle, ol' Dobbin took off like a shot! Not that I would have, but he didn't even wait for "Giddap!" or whatever you're supposed to say.

Before I knew it, I was circling the track at breakneck speed (bad choice of words), hanging on for dear life, and screaming "Whoa! Whoa! Whoa!" But it was no use. Ol' Dobbin had me where he wanted me, and he knew he was in control! I began to pray and confess (all) of my sins.

On the humorous side, Andrea told me later that I did a pretty good job for a novice. According to her, they were enjoying my form so much, they waited until I made a few rounds before they let Andrea mount up. In fact, the stable keeper even commented to her as they were watching me circle the barn, "Wow, that guy can really ride! I thought you said he couldn't ride very good!" I guess I had 'em fooled until I passed by the last time, and they heard me screaming my brains out in fear.

I don't remember too much after that, except quaking to Andrea when they finally reeled ol' Dobbin in, "Don't you ever expect me to get on another horse, EVER!" I think I gave new meaning to the term "laughing stock" (not to be confused with livestock).

OK, enough about horses. There were a couple of other incidents on the motorcycle that stand out. One of them happened on my last motorcycle, a beautiful red and black Yamaha Classic V-Star 1100 I had dolled up with American Eagle decals, saddlebags, and a Dukes of Hazzard horn that played Dixie! Most people mistook it for a Harley, so I had dubbed it my "Yamaharley."

It was on a Friday morning in November. I didn't usually work on Fridays, but I needed to go to the office to tie up a couple of loose ends, hoping to ride that afternoon, as the forecast looked like a great fall day. I had let time slip up on me and realized at the last minute that I would have to rush to get to the office before it closed. When traffic is right, I can make it from my house to the office in five minutes or less. It was about 11:40 A.M. and the office usually closed at 11:45. My house is the 3rd from the corner at which I had to turn right, and as I approached the red light where my street butts into the main drag, I pulled the choke back half way, reasoning that the motor had been running long enough to have warmed sufficiently. Usually, I would let the bike run for several minutes before cutting the choke completely off. I almost always have to stop for this particular light because it rarely changes even when driving a car, and I've never had the bike trip the light. From my house to the light, the street is on an incline, so I'm always faced with whether to keep moving slowly in hopes of the light being tripped on the other side by oncoming traffic or stop completely. Unfortunately, as fate would have it, everybody in Montgomery was headed to lunch on the main drag, forcing me to come to a complete stop. Knowing that the light would not change without other vehicular assistance (or divine intervention), my only hope in making it to the office before closing was to wait for a break in traffic to my left and then proceed by turning right on red. This time, fate was on my side, as the break came within seconds. Gunning the engine with my right hand while simultaneously easing my right foot off the brake and letting out the clutch with my left hand wasn't the tricky part. My left foot steadied the bike as I leaned to the right, assuming that full throttle would take me through the turn. The operation was performed—as it had been probably thousands of times before—with flawless perfection. Then, without warning, halfway through the turn, the engine died, and 800 pounds of dead weight motorcycle instantaneously pulled me down toward the pavement. It was a split second decision (or maybe it was a reflex), and my right arm instinctively jerked the handlebar upward as both legs shot out for balance. I knew that, if gravity won, several scenarios could unfold. First, I would probably break my right arm and/or shoulder, complete with lacerations, not to mention the damage to my right leg as the weight of the bike smashed it into the asphalt. Gravity would also pull me back down the hill, with the bike on top of me, possibly breaking my neck, or worse, cracking my skull if I lost the helmet. The other option (which would be worse...?) could possibly put me down in the middle of the street, with rush-hour lunch-goers unable to stop before running over me!

My right bicep took the brunt and snapped under the strain as I struggled to keep the bike upright. I felt the muscle separate from the bone, just above my right elbow. My right leg took over as sheer adrenaline steered the machine onto the grassy knoll to my right and out of harm's way. While I knew I had miraculously escaped major injury, I also knew my arm was hurt badly. Still stunned and trying to assess the damage, I pretended I was OK, but angry at myself for letting my haste over-rule my logic. After several seconds of painful silence, I decided to do the unthinkable and continue on to the office. *Maybe it wasn't as bad as it seemed*, I reasoned. *Or, maybe I'm just being a baby.* And, logically, it seemed that it would be more trouble to turn around from where I was than to keep going the way I had started.

Somehow, I made it to the office (on time!), and no one was the wiser as to my condition. I finished the job there, and after about 10 or 15 minutes, I drove the bike back home. I went straight to my car and drove immediately to the emergency room, afraid to pull my sleeve up for fear of what I would see. I could feel the muscle actually swinging back and forth under my skin. Within minutes, the doctor announced his "rule out" diagnosis: a torn right bicep tendon. They needed an MRI to confirm the diagnosis and, arm in sling, I sped to the imaging center for what I was sure would be more bad news. Before leaving the imaging center, I had an appointment scheduled to see an orthopedic surgeon on Monday.

Needless to say, the rest of the weekend was a wash, but the pills carried me through. On Monday, Dr. Freeman scheduled surgery for the following Friday, exactly a week from the day of the mishap. The doctor told me later that he was trying a fairly new procedure on my arm and hoped it would work. Apparently, it did, and with my work to keep my mind occupied and off the injury, and a trip to Phoenix to visit my daughter and granddaughter for Thanksgiving, the cast came off on Wednesday, November 28th. Several physical therapy sessions followed, and my final follow-up appointment with the doctor on Monday, January 4th netted a clean bill of health for the old right bicep tendon. The moral of the story: Don't bite the hand that feeds you, but rather use it to choke your motorcycle.

The final straw that unofficially ended my motorcycle riding career happened on a Saturday of Labor Day weekend a couple of years ago. Mike, a long-time "biker" buddy of mine, had asked me to go riding with him to see a friend of his. I had told Mike that I was maybe considering getting a "trike," because I had been dealing with some health issues, and I wasn't getting any younger. I though I might feel a little steadier on three wheels, so I had been shopping around for one. Mike had a friend, Jim, who had also had some health issues and had retired to the lake. He had a trike he wanted to sell and thought I might be interested in it.

Mike had another friend, Chris, he was going to pick up on the way, and I had some errands to run that morning, so I wouldn't be able to ride my bike over, but I did agree to meet them later at Jim's place.

It was a beautiful, pleasant fall afternoon by the time I left, and even by car, it was still a nice drive, which took me about an hour.

I didn't really know if I wanted a trike, because I had heard things about them I didn't like. You can't bank into a curve like you can on a two-wheeler, and it just doesn't have the same "feel" as a true motorcycle, I was told. Nevertheless, I was willing to try it out.

By the time I got to Jim's house, the rest of the gang was already there on Jim's back deck on the lake, telling war stories about motorcycles. After about an hour, Jim asked if I was ready to try out his trike.

To be honest, I wasn't too impressed with it from the start. First of all, even though it had low mileage, it looked much older than it was, which indicated to me that it hadn't been very well taken care of. Also, Jim had installed a "kit," sort of like training wheels for a bicycle, which meant that the vehicle now actually had four wheels, one in front and three in the back. Plus, the wheels on the kit didn't appear to have been installed properly as they were both about two to three inches off the ground, making the bike feel quite unsteady, even wobbly. Since I had never driven a trike, I asked Jim if he would back it out for me and let me take it around the block.

The trike was the same model as my Yamaharley, so I was familiar with its operation. The problem was, Jim lived on a fairly steep hill, so that I would have to pull out of his driveway and immediately turn hard right *up the hill*. Naturally, I wasn't too comfortable with this, but I didn't want to let Jim or my friend Mike down.

I had been told, "Whatever you do, *don't put your feet down.*" Jim had told me that I would feel like I was going to flip over, but under no circumstances should I put my feet down. The rear wheels would keep it upright, he assured me. He was very emphatic. I nervously edged the trike out onto the pavement, slowly pulling the right handlebar back to turn right, as I eased out on the clutch (and remembering my previous right bicep injury).

Within seconds and without warning, I found myself careening *down the hill toward the lake!* The trike had somehow decided, on its own, to take a sharp left as soon as I left the driveway! Immediately, I realized that I had absolutely no control of the trike, and even the brakes didn't seem to be working properly. Since I had never learned how to swim, I knew I couldn't end up in that lake. Fortunately, my right arm had healed enough to allow me to pull with all my might toward the right edge of the road. It must have rained recently because the ground was soft and the grass was lush and about six inches high, which slowed me down considerably.

Having ridden motorcycles for close to 50 years, my instincts told me to prepare for landing, and forgetting Jim's warning, I thrust both feet out to bring the trike to a stop. The consequences of my decision became grimly clear as the trike literally ran over both of my feet, bending them excruciatingly backwards trapping them under the trike's "running boards" before coming to a slippery halt on the wet grass!

I guess adrenaline kept me from realizing I was hurt, but when I looked down, I knew it wasn't good. The tops of both feet were embedded in the grassy soil, with my toes pointing backwards in a grotesque pose. I was so thankful I hadn't ended up in the lake that I didn't fully realize how dire my situation was until I tried to pull my feet out. The pain started to kick in about the same time panic set in. I desperately tried to rock the 800 pound trike from side to side in an attempt to pull one foot out at the time.

I was several yards from Jim's house by this time, but it seemed like hours before Jim had reached my side and started trying to help me pull my feet out of the bog. Apparently, the soft earth was the only thing that prevented both feet from being broken. Not realizing the pain I was in, and still not knowing for certain how badly I was injured, I heard Mike and Chris laughing hysterically from the deck on the back of Jim's house.

Slowly, panic turned to rage, accompanied by more adrenaline. Chris was next to arrive on the scene by the time I had freed my feet. He was a big burly guy and had driven trikes, so he offered to pull it out for me. I'm now hobbling away from the trike, trying to determine the extent of my injuries, which miraculously turned out to not be as bad as I had thought.

I was more incensed at being laughed at than I was afraid of my injuries. I even faked it enough to give the test drive another try, this time on flat ground. The trike performed no better the second time, so I figured it was time to give up on the idea. With almost unbearable pain in my feet, I was nonetheless determined to let no one know I was hurt. I remembered a Pee Wee Herman movie in which he was riding his bicycle past some of his "friends." He unexpectedly hit the curb, which sent him sprawling. As his friends rushed over to gloat and laugh, poor Pee Wee looked up with self assurance and declared confidently, "I meant to do that!"

Mike and his friends spent the next half hour or so chiding and chastising me for "putting my feet down." After convincing myself that I had fooled them all, I put on my best Pee Wee Herman face and proudly proclaimed that I needed to be getting back because I had some other "stuff" I had to do.

With pain still plaguing me, I finally went to see the doctor a month later. He told me that neither foot was broken, but gave me some "braces" to wear at night. The impact of the running board had lacerated my left ankle, above my Achilles tendon. It took several more months for the wound to finally heal, but the pain in my left heel had worsened to the point I actually considered getting a cane or a walker. My regular "podiatrist" had given me a different brace and sent me to physical therapy, but the pain got worse. I eventually saw a specialist at the Kirklin Clinic at UAB in Birmingham, who diagnosed my condition as Achilles Tendonitis. I was given still a different "boot" to wear and was told that, if this didn't work, I would need to have surgery.

Fortunately, after a few weeks, the pain was gone, and the whole incident began to fade in my memory. As fall turned to winter, and later spring, I tried riding a couple of times, but it just wasn't the same. I loved riding and still have fond memories of the great times on the road and the trips I took on my Yamaharley, as well the eight previous motorcycles.

    I sold the bike three months later, and although I miss riding, I know my mother is breathing easier in Heaven, knowing that I will be safe until I see her again. I never heard from Mike or his friends again.

CHAPTER TWENTY-FOUR

REMEMBERING FRIENDS

THEY SAY THAT, as a rule, the average person will end up having no more than three or four good friends in his or her lifetime. That doesn't mean just "acquaintances." Most of us have plenty of those. The first definition (out of five) of "friend" in my Webster's Unabridged Dictionary reads as follows: "a person whom one knows well and is fond of; intimate associate; close acquaintance; applied loosely to any associate or acquaintance."

My personal definition goes a little deeper. I have often defined a friend as "someone who is still there for you when everybody else walks out on you." And those of you who have true friends (a redundant term?) know who yours are. You've probably heard people say, "I hadn't seen (Susan) in over five years, and last week when we met for lunch, we picked up right where we had left off…just like it was yesterday!"

I think a person is very fortunate this day and age to have friends like that. As the years have passed, I've seen acquaintances in the obituary section, which saddens me. But when it is a friend (by my definition), I typically don't read about them in the paper. Usually, the family or a mutual friend has already contacted me, giving me time to try to prepare for the worse.

Thankfully, those of us who are still around manage to get together whenever we can, usually to talk about nothing in particular. It's the fellowship that's important, and just being there for each other. It reminds me, in a way, of Dolly Parton's song, "In the Good Old Days (When Times Were Bad)."

The following five special friends never met each other, but I knew them well. And they are representative of the wonderful memories I have of them all.

Meet Barbara...

It's not often one can say they remember vividly the first and last time they saw someone special to them. I can, however, say that about my friend, Barbara Cain. I first met Barbara in August of 1989. Barbara and two friends, Jeri and Norma Jo had placed an ad in the Bulletin Board, a local advertising "rag," inviting three gentlemen to write letters of application to attend their "dinner party." I, along with two other total strangers at the time, Billy and Jimmy, were the lucky winners. I won't say that we overstayed our welcome, but let's just say that Barbara and the girls had to literally run us off that night!

I can't speak for the other two guys—but, then again, I think I can—we left that night feeling that we had known the other five attendees all of our lives. Sadly, Barbara was never again able to get all six of us together at the same time, but over the years, she kept our friendships going with phone calls, cards, letters, and simply "being there" when we needed her.

When Barbara had cancer several years later, I was privileged to help care for her during chemotherapy, prednisone, nausea, bald head and all. She, of course, returned the favor when I was diagnosed with cancer in August of 2003. I always prided myself as never being at a loss for words, but when Barbara sent me a check for $100 when I lost my job, words failed me. I knew she couldn't afford it, but when I attempted to pay her back, she let me know in no uncertain terms that a gift from the heart is never to be repaid.

Barbara was one of the first to visit me in the hospital after my cancer surgery, and one of the first to read the book I wrote in 2005. I can't begin to do her justice by trying to summarize what Barbara Cain meant to me. I could write another book about the goodness I saw in her. Through all of her trials, I never heard Barbara complain, and when I was at my lowest, she made me feel at my highest with her bright smile and infectious laugh.

I think sometimes we don't know what we have until we lose it. I'll admit that I took Barbara for granted, somehow knowing she would always be there for me if I needed her. Then suddenly the world changed on that fateful Tuesday afternoon while I was at work. My phone rang. It was a mutual friend, Dolores, calling to let me know that Barbara was in the hospital.

"Oh, my gosh, Dolores, is she OK?" I asked, not expecting the dreadful answer.

"No," Dolores replied, her voice quivering, "I don't think she's going to make it."

Surely, I must have a bad connection, I thought. "Wait…what do you mean…?"

Dolores went on to explain that Barbara had been battling respiratory issues the past few weeks and that her condition had worsened the last several days. *Why hadn't Barbara called me? Why hadn't I kept in touch with her? Did she just not want to bother me or worry me?* Too many questions.

I asked Dolores if I could see her, and she told me I didn't need to rush, that she was resting comfortably. She was sure it would be fine if I came after work. It was around three o'clock, but I didn't want to wait, so I wound things up at the office and left early.

I got to the hospital before rush hour had set in. I wasn't prepared when I walked into Barbara's room. She was struggling for breath and unable to open her eyes. I suddenly felt a lump in my throat as I approached her bedside. I slowly reached for her hand as my eyes filled with tears. I wasn't sure she would recognize my voice, and with all the courage I could muster, I told her simply, "Barbara, it's Mike; I love you." Her eyes remained closed, and I was almost certain she wasn't aware of who I was.

Surprisingly, however, without hesitation, she answered back, "I love you, too." I continued to hold her hand, gently stroking it and praying that she was somehow comforted by my presence. I'm not sure how long I savored our last moments. I only know it ended all too soon. I gave Barbara a lingering kiss on her cool brow; my tears flowed freely, burning my eyes as I stifled my sobs.

Although I still wasn't ready to let her go, I knew Barbara was a dedicated Christian and that she was at peace with the world and ready to meet her Savior. As I stumbled into the hallway, I remembered the night Barbara had brought us all together. It seemed like yesterday, and I remembered thinking that life is much too short.

Barbara died peacefully in her sleep early the next morning. The date was June 16, 2010. Barbara had graced me with her friendship for nearly 21 years, and it seemed I had known her forever. As I got up to go to work that morning, I spoke with her one last time in my mind. "Enjoy singing with the angels, Barbara. We'll see you at your next 'dinner party'."

Meet Dean...

Don't let the name fool you. Although a typically masculine name, this "Dean" was a woman through and through. Blessed with beauty and moxie, she challenged everyone she knew, making new friends wonder why they hadn't become friends sooner.

My family and I had just moved into a neighborhood of mostly young to early middle-aged couples raising their children, working, and being good neighbors. The area was beautiful and vibrant, with tree-lined streets and well manicured lawns tended usually by the "man of the house." Andrea and I often took walks, occasionally meeting a neighbor here and there.

One particular home intrigued us, as it was on the corner of our street, with "everything in its place," so to speak. As we approached the Faulkner home, we noticed a striking, very pregnant, auburn-haired lady strolling the yard. Almost immediately, we were in conversation with Dean, who was expecting her first child. Our walk went no further than the corner, and we agreed to get together with Dean and her husband, Buddy, as soon as we could arrange it. And thus began an incredible friendship filled with fellowship, singing, dining, storytelling, and just plain fun.

The marriage was the first for Dean, the second for Buddy. They seemed to be a good match, with Buddy's laid-back and charming manner and Dean's sometimes fiery, take-no-prisoners presentation. Buddy was a pilot, usually in great demand, and flew both helicopter and fixed-wing planes. He had worked for the Alabama Drug Enforcement Agency, and listening to his stories of flying around the state, searching remote areas for marijuana plants and suspicious drug dealing activity was always a favorite pastime. He would sometimes freelance and fly various local businessmen to meetings, conferences, and other functions around the state. He even showed us a picture of him actually pulling his small Cessna (true story!) with a rope off the interstate highway one night after an emergency landing. With some help from a couple of Good Samaritan passing motorists, he was able to move the plane out of harm's way. One of them took a picture of the eerie scene and sent it to Buddy later for his "scrapbook." Never a dull moment!

Buddy was also a musician of sorts, and to my way of thinking, he was an excellent guitar player. Many nights, with our two daughters in tow, Andrea and I would trek to the Faulkner home to enjoy a relaxing night of singing and laughing. In fact, none of us (including Buddy) were accomplished singers, but we certainly had fun trying! And Dean always managed to have some festive snacks and other goodies to add to the mix.

Dean had left the work-a-day world to be a stay-at-home mom to "Angel," who was born only a few weeks after we met. Although Dean was our age (Buddy was a few years older), Andrea and I had become "old hands" (or so we thought) at parenting. We would often exchange war stories of things to come for her and Angel.

As the years passed, Dean enjoyed finger-wagging as our daughter, Ashley, entered her teen years. She would remind us of "advice" we had given her early on as we now struggled with adolescence and sibling rivalry.

Eventually, both the Moodys and the Faulkners moved on, leaving the neighborhood as the city adjusted to demographic change. Occasionally, we would run into our old friends and reminisce about times spent in the old neighborhood.

Time waiting on no one, our respective marriages unfortunately ended in divorce and our children grew up and moved away. Understandably, Andrea and I lost touch with the Faulkners but held on to the fond memories. Buddy had provided generously for Dean after their divorce, and we had all adjusted to our new lives.

I later had to deal with cancer and accompanying chemotherapy, hair loss, depression and adjustment to living alone. Then suddenly, Dean reappeared.

I was mindlessly watching TV when my doorbell rang. The Dominos Pizza delivery guy looked somewhat confused as he asked my name. I confirmed that I was who he was looking for and that my address matched his paperwork. However, I told him that there must be a mistake and that I hadn't ordered a pizza.

"Yeh, I know," he said, "but this isn't a pizza." At this point, I'm starting to think that maybe I was hallucinating from the effects of chemo, or maybe I wasn't fully awake from a dream I was having. *I must have fallen asleep in front of the TV, I thought.*

Sensing my bewilderment, the pizza guy explained. "You see…this lady came in tonight as I was loading my car for my deliveries, and she asked me if I wanted to make some extra money. She asked if she could pay me for a pizza box and would I deliver it to you at this address."

None of this was making sense, so still confused, I pressed him for more information. "What do you mean? Who was it?" I asked. "Are you telling me that some strange woman approached you to deliver an empty pizza box to me?"

"No…I don't think it's empty…she put something in it. I think you should take it. There's no charge; she already gave me the money."

I'd never been a suspicious or paranoid person, but I was starting to wonder if this was a joke, or maybe an "enemy" I must have made somewhere along the way. I took the box to the kitchen and slowly opened the lid. Inside was a neatly folded, obviously new Tommy Hilfiger shirt with a small white envelope which concealed a note from Dean.

Mystery solved. Dean had somehow heard of my health issues and had "tracked me down." Because Dean and Buddy shared a strong Christian faith with Andrea and me, she wanted to reach out to me, but she wasn't sure how I might take her efforts. She decided this would be a clever way to let me know she was concerned about me without being too forward or presumptuous. It was classic Dean! And I loved it!

Over the next several months, we did "reconnect," and we saw each other as friends. I still considered Buddy my friend, so I didn't want to damage that relationship. Andrea had remarried and I was "rebuilding" my life and my career. Dean remained my good friend, and, in a sense, we became each other's "counselor." Dean eventually moved back to her parents' home 50 miles away to take care of their affairs after their deaths. Then one day, Dean called me with the devastating news. She had cancer, and the prognosis wasn't good.

Being the strong, independent person I knew her to be, she didn't ask for help, but I knew she was in for a fight against this horrible disease. She had been diagnosed with lupus years earlier and had dealt with it off and on for some time. Although not the same as cancer, the treatment sometimes includes immunosuppressant drugs that are also used in chemotherapy.

I made it a point to help Dean as often as I could during chemotherapy. The Cancer Center where she was being treated was within a couple of blocks from my office, so I would meet her there as my work schedule permitted.

Amazingly, she made it through chemo, and I never heard her complain about her bald head. The beautiful red hair was gone, but her fiery personality was still there! I visited with Dean at her home several weeks after her regimen of chemo was completed, and I was stricken with how well she seemed to be doing. Her auburn hair has replaced with short, curly (and might I add, stylish) salt and pepper that was quite becoming! She was upbeat and cheerful and talked about the future. I left thinking that maybe things were looking up for her. Then the call came from Angel.

Dean had died peacefully at home, and had earlier asked Angel if she would see if I could serve as a pallbearer. I was devastated, and of course, I gladly accepted the honor of seeing her this one last time. I was sorry I hadn't been there for her when she needed me the most, but I was also sure she simply didn't want me to see her "that way."

The church was small and, when I arrived, was already overflowing with family, friends, and acquaintances coming to pay their respects to this incredible woman. After the service, I had a nice visit with Angel and her father, my old friend, Buddy.

We all agreed that, today, Dean was probably combing that new shock of auburn hair and planning her next "pizza delivery!"

Meet Harry...

And then there was Harry. Harry Wallis gave new meaning to the word flamboyant. I met Harry in 1971, shortly after my family and I moved to Birmingham. But first, a little history.

We had been living in Lexington, Kentucky for the previous two years, where my wife and I had gotten involved in the "conservative movement." Although Andrea and I were from different parts of the country (she was from Wisconsin and I was born in South Alabama) both of our families raised us in traditional American style. We were taught to respect our elders, do as our parents told us, go to church, pledge to the flag, and don't smoke and drink. I don't really remember being taught all that; we just learned it somehow. And it made sense to us. Admittedly, there was some culture shock for both of us when we started dating. Her parents had moved South where her father, Roger (a brilliant and kind Christian man), had gotten a job at NASA in Huntsville. Andrea and her mother, Janet, attended the University of Alabama in Tuscaloosa while Roger worked in north Alabama, some 120 miles away. I had enrolled in graduate school at UA and met Andrea in one of my first classes.

Andrea was under the impression that anybody who lived in the South was a snaggle-toothed red-neck hillbilly, and I was pretty sure she was a Damn Yankee because, frankly, my daddy believed anything north of Montgomery, Alabama was "enemy territory." I guess we were both bigoted in our own way, but suffice it to say, we both learned a lot from each other.

Fast forward back to the future approximately seven years. Although Kentucky was a beautiful state, a good part of the economy was driven by distilleries, tobacco farms, and gambling (on the horses at the Kentucky Derby). Neither Andrea nor I had anything to do with those three (except that Andrea liked horses), so we headed back to Alabama, closer to our family and friends.

And that's where we met Harry. He was an accountant by trade. I don't think he had an "advanced degree," but it didn't matter. He was so good at his trade after many years of "practice," that he actually was instrumental in putting together the requirements for becoming a certified public accountant (CPA) for the state of Alabama. He was also big in the "conservative movement," which is how we came to know him.

Through our connections with some of the local conservative leaders in Birmingham, I managed to land a job managing the American Opinion Bookstore on the south side of Birmingham. The store was quite the political establishment, as it was actually set up to distribute books, pamphlets and other information about the John Birch Society, and it operated on a shoestring budget. Even though Harry was never a member of the Society, he was sympathetic to the cause, and most of the members considered him an "honorary member" who paid his dues in service to every one he came in contact with. Harry actually donated his time as the store's bookkeeper, and after working at the store for several weeks, I met Harry for the first time.

As soon as he walked in, I immediately liked him. Harry didn't work on a schedule. He'd just show up when he was "in the neighborhood," take a look at the books (both financial and the ones on the shelf). And then we'd talk politics. Harry must have known everybody in Birmingham, because by the time he would leave, he had educated me about all of the people he knew who were "anybody" in Birmingham.

Although Harry was as serious as they came when it had to do with the plight of America (even in 1971), I never saw him without that devilish smile that made you think he surely was up to something. And he usually was. An hour with Harry seemed like minutes as he would opine about whatever came to his mind. Needless to say, we became fast friends. He was probably 25 years older than me, but Harry was the kind of guy who could talk to anybody of any age, and make you feel like you'd attended high school together. He was dashingly trim and dapper, with a shock of wavy white hair that was as wild as the wind. Even at age 52, his silver coiffure looked like a cross between Dr. Emmett Brown from Back to the Future and Albert Einstein. But, believe me, his hair was the only thing "old" about him! He and his wife were members of a dance club, and I soon learned that dancing was a passion of his. He was devoted to his wife, who shared his interest in dancing and accounting.

During the time I got to know Harry, he started helping me with my tax returns. I don't know how much he charged his other clients, but I always felt like he was charging me much less than he could have. I do know that he knew how to pinch a penny if he had to and was an excellent manager of his business. He even employed his wife, Janet, and a couple of his daughters, along with a couple of other accountants.

The first time I went to Harry's office, I was surprised to find that it was actually in his basement! Well, that's actually not totally true. Harry had a beautiful home in an upscale suburb of Birmingham, and it just sort of evolved that he was doing accounting in his home, so he figured why not just convert his (unused) basement into an office. And that's what he did.

This worked OK until one year an irascible neighbor decided there were too many cars at his house and complained to the zoning board, forcing Harry to rent an office nearby in the business part of town. But Harry never missed a beat. He didn't like the arrangement, but he complied until he could work the matter out with "the authorities." He was eventually allowed to move his business back to the neighborhood after fixing a separate entrance to the basement and designing a parking lot hidden by the trees to accommodate the traffic. I think the neighbor finally moved anyway.

I later "moved on" from my job as a bookstore manager, but Harry and I kept in touch. When I told him I would be leaving Birmingham to accept a job managing a radio station in Troy, I asked him if he could recommend someone there to do my taxes. In typical Harry Wallis style, he asked, "Why don't you let me do it?"

And so began our long distance relationship that lasted another 30 years. The drill was consistent. Each year, around February, I would get a letter from Harry, reminding me it was almost time to get my "tax stuff" together. He would always include a "packet" for me to complete (which I never did) before our appointment sometime before April 15th. I would make the annual trek to Birmingham, where Harry and I would sit around and talk politics, lamenting the good old days, and blasting the evil IRS.

Eventually, I'd pull out the packet (which I hadn't looked at until that day), and Harry would go to work, asking me questions about my deductions, donations, car tag receipts, and any other pertinent information we could use to make my tax burden lighter. Harry was the quintessential tax man, never missing an opportunity to save the beleaguered taxpayer a few cents.

After a couple of hours (or more), we would wind up our meeting. I would always joke about how I wasn't paying him enough and he was spending more time than I was worth, but Harry always shrugged me off with a hearty handshake and that familiar Wallis grin.

Harry saw me through a lot of personal and financial history, guiding me and advising me the best course to stay out of trouble with "the beast." As the years passed, I wouldn't let myself think about the inevitable. Then, in November of 2008, I got the letter.

I knew it was too early for Harry to be reminding me about "tax time," and the envelope wasn't the familiar large brown envelop I was used to. I finally opened it two months later.

The first three words confirmed my worst fears: *"We are saddened..."* Through the mist, I read *"...passed away on September 5th...a tremendous loss...will be surely missed..."*

I immediately felt ashamed that I hadn't read the letter sooner, so I labored over how to respond. I sent his wife, Janet, a letter on January 30, 2009, in which I tried to sum up what Harry had meant to me: It read in part as follows:

> *Words cannot express the sadness I felt when I received the inevitable letter with the news that my dear friend, Harry, had passed away. Since I first met him at the American Opinion Bookstore in 1971, Harry has been my friend, father figure, mentor, political ally, counselor, confidant, and, of course, my "tax man" for the past 36 years, getting me out of more than one tight with the dreaded IRS. As you know, during that time, we rarely saw each other more*

than once a year when I made the annual trek to Birmingham to catch up on all the news, talk about the good times (and the "bad times" in politics!), and just renew the friendship that had grown so strong over the years. Harry and I had a connection that made me feel each time I saw him that I had just seen him yesterday. You and Harry and the staff were a permanent part of my Birmingham family. He and I used to joke that it cost me too much and it took him too much time to make it profitable for either of us. Yet, we continued to do it year after year. My greatest fear—besides the realization that one day it would all end permanently—was that, because it wasn't an economically wise arrangement for Harry, he would just cut me off and tell me to get my taxes done locally. But he never did. And I always told myself it was because he just enjoyed seeing me too.

Although I received your letter in November, I still have not fully accepted Harry's passing. They say that denial is the first stage in dealing with grief and loss. To say that he will be missed is a gross understatement. I didn't lose a tax man; I lost a buddy. A tax man can be replaced, but there's no way to replace Harry.

My friend was 89 years old, and as far as I know, he never stopped working. If heaven ever needed an audit, I'm sure Harry Wallis is the man for the job!

Meet Wiley...

I always associate Wiley Perry with Birmingham, because that's where it all started with him. I had already done one stint at WDJC-FM from 1972 to 1977. I left for seven years to try my hand as an entrepreneur in Troy, about 20 miles from my home town. I knew a few people in that area, so I had some "connections." I had gotten interested in the idea of an old-fashioned ice cream parlor after becoming intrigued with Baskin Robbins Ice Cream (with 31 flavors) in

Birmingham which my wife and daughter would often frequent.

Unfortunately, I had no idea what I was doing, and I had a lot of competition from a local merchant in Troy who had been in business for years with a shop nearby called the Tastee Freeze. Just in case my little venture didn't make it, I had taken a management position at WRES-FM in Troy. To complicate matters (but really, in a positive way), my wife had become pregnant with our second child, and by the time we opened Moody's Old Timey Ice Cream Parlor and Sandwich Shoppe, she was already about seven months along. We specialized in old-fashioned dip ice cream, and Andrea's tummy started to get in the way. Long story short, we closed the store four months after the grand opening, and the following year, the radio station was sold and the new owner no longer needed my services as a manager.

This was followed by four or five more years of floundering aimlessly in the work force, so I was glad to get the call from Birmingham in 1984. After some restructuring, WDJC's owner had decided to start over with as many of the original staff as possible, and I was asked to come back as Director of Station Operations. That was the good news. The bad news was that my wife had finally gotten her first real job as a teacher (after returning to school to become certified), and my children were well established in the school system in Montgomery. So the decision was made for me to commute to Birmingham from Montgomery. I would leave on Monday mornings for Birmingham, drive back home on Wednesday nights, back to Birmingham, then home on Friday nights.

Basically, I was responsible for the on-air sound, including programming of the music, production and scheduling of commercials, and hiring, training, and (unfortunately) sometimes firing on-air personnel.

I have to admit I wasn't that impressed with Wiley when I first met him. A former newspaper reporter, he had "reinvented" himself five years previously after struggling for decades with alcohol addiction. He had been clean and sober since then, and had married a very sweet young lady 15 years his junior. Mary was definitely a keeper, as she supported Wiley in whatever he endeavored to do. Theirs was truly a touching love story. She was employed by the University of Alabama in Birmingham and was responsible for maintenance of all of their buildings, and in addition to supporting Wiley during his "recovery," she was also his most ardent "cheerleader."

Wiley was a talented musician and photographer, and before starting his journey into sobriety, he played gigs at most of the popular night spots in town with his own band which he called "Periscope." He had his own photography studio in their small apartment, and its walls were adorned with a large assortment of his professional photographs. Wiley was also a passionate motorcycle enthusiast, and after his spiritual awakening, he and Mary would attend Hell's Angels and other rallies, witnessing and preaching to the bikers of Jesus's saving grace!

I had advertised for someone to fill the early morning, pre-drive time slot, and Wiley showed up for an interview. "So, how much radio experience do you have, Wiley?" I asked. "Well, I don't really have any experience in radio, but I used to work at a newspaper in Macon (Georgia)," he responded. And thus started a very long conversation with one of the most interesting applicants I had ever had.

I still can't explain why I hired him. I think I just liked him. As he had pointed out, he had no experience, but his sincerity and, dare I say, his brashness, impressed me. The early morning slot was typically not a heavy audience, and I figured, with Wiley's zeal, maybe he would learn the ropes fairly quickly.

To say that his first several weeks were challenging would be an understatement. There was no getting around the fact that Wiley was a "country boy." He even came up with his own moniker, and called himself, "The Old Preacher's Boy." His father had been a Baptist minister, so the name stuck. As sincere as he was, though, Wiley had difficulty developing an "on-air personality," and I eventually started having him perform other necessary jobs around the station. And this is where he excelled.

One of my duties as Director of Station Operations was scheduling the full-time and part-time announcers to fill 24 hours, seven days a week. It was an arduous task, and I had been writing it out on a lined piece of notebook paper. It was messy at best, and I was constantly frustrated with having to make last-minute corrections by hand, which was often confusing to the staff.

Apparently Wiley took note of this, and one morning he came in and handed me a piece of paper. "What do you think of this?" he asked. To my amazement, the complete schedule was neatly typed on an easy to read grid, with every slot filled in as I had written it out the previous week!

"What…? Wiley, how did you do this? When…?" Wiley cut me off in mid-question and with a sly grin replied, "I used my computer."

Somewhere in time, I must have heard the term, but I had no idea what one was. "Computer…what's that?" I asked. Oh, I forgot to mention that Wiley was an IT person before there was a name for it. Truthfully, he was a computer whiz, and after about 15 minutes of attempting to explain what he could do with this new fangled invention, I stopped him with a wave of my hand. "Well, never mind, just keep doing it." *One less thing I'll have to worry about, I thought.*

So, with Wiley in the background, and me taking credit for it, I became probably the best Director of Station Operations WDJC ever had! It didn't matter to Wiley; he was just glad to have the job and to be able to prove to me that I hadn't made a mistake in hiring him.

Over the next three years, Wiley Perry became my right hand man, rescuing me from many a tight spot precisely when I needed it, taking a burden off my shoulders when it all seemed too much to handle, and best of all, just making me look good! And the amazing thing about Wiley was that he never had a desire to take credit for any of it, and he never complained about anything I gave him to do. In short, Wiley made me forget the age-old admonition in management: *Never be friends with those who work under you.*

To the contrary, I came to depend on Wiley more than I realized, and my family and I developed a rock solid friendship with Wiley and his wife, Mary.

Sadly, due to circumstances beyond anyone's control, Wiley's position was eventually eliminated by "corporate," and I had to tell Wiley that we no longer needed him. I had had to fire employees in the past - which was never pleasant - but this was probably the most difficult "pink slip" I ever had to deliver. Instead of my consoling him (which I tried to do), Wiley shrugged me off, expressing thanks for believing in him when no one else would.

"What am I going to do? How am I going to make out my schedules?" I wailed.

"Just get your own computer," he said.

"But I don't know anything about computers," I moaned.

"That's no problem," he stated, in typical Wiley fashion, "I'll show you how to find one."

We remained friends through it all, and Wiley and Mary eventually moved "back home" to care for Mary's elderly mother in Alexander City. Several years later, when I started working on my book, Mules In The Fast Lane, I contacted my good friend, Wiley, and made several trips to his house to get help with layout, editing, and picture placement, drawing on his newspaper background for inspiration. Wiley was 10 years older than me and by now, I could tell that something just wasn't right. Although I didn't know it at the time, Wiley was beginning to suffer with early onset Alzheimer's, and, as much as he wanted to help me, it simply wasn't working for him.

I talked to Mary and she and I agreed it would be best if I bowed out and tried to make it without Wiley's help. I thanked Wiley for being such a good friend and for agreeing to help me with such a daunting project. I said my goodbyes, knowing that it was just a matter of time before the dreaded disease would take him from us.

Several months later, I called to check on Wiley, and as expected, Mary told me he wasn't doing well. I made plans to drive over and have lunch with them that weekend. I knew it would be hard, but I wasn't prepared for Wiley's condition. It was heartbreaking to see how much my friend had deteriorated since I had last seen him.

The meal and the fellowship were great, but I could tell Wiley was struggling with his memory and even his words, asking questions that had already been answered and periodically lapsing back in time, talking about old times as if we were still there.

I knew I wouldn't be ready for the call from Mary, which came only a few weeks later, letting me know that Wiley had passed away. As I hung up the phone with her, I was reminded of the song by Luther Vandross: "If I could steal one final glance, one final step, one final dance with him; I'd play a song that would never ever end…'cause I'd love, love, love to dance with my father again."

Although I was very sad, I knew that, at last, "the old preacher's boy" was reunited with his family. And, undoubtedly, dancing with his father…again.

Meet Jerry…

Over my lifetime, I estimate that I've purchased probably a couple dozen or more cars or trucks. All but three have been used. I have never leased a car, although I have rented a few. I've also rented trucks when I would move. There have been only two salesmen that I have trusted without question. One is my brother-in-law, Don (married to my sister, Jean), and the other was Jerry Lanier. I use the past tense, because my good friend, Jerry, passed away unexpectedly a few months ago.

I moved to Montgomery 38 years ago and met Jerry about seven years later. He and his (later) partner, Joe Harrison, were independent dealers and had separate car lots next to each other on a prominent corner on the Atlanta Highway. CVS needed the corner, so Jerry and Joe formed a partnership after CVS bought them out, and moved their lot across the highway.

Jerry and Joe worked well together. One would watch the store while the other went to the auction, then vice versa. I had actually met both of them before the move, but hadn't bought a car. When they got "established," I found myself stopping by occasionally just to chat. They were just nice, friendly folks, and our friendships grew. Before long, I had bought my first car from Jerry. Later, both of my daughters bought a couple of cars each from Jerry or Joe.

After Joe retired and moved back to South Alabama, Jerry and I got to know each other better, even riding our motorcycles together when time and weather permitted. Soon it was understood that I had no need for any other car salesman but Jerry. He was the proverbial good ol' boy, about my age, and the most amazing thing about Jerry was that he never tried to sell me a car. But he always did.

Jerry would often encourage me to look somewhere else before considering getting a car or truck from him. He would even help me look elsewhere if he didn't have the particular model I was looking for. But I always came back to Jerry. And I always bought my car from Jerry. He would even help me figure out purchases my daughters were interested in as they moved from Georgia, Arizona, Massachusetts and California.

And if I ever wanted to get rid of my vehicle, he would let me park it on his lot at no charge. If I couldn't come over when someone was interested in it, he would call and ask how much I wanted for it, and he would sell it for me, never charging me a commission. And he never required I buy my next car from him. But I always did.

It wasn't uncommon for Jerry to catch me out on his small lot kicking tires and hand me the keys to a particular model. "Here, take it home with you and drive it over the weekend." I didn't always buy it, but he knew I'd come back. That had never happened to me before I met Jerry.

One day I purchased a Dodge Ram from Jerry. Several days later, I was purchasing the license plate for it and the clerk told me the seller had made an error in figuring up the sale. She didn't tell me what kind of error it was, so I didn't really give it much thought. I knew that, whatever it was, Jerry would make it right, so a couple of weeks later, I stopped by the lot and nonchalantly told him he owed me lunch.

"Really, why is that?' he asked. I explained what the clerk had said, and Jerry immediately told me to go get the paperwork out of the truck. Thumbing through the documents, he paused to scratch his head, and declared, "She's right, buddy, I owe you $300," and proceeded to write me a check right there on the spot!

One of the last conversations I had with Jerry turned out to be somewhat prophetic. We were "visiting," as usual, and I asked him, "Jerry, when are you going to quit all this and take some time off?" "Well," he replied jokingly, "when I hit the ground, I guess."

We both stayed busy, and it wasn't unusual for us to go fairly long periods of time without seeing each other. Several weeks after that conversation, I passed by the lot and noticed it was nearly empty. Hoping his inventory had just gotten low (which would have been very unusual), I waited a few days before I made the phone call. His trusted friend and jack-of-all-trades right hand man, Johnny, answered the phone. "Jerry passed away, Mike...he fell...it happened real quickly..."

Jerry was my car salesman, my confidant, my advisor, my buddy, and I miss him immensely. But, sometimes God forces us to get the rest we need. So...rest in peace, my dear friend. And please...slow down.

Honorable Mentions

I've lived long enough to appreciate the wonderful life I've had and to take time to celebrate the time I have left. Unfortunately too many of my dear friends have passed away, and from time to time, I still pause to celebrate their memory and all they meant to me. Each one would make a book within itself. And to say that they deserve an "Honorable Mention" wouldn't even come close to expressing what they meant to me. Although I could write a book about each one, I selected the preceding five as representative of the richness they brought to my life.

Other wonderful friends I still hold in my heart are no less precious than the ones I chose to honor in this chapter. Each chapter of my life has special meaning, and each has been filled with wonderful people and experiences that cannot be measured or bought at any price. For example, one chapter alone, "the broadcasting chapter," would contain volumes. To mention a few, my dear friend, Gordon Tucker was an incredible radio man, with a booming voice that I could only dream of emulating. His unflagging optimism and dedication to broadcasting was an inspiration to all who knew and worked with him. One of my fondest memories of Gordon was when we traveled around Alabama and Georgia marketing (or attempting to) his own radio series he called "Just a Minute, Mr. President!" During one of our travels, we actually "discovered" an AM radio station in Dallas, Georgia with the call letters, WKRP!

And Don Markwell, radio disc jockey and pioneer, manager, intellectual, "political acitivist" (and friend of Gordon Tucker) honored me by having lunch with me every Thursday for the last several years of his life. I was with him at his home when he passed away in 2011, and I still remember graphically our stimulating lunches.

My tenure in Christian radio afforded me associations with virtually every preacher, minister, pastor, evangelist and Christian "crusader" in the city of Birmingham during the 1970's and 80's. WDJC manager, Larry Adcock believed in my ability as a program director, copywriter and producer and gave me my first "real job" there. Wayne Wallace was at WDJC when I started and was host of the popular "Dixie Gospel Caravan" from 6:00 until 10:00 P.M., his career spanning 45 years from 1968 until his death in 2013.

I could go on and on and never succeed in honoring them all. So, I'll simply end this "chapter" with the words from the movie "Titanic" and hope it will suffice:

> *Near, far, wherever you are*
> *I believe that the heart does go on*
> *Once more you open the door*
> *And you're here in my heart*
> *And my heart will go on and on*

CHAPTER TWENTY-FIVE

THE ROAD IS LONG

AUTHOR'S NOTE: It seems appropriate that any writer of any book, story, or recollection would want to leave the reader with a desire to want to read more, to know more, and to perhaps even write their own book. Any book, after all, will be history after it is written. I've often said that every person has a book in them; for most people, it just hasn't been written yet.

This "final chapter" is not really the end of history. It is only documentation of the past and a continuation of a past that others can hopefully use to inspire them to do their own "personal work." As a counselor, I encourage people to "write it down," whether it be in an "official" journal or on a piece of scrap paper. Because you never know who might find it useful after you write it. It might even be you.

The story behind "The Road Is Long" spans almost 54 years. Although it has been a "work in progress" for that long, its official "recording" (writing it down) started Thursday afternoon, September 21, 2017, and still it is a work in progress. As a result, the reader may find that parts of this chapter are duplicated from previous chapters.

In relating this story, I have attempted to include enough detail so as to report it as accurately as possible. At the same time, I have taken great pains to respect the privacy of each individual who has made this incredible journey with me. Some names have been changed to accomplish that goal. I apologize in advance for any errors in reporting or for any disclosures that I overlooked when including or excluding them that may appear inconsiderate or lacking assiduousness.

January 6, 1964. It was my 20th birthday and the first day of my last quarter in college. I could almost feel the light at the end of the tunnel. I had been in college since June of 1961 (a week or so after high school graduation), taking no breaks, except for those between quarters and the various holidays. My purpose in going "straight through" was three-fold: (1) I wanted to get away from my father, who was, by this time, what appeared to be a hopeless alcoholic. (He did eventually quit drinking on October 18, 1975, never to take another drink.); (2) The Vietnam war was starting to heat up, and I wanted to see what the real world was about before I got drafted and got my butt blown off in an undeclared, no-win war on the other side of the world; and (3) I simply wanted to get a job and get out on my own.

However, a lot of other things were going on at the time. (Several years later, I tried my hand [voice] at being a disc jockey, which is why I bring up the following.) For one thing, within a month of registering for my final quarter, the British Invasion slammed into the U.S. with full force. "I Wanna Hold Your Hand" went to the top of the charts, it seemed, almost overnight. It "charted" at Number 45 on America's Billboard Hot 100, and by February 1st, it hit Number 1, staying there for another seven weeks. It was recorded by a group of four shaggy-haired Brits who called themselves The Beatles. The song was so awful compared to the music genre of the day that I thought it was a joke the first time I heard it! Ray Stevens had made several splashes by this time with several quirky and goofy tunes, and I thought this must surely be just another "novelty record" destined soon for the trash bin. In my naiveté, I had no way of knowing that, not only were the Beatles to change the world of music, my world was poised to dramatically change as well.

But, I digress. January 6th was on a Monday, and I was at the end of a very long day. My last class of the day was an art class. I didn't actually know at the time how close I was to graduating and realized later that, if I had doubled up and taken an extra course or two here and there, I could have finished in 10 quarters rather than 11. This final quarter, I was coasting, and taking only enough courses to complete the required number of credit hours for my diploma. By this time, I had enough credits to earn a major in economics, and a double minor in business administration and art. So, of course, one of the courses I chose was an "art" class. Although I don't remember the exact name of the course, it was what students called a "CRIP." I'm not sure if it was an acronym or just a name students had given a class that was fairly easy and almost a guaranteed "A." This particular class consisted of an hour of sketching "still life" in charcoal (fruit and/or various objects accented by light and shadow). It was in this class that I met Joane, a strikingly beautiful, tall blond who captivated me from the start.

The bowl of fruit was already positioned on a table in the center of a circle of chairs as I entered the room. Although students weren't "assigned" specific seats, I had hoped I'd find one near the window and away from the noisy door to the hallway. The deafness in my left ear since the age of 10 had always been a determining factor for me in any seating arrangement—school, church, restaurants, parties, etc.—anywhere where I would have to listen to people speaking to me. Fortunately, the only chair left unoccupied was one near the window and actually farthest from the door. I knew this was going to be a good class, because it was not only my last quarter, it was my last art class. Little did I know that meeting the alluring and mysterious Joane would be the beginning of a relationship that would take us through personal and professional highs and lows, parenthood, fears, disappointments, jubilation, a secret romance, health challenges, and ultimately our final moments a short 53 years later.

The 20 or so class members were already seated in a circle—sketch pads in hand—around said still life, and, moments after taking my seat, Joane's eyes met mine. From my vantage point in the circle, I was directly across from Joane and was immediately taken with this incredibly striking young lady with a perpetual pout. At a time when bee hives dominated the girl-hair fashion scene, this goddess-on-the-other-side-of-the-room sported a unique "do" which swept her straight blond locks from just above her right ear completely over the top, cascading down, covering her left ear, and stopping short of her inviting shoulder. *WOW!* I was hopelessly smitten, and my final art class became no longer about art, but about the beautiful Joane.

Class after class brought Joane closer in my mind, and I began to study *her* rather than the art I had signed up for. It must have been the realization that, in a couple of months, it would all be over, including any chance I might have to get to know Joane. Whatever it was, *something* caused me to follow her out that fateful day and to stumble my way to her side as she made her way to the parking lot, and out of my sight once again.

"Hi," I stammered.

"Hey," she answered, her blue eyes looking suddenly bluer.

"I, uh, noticed you across the room." *Not the most brilliant pick-up line, I thought.*

"I noticed you, too…"

Thus began a roughly hour-long fact-finding expedition into Joane's life, in the front seat of her '55 Chevy, which made it no further than said parking lot. Coincidentally, my apartment was a stone's throw from the parking lot, so it didn't look like I was stalking her. I had already noticed that the ring finger of her left hand sparkled with a telltale diamond and was hoping that it wasn't what I thought it might be. Joane's admission hit me hard, as she reluctantly confirmed that she was engaged, and that her parents really liked "Sam." As the discourse became more personal, however, it was obvious that, while she cared deeply for Sam, Joane didn't share her parents' enthusiasm for him. Yet, Joane felt she had gone too far to turn back. Rather than disappoint her parents (and apparently everyone else who had "chosen" Sam), Joane had been playing the part of the happily-engaged, soon-to-be-married-wife of Sam. Problem was, Joane was not sure this was what she wanted, and it was obvious that she was conflicted about it.

Sensing this, I started making it my quest to break Joane free. Free to determine her own destiny. Free to pursue happiness on her own terms. And free to be with me—if that is what she wanted.

Then, an incident took place that ramped up our "relationship" another notch. Having been a life-long teetotaler, I was opposed to drinking of any kind of alcoholic beverage. One of the things that had attracted me to Joane was that she felt the same way I did about alcohol. However, one of my roommates didn't share my disdain for liquor and would often have other imbibers over to our apartment where they would drink themselves stupid. I came in one night after class to find that the apartment had been trashed by this drinking mob, who had gleefully destroyed all of my artwork which I had proudly displayed on the walls over the course of my studies. I don't know that I would have been considered necessarily a good "artist," but that wasn't the point. I had spent most of my growing up years dealing with my father's drinking, and this was the last straw. To say that I was livid would be putting it mildly. I had to have a talk with my roommates.

I simply explained that, when I was living at home, I didn't have a choice—nor anywhere else to go—when my father would come home drunk. This time I did. I unceremoniously moved out the next morning to a motel, making enemies out of my two roommates, who were upset that they would have one less person to split the $50 a month rent with. Even though I would have to pay $35 a month for the hotel room, it was better than living with a horde of marauding drunks, I reasoned.

The next time I saw Joane, I told her what had happened. After some consoling, I noticed a twinkle in her eye. Joane had a solution to my problem, and she thought she could help me. It would be good for both of us, she said. Her best friend, Sandy, lived within walking distance of the campus and only a little further out from my apartment. Sandy lived with her grandmother, who often rented out the spare bedroom in their small apartment to students. It had just become available, and the rent was $25! I met Sandy and her grandmother that afternoon and moved in as soon as I could get the refund from the hotel!

Obviously, Joane and I would be seeing a lot more of each other now. The next two months blurred into a cacophony of emotional ups and downs, with classes and grades taking low priority and my waking and (rarely) sleeping hours consumed with Joane. Innocently meeting Joane as she "visited" Sandy. Clandestine trips to a local "getaway." Plans to drive to a neighboring state (between classes?) to secretly get married. Offers of meager financial assistance from my family should we decide to run away. Even threats from Joane's mother and sister, and ultimately her father threatening to kill me. The list goes on.

In retrospect, I now understand the hostility from parents, family and friends toward me and my naïve, but doomed-from-the-start efforts at winning Joane. We had been ignoring the obvious, which was that we were on borrowed time. Somehow, we just couldn't face that fact. The saga came to a climax the night Joane gave me a lift to Sandy's apartment, and she asked me the following question: "What does a person do when they're always thinking about someone they know they shouldn't be thinking about…?" This followed a somewhat stressful day for Joane, as I learned later that the announcement of her marriage to Sam would be published the next day in the local newspaper. My insistence to Joane that she follow her heart and immediately call the newspaper and cancel the publication became a critical turning point in our relationship.

Of course, cell phones were non-existent at the time, so when Joane and I walked in, she asked to use Mrs. Larson's phone. With Mrs. Larson and Sandy by her side, and with me holding her hand, Joane shakily dialed the number to the newspaper. Although I didn't hear the other side of the phone conversation, the news was obviously not good. It was too late. Joane collapsed onto the floor. I had never seen anyone faint, but somehow I must have known what to do. Suddenly, my arms were under her, and I was lifting her, carrying her to a nearby sofa. It had all been too much for Joane. It was then that, for the first time, I feared for her life, not mine. When she regained consciousness, I drove Joane home in her car, and walked, ran, and stumbled the three-plus miles back to my apartment, my heart breaking with each step. The words of Joane's father—who had met me at the door—rang in my ears as I recalled his previous threat that, if I didn't stay away from Joane, he would kill me.

Joane and Sam were married two weeks later, and I resolved to "see" her only from afar, the realization finally sinking in that my life with Joane was over even before it began. To see her still directly in my sight, while pretending nothing had ever happened, was surreal. And, I thought, impossible to do.

I officially finished college two weeks later and started my new life without Joane. To my surprise, I received letters from her for a short time, but I knew that any attempt on my part to answer them, or to contact Joane, would make matters worse for all of us. And somehow, at the tender age of 20, as much as I loved Joane, I knew it was wrong to be involved in any way with a married woman.

If the story ended here, it would have made an incredibly sad movie. But it didn't. I was not to see Joane until years later, when fate would once again bring us together.

I was working at a "job between jobs" at a tiny convenience store, having struggled to find a permanent position in the work force due to factors beyond my control, including complications from my National Guard Service, and general dissatisfaction with my vocational field of endeavor. I was working the day shift when a familiar looking customer walked in.

As we embraced, I whispered, "It's been a long time, Joane." And, as though she had been keeping track through time, she answered without hesitation, "Yes…16 years."

Our attempt at recapturing those years ended all too soon, but we did learn that, as we raised our respective children (who were attending the same elementary school), we were living only a few blocks away in the same neighborhood!

Now that I was aware of Joane's presence in the neighborhood, I would sometimes see her drive down our street. On a rare occasion, I would "flag her down," walk over to her car and chat for a precious few minutes. Once again, however, my "relationship" with Joane would take another hit when my wife and I were forced to sell our house in that neighborhood, due to circumstances beyond our control. Just as well, I thought, we both had moved on. And, being still from the "old school," I didn't feel it was right for either of us to pursue the relationship any further than what it had been.

Years passed, as I toiled at many jobs (to steal a phrase from the 1960's hit TV series, "The Fugitive"), none of which led anywhere. This, even after I had returned to school at the University of Alabama and worked on a Master's Degree in Broadcast and Film Communications. I worked in Educational Television in both Alabama and Kentucky. Because money was always tight, I was a radio disc jockey for a time and supplemented my income by playing "DJ" at birthday parties and class reunions. I eventually taught a course at Auburn University in Montgomery, the course based on a booklet I had written entitled, "How to Break Into Broadcasting." Ironically, I never seemed to hit it big, but I did have several students who went on to successful careers in radio after taking my course. Although my wife had earned an undergraduate degree in Broadcast and Film Communications, she had never really "used" her degree, and back in the day, a wife wasn't really expected to work outside of the home unless she wanted to. Andrea had had some emotional issues that caused extreme anxiety, but we had worked on those, and I hadn't really pushed her to get a job. Meanwhile, even though our older daughter, Ashley, enjoyed having her mother at home, expenses always seemed to outrun revenue in our family. So, the decision was made for her to pursue a degree in elementary education and become a teacher. It would relieve some of our financial burden, and the job would offer benefits (which most of my jobs had not), and she could be at home when our children got home from school. I worked a night job as a dispatcher at a trucking company while Andrea attended school. Ashley was already in elementary school, so this arrangement allowed me to watch our 3-month old daughter, Crystal, during the day while Andrea attended classes, thus saving us a ton of money. I would go in to work at 8:00 P.M., get off at 6:00 A.M., and get home around 6:30, just in time to have breakfast with my wife and Ashley. They would leave at 7:00, and I would spend the next 2 ½ to 3 hours trying to keep Crystal asleep so I could get some sleep myself. Invariably, she would be ready to rock and roll by 9:00 or 9:30. The drill would continue the rest of the day, with me trying to get Crystal back to sleep and me taking precious cat naps when possible. I would pick up Ashley from school in the afternoon, and Andrea would get home about 5:00, at which time I would grab a quick sandwich (and another nap, if possible) before going back to work at 8:00.

After a year and a half, our hard work paid off, and Andrea landed a job in the public school system in Montgomery. Things were finally looking up. The year was 1984, and computers were still in their infancy. I thought I'd "ride the wave," and I had just gotten an associate degree in data processing from a local trade school. However, after a week on my first (and only) job as a computer person, I received a much needed paycheck, which promptly bounced. Things were looking down. I quit that job (for which I never got paid) the next day.

Then, by some miracle, I got a call from a Birmingham radio station where I had worked in the 70's asking me if I would be interested in being Director of Station Operations (aka station manager). The station was "re-inventing" itself, and the sales manager (with whom I had worked in the 70's as program director) recommended me for the job. The station needed someone with experience and who knew the market. I had worked there for almost 5 years, so I knew I was a shoo-in.

So...what to do with my wife's new job and the fact that our children were finally settled permanently in school after years of Dad chasing the rainbow and moving from one dead-end job to another? Answer: I would commute the 90 miles from Montgomery to Birmingham, coming home on Wednesday nights and Friday nights. No one, including me, the station owner, my wife or children, was satisfied with these terms, but I saw it as a way to revive my career and finally be happy in it.

After four and a half years at the station, the stress of the job and being away from my family took its toll, and my marriage of 22 years fell apart. I became depressed, even suicidal, but in April of 1990, I vowed to "get better or kill myself," and so, returned to school once again, earning a Master's Degree in Counseling and Human Development. I earned my degree in 1991, but by this time, I was dead broke and moved back in with my parents, fifty miles from my children. Shortly, however, a former classmate recommended me for a job at CSA (The Council on Substance Abuse). Although this meant more long distance commuting, this job would connect me with many professionals in the field. On the local scene, I was juggling a semblance of a social life and helping manage my aging parents' Mom and Pop grocery store and service station. But, I had become increasingly worried about my mother, an angel from heaven who never complained about anything. She had started suddenly going to bed during the day, and nausea and vomiting were the order of the day. One particularly bad day for her, I decided to take her to the ER in Montgomery. My mother had had several bouts with cancer and other health issues over the years, and although I was concerned, I hoped this was going to be just a routine examination with probably some medication, and that she would be back on her feet, working in her flower garden, cooking those good Southern meals, and making her customers and her husband happy.

My mother died eight months later, the day before Valentine's Day, after lapsing into a coma and succumbing to the bone cancer that had ravaged her body. My mother had always told me, "You can give out, but you can't give up!" And she never did. The night she died, my father had already gone to bed, and I had to go in and tell him that mother was gone. Through his sobs, he clawed at me and screamed, "I'm not going to make it!" I knew I was lying when I told him that sure he would; we'd all pull together and we'd all be fine. Mother would want that for us.

Daddy committed suicide eight months later on October 7, 1992. My mother and father had been married 53 years when she died. With my father's word's ringing in my ears, I began to wonder if I would make it myself. While not prone to superstition or seeing God in every familiar sequence of numbers, I had to believe that somehow God was trying to comfort me when my beautiful granddaughter, MaKayla was born exactly five years later on October 7, 1997. And again in 2014, my second precious grand-daughter, Vox Vivienne's birthday on July 10th held a special meaning when I realized that day was the transverse of MaKayla's (10/7 and 7/10). Perhaps just coincidence…but perhaps not.

I began to take inventory and was struggling with the reality of it all. I had lost virtually everything in my divorce; I rarely saw my children and had been told by at least six lawyers that gaining custody would be virtually impossible. However, once I had gotten established with my work, my generous parents gave me enough money to make a down payment on a house in Montgomery. And, incredibly, within a few months, I gained custody of my children. Ashley was 17 by now and had just graduated from high school. Crystal was 11 and going into an "awkward" stage. I knew that my mother would want me to continue on with my life, so at CSA, I quickly advanced to manager, and soon a co-worker at CSA asked if I would be interested in working with a new program at the State Youth Facility working with addicted teenagers. Her father was the director, and they needed seven counselors, and I suppose because of my age and gender (there were very few guys my age doing this kind of job), I was immediately hired! This led to a former classmate again recommending me for a job as counselor at the "big house," Kilby Correctional Facility, around the corner from the Youth Facility. I started March 2, 1992. (My first day on the job, a giant schizophrenic spit in my face, and I wondered if I had again made a bad decision in job choices.) In the almost nine years there, I learned a lot about being a counselor to people with every possible mental disorder in the book. I even got remarried, but with too much baggage for my wife, we divorced 5 years later. I was devastated and wondered how I could be any kind of counselor with such a record. Then, my mother's words came back to me and I knew I couldn't give up. I eventually obtained a license as a Licensed Professional Counselor and later became a supervising counselor, helping other graduates earn their licenses as well.

Although I was happy working in the prison system, my sister told me that the elementary school where she taught was looking for a school guidance counselor (again 50 miles away!). The Alabama Board of Examiners in Counseling had worked hard to have LPC's accepted by the public school systems. An LPC had only to work as a counselor for two years, at which time he or she would be tenured and receive benefits as though they were certified teachers. It was a nice drive and I did a lot of self-counseling during the commute!

I had worked at Goshen Elementary School for a year and a half and had almost "learned the ropes" when a dear counselor friend and former coworker called me from Montgomery and asked if I would be interested in working with her again. There were two openings at Behavioral Medicine, Inc. where she worked, and the terms of employment were outstanding. I would start at a salary much higher than I had ever made, with increases which would top out after three years, to be re-negotiated after the third year. I turned in my two weeks' notice, and after many tearful goodbyes, I started my first "real" counseling job, back in Montgomery, sans the commute, of course. This was in January of 2002.

Everything seemed to be going well, until I took a nasty spill at lunch about a year and a half later. I wasn't really hurt, but my "arthritic" left hand had taken the brunt of the fall, causing pain that simply wouldn't go away. I was involved in a relationship with Reba by this time, and she suggested I see her parents' crabby rheumatologist for an evaluation. During the office visit, I explained to him that I didn't think there was anything wrong, and I just wanted him to tell me I was getting old. After a brusque examination of said wrist, the doctor promptly told me that I was just getting old. He took me literally!

Before I left his office, he asked me if I was having any other problems, and I told him that the only thing I had noticed was a sort of weird discomfort around my belly button. It hadn't really bothered me but since he asked, I thought it wouldn't hurt to mention it. After more questioning, including when was my last colonoscopy, I timidly told him that I had never had one. Knowing my family history, he immediately made an appointment for me with a gastroenterologist, which I delayed a month due to a motorcycle trip Reba and I had planned for some time.

On the day of the "procedure," I was joking with the doctor, who asked me if I had ever had a colonoscopy. "No," I replied, "I'm a virgin!" As I came out of the anesthesia, however, there was no laughter. The somber look on his face told me the news wasn't good. "There's something in there, but we're not sure what it is. It's got to come out." The date was August 4th. Two days later, I got the call with the diagnosis: Non-Hodgkins Lymphoma. It was an orange-sized tumor in my lower intestines and would require immediate surgery, followed by 4 months of chemotherapy. On August 23rd, I had a "right colon resection," and my doctor wanted to start chemotherapy right away. I suppose I just wasn't mentally prepared, so I asked if I could get a second opinion, hoping that another doctor would tell me I would be fine without it.

To the contrary, this "second opinion" doctor told me, in effect, the sooner the better. By this time, all of my family had moved out of state, so I decided I could do this on my own, with help from my friends and, of course, from Reba. I started chemo on October 13th.

I also determined that I couldn't afford to lose any more time from work, as all of my sick leave, personal leave, and vacation time had been used up. I would go for a round of what looked like red Kool-Aid (actually poison) slowly dripping into my veins a couple of days a week every three weeks. These sessions would sometimes be scheduled in the morning, sometimes in the afternoon and would last from 5 to 6 hours. I would faithfully attend these sessions, then faithfully meet with my patients/clients for as many hours as I had left on that particular day. This schedule began to take its toll, and by Christmas, I was totally bald and so weak that I was in bed for 10 days, getting up only to drive to the Cancer Center for fluids. My family came from Boston and Phoenix. I wasn't sure I was going to make it, but my mother's words kept ringing in my ears: "You can give out, but you can't give up."

By April, I had missed so much time at work, I was sure I was going to lose my job. My friend (who had helped me get the job) assured me that I would be fine and that the manager (and part owner) of BMI was not going to fire me. On at least three occasions, I had asked him if I could cut back to part time at a reduction in pay, as I didn't see any way I would ever be able to make up the time I had lost. Each time, he continued to reassure me, stating at one point, "Don't worry about it; we love you; we just want you to get well." (his exact words)

It was a couple of days after our last conversation that my "boss" suddenly called me into his office and, in a rage, asked me how the f*** I was going to pay him the $8,000 I owed him! This was so unexpected and cruel (my hair had just begun to grow back, and although weak, I had continued to work up to this point), I thought at first I had surely misunderstood him. He then made it abundantly clear what his intentions were as he literally threw a stack of papers at me and ordered me out of his office and out of the building. I was in shock as I drove out of the parking lot, not even having time to tell my coworkers what had just happened.

Knowing that unemployment was not an option, I immediately

drove down the street and made arrangements to rent an office of my own. Fortunately, I had saved all of my records of patients I had seen since joining BMI. I contacted as many as I could over the next two weeks, and with only my license in hand, a wing and a prayer, I opened my own practice. Still reeling from the effects of chemotherapy and a profound sense of failure, I began to doubt my ability to pull off the impossible. Then, I received a call from a former coworker. She wanted me to contact a friend of hers, Dan Clark, a psychologist whom she had worked with. Unbelievably, it turned out that Dr. Clark had opened a practice, Associated Psychologists, with another psychologist, Dr. Marnie Dillon around the corner and two blocks from where my office was! He needed someone to do therapy and Medicaid evaluations on a contract basis, and after agreeing on terms, I started immediately, working with patients/clients at AP in between my own clients at my office around the corner. That was in May 2004, and after three months or so, I was doing more work with Dr. Clark than at my own office, so I started full time at AP on September 1st. It was the most nearly perfect situation, as I could work at my own pace, seeing both children and adults. AP would provide scheduling, bookkeeping, insurance, phone, office staff—all the amenities. All I had to do was show up (and do a good job, of course!). Space was limited, so I had to work in the "Play Room," complete with "live therapy gerbels" as gifts for children if their behavior improved with counseling. This was fine with me, because I loved animals (early on, I thought I wanted to be a veterinarian), and considering what I had been through, this seemed like a dream job. Things were going very well and my case load of patients was steadily increasing. I really felt that, for the first time in my life, I was doing a job that needed to be done and that I was genuinely helping people "get better." I had no way of knowing that this was just another decision that would once again lead me to Joane. Much more was to happen before we would actually meet, however.

  Since I was in 6th grade, due to a playground injury, I had had back issues that would unexpectedly recur for no apparent reason. On December

1, 2004, I started to feel a strange uncertainty in my back when I went to bed that night. (That's how it would usually start.) The next morning, I awoke in such pain, I was clawing the walls and almost delirious when I called Reba, who rushed over and took me immediately to the ER. Surgery was scheduled for January 27th. With some serious medication to quell the pain for the next two months, I had major surgery on my lower back, including hardware imbedded to keep it in place. Instead of threatening me with dismissal, Dr. Clark unhesitatingly paid my estimated salary for the five weeks I was off recuperating.

I shakily returned to work on March 1st to probably the biggest surprise of my life. Dr. Clark had consulted with Dr. Dillon and they agreed to take over a major portion of the adjoining office (occupied by the company that managed the entire building). A huge undertaking, to say the least, as it included making our existing office accessible to the addition by knocking out a wall, installing a new door and window, and reconfiguring the addition to accommodate a second waiting area and three offices for testing and therapy. Dr. Clark gave me the "grand tour" before the work day started. As he led me down the steps to the new addition, he opened the door to the largest (corner) office, complete with new furniture and a view from two sides! I cannot describe the rush of emotion I felt when Dr. Clark told me the office was mine. I think (no, I know) I unashamedly cried like a baby. For someone 61 years of age who thought he might die a year earlier, I felt at that moment that I must surely be the most blessed and fortunate person in the world. I had literally won the lottery. Later that summer, I had surgery to repair a left inguinal hernia—a piece of cake compared to the six previous surgeries I had had. In fact, I had surgery on a Thursday and returned to work the following Monday.

As my life fell back into place, I was at peace with the world. I even wrote a book entitled "Mules In The Fast Lane," a sort of autobiographical account of life lessons I had learned growing up in rural South Alabama after World War II. The only time I worried about anything, it would usually be about my children and granddaughter, who were still far away in Boston and Phoenix. Each of my patients was special and I cherished the relationships I developed with each one. I was seeing new patients weekly, so I expected nothing out of the ordinary when I saw "Martin" on my schedule in October of 2006. Martin was there with his mother, Danielle, to work on some family issues and adjustment to adolescence. I saw him several times, learning, as I typically do, about his family, his friends, his life. I still suspected nothing, even when he told me that he thought his grandmother knew me. By this time, I had seen a lot of mutual acquaintances over the years whose paths often cross. Then he told me her name was Joane.

I usually don't leave a stone unturned when it comes to finding out about any and everything that will help me help my patients. Martin was especially close to his grandmother, and we had talked about Martin bringing her in with him to one of our sessions. By this time, however, I had begun to put two and two together and was almost certain that this was not just another "Joane." This was going to be a problem for Martin and me, because patient/client confidentiality is sacred and "dual relationships" are strictly forbidden. I was walking a tightrope, so I decided to talk to Danielle and to disclose that I did know her mother and that we had a "history." To my relief, she told me that she had already figured it out some time ago, that she had told her mom about Martin's counselor and that he really "liked me," etc. She told me that it didn't matter to her and that she thought we were doing some good work, and that she was pleased with Martin's progress as well. They had all agreed that absolutely nothing of a counseling nature would ever be discussed with Martin or with Joane, and that they had rather I continue with him than to be overly concerned about the confidentiality factor. In retrospect, this turned out to be the right decision, and after Martin and I finished our work, I decided to contact Joane, having found out that she and Sam had divorced and he had subsequently passed away. This time, we actually got to know each other, but without having to rush.

Unsure how to approach our relationship after such a long period of time, Joane and I decided it was more important to try to catch up on how we didn't know each other than how we did. We visited many times over the next several years. Then one day, Danielle called to tell me that the family had planned a surprise 65th birthday party for Joane and asked would I please come. It was a wonderful occasion. Joane wasn't into surprises, but she seemed happy that everyone had made an effort to help her celebrate. Although we both felt somewhat awkward, as this was the first time we had ever met in a public venue with family and friends who knew both of us, but did not know our story. There was one, however, who knew, and she was there. Sandy seemed to have entered a time warp, and looked much the same as I remembered her years before. I had unexpectedly run into Sandy not too many years after Joane got married, and she told me that Joane still had strong feelings for me. I wasn't sure how to handle this flattering disclosure, so I never mentioned it to anyone. Joane's father was also at the party. Since Joane had not known about the party, nor who would be there, I think we both realized as soon as he walked up that we would be the only people who would know why he might react negatively to someone who was supposed to be just another one of Joane's many friends. I'm sure he remembered the troublesome young man from 46 years ago, but thankfully, he must have not made any connection to me and our past history. I was, of course, relieved and, in my mind, had made peace with myself and Joane's family years ago. Surprisingly, when I was "re-introduced" to Joane's sister, Cassie, she apparently remembered me and later took me aside and apologized for her treatment of me. It was a very special day for all of us.

After the surprise party, Joane would often have me over for dinner, preferring to cook for me at her place than going out to a "fancy restaurant," although I offered many times. We would often visit and discuss gardening. She had a beautiful lush garden out back, with a new plant almost every time I went over. She would graciously give me a "cutting" of anything I saw that I liked. She had even, on occasion, bought some plants for my back yard (which was an unattended jungle compared to hers). Each Christmas, I would receive a small, but significant gift, and of course, a card. In fact, I would receive a card from Joane for virtually every possible occasion—Easter, Halloween, Valentine's Day—you name it. Each would contain a special hand-written message and would always be signed, "Love and Prayers, Joane." And I saved every one. Although our bond had remained strong over the years, because so much had happened to us respectively, we didn't see each other regularly. But we kept in touch. She and I both knew that if one needed the other, one needed only to pick up the phone.

One particular "Joane" incident, I remember vividly. Joane was a talented and creative artist, and much of her work was done with pieces of colored/stained, broken glass, which she sometimes fired in a kiln to create beautiful masterpieces of flowers, landscapes, birds, etc. She was a true artist, rarely receiving compensation for her work. (Much of what she learned about this technique was in art classes she had taken before we met.) One such creation was a leaded and framed stained glass piece depicting a simple but impressive sunset over water, surrounded by foliage, lighting up an evening sky of brilliant orange. Although she would spend hours on such creations, she was never totally satisfied with them and would point out perceived imperfections in describing any of her work. She presented "The Sunset" to me unexpectedly one evening after dinner; it hangs in an east-facing window as a constant reminder of Joane's beauty and selfless generosity.

Another incident, again totally unexpected, comes to mind. I received a call from Joane with a strange request. She had "something" in the back of her car and needed help unloading it. Being fiercely independent, she rarely asked for such help, so I was glad to accommodate. "Would you like me to meet you at your place," I asked. "No," she responded, "I'm coming over there." Of course, I assumed she was coming "over here" to pick me up.

Ready to go when Joane drove up, I hurried out to her car, but she had already opened the back of her SUV. "I...I thought we were going to unload something at your house," I stammered. "No..." she replied, the twinkle in her eye finishing her sentence, "I never said that." Peering into the back of the SUV, I saw a familiar piece of artwork. I recognized it as a heavy, stone "park bench," with an intricate pattern of brilliantly-colored hummingbirds feasting on an array of equally brilliantly-colored flowering plants - the same piece I had seen in her studio (which she called her "junk room") several weeks earlier! I had commented on how beautiful it was and how much I liked it, as she explained how each piece of colored glass had to be individually and meticulously cut, sometimes several times, to get the pattern just right.

I was so taken aback by her gift, I never determined if it was something she had been working on all along especially for me, or if she decided to make it a gift to me after I told her how much I liked it. In either case, that summed up Joane.

The last time I saw Joane, she was in the hospital. Danielle had called to tell me that she was OK, but that she would worry each time she got sick because of her history of cancer and other health issues. She had been a smoker since her teen years, which further complicated her health. The small hospital room was full of friends and family. I knew only Danielle and Cassie. Joane was alert and in good spirits and was released the next day to continue her job teaching art at a local private school. She was glad I had come. Anytime we would see each other, we always assumed we would talk later.

My health issues had prevented me from working more than two days a week by now, and I had already had more surgeries than I wanted to count. Several weeks after Joane left the hospital, I was facing more surgery, and we always mutually agreed to pray for each other. After a particularly busy weekend, including the death of a former high school teacher's wife, I didn't really feel like attending the funeral, which was on Monday. I did go, however, which was a 50 mile trip down and 50 miles back. Exhausted when I went to bed that night, I was looking forward to going back to work the next day, my regular days being Tuesdays and Wednesdays. I didn't have anyone on my schedule in the

8:00 A.M. slot that morning, so I was busy organizing my day when my phone rang. It was Danielle. Joane had gone to work on Friday, not feeling well. She convinced her mother to go to the ER on Saturday, and Joane was immediately admitted to the hospital. Danielle's voice began to break. "Mike, she didn't make it. She passed away last night."

They say that a person's life passes before them right before they die. I don't remember what I did after Danielle told me the bad news. I only remember seeing "our" life instantly pass before my eyes. Services would be at a local Catholic church on Thursday, September 21st, with visitation at 11:00 A.M. and mass to follow at noon.

I had promised myself I would be brave and not "break down," but I wasn't sure I could keep my own promise. I arrived at the church around 10:45. It was a beautiful fall day, the kind Joane loved. The parking lot was already full as I drove in, and I scanned the parking lot, searching for familiar faces. The lump in my throat would not go away, and tears were already a problem. *"You can do this, Moody. You have to,"* I told myself. Entering the church, I approached the guest sign-in table with Joane's picture. Still, I was strong…for Joane. My first handshake was a tall handsome young man with neat blond hair. I heard myself say, "You're Michael, aren't you?" "Yes…and you're Mike…?" He apparently remembered me from Joane's surprise party.

Danielle's hug was warm, lingering, and heart-felt. She was being strong too. Then there was Martin, who told me after the obligatory greeting, with tear-filled eyes, "She was my best friend." I had to turn away, lest I betray my own pain, which would seem out of proportion to Martin. Some idle chit chat followed with a mutual friend, Sharon, a counselor with whom I had done some work years earlier. We talked about the recent death of her husband. But we didn't delve too deeply into my relationship with Joane. It would complicate things. "We knew each other in college," I told her.

When I saw Sandy, it was as though we both flashed back to the night Joane fainted in her living room. I was still being strong. Sandy was Joane's best friend. I had to be strong…for Joane. After a couple of minutes of idle talk about her hundred-mile drive up from her home in Dothan, we found ourselves in our own private conversation. "Mike, I have something to give you," she started. Totally unprepared, I responded, "What is it?"

"It's out in the car. It's something Joane gave me 43 years ago. She told me if anything ever happened to her, she wanted me to promise I would give it to you." My silence was deafening, and I could hear only my heartbeat, wondering if I was going to pass out. "Do you want to go out and get it now?" she continued.

The sun blinded me as we walked out to Sandy's car, which was only a couple of spaces from mine. Neither of us spoke as Sandy reached for her keys. The trunk popped, and Sandy reached inside to retrieve her purse. The mild fall day seemed suddenly much warmer as Sandy reached slowly into her purse and pulled out an obviously old and tattered long white envelope. "Joane sent me this 43 years ago," she repeated. Reaching inside the envelope, Sandy pulled out a much smaller, sealed plain white envelope with no writing on it. "What is it?" I repeated. "I don't know; it's for you." "What…you never opened it?" I asked incredulously. "No, but I'll read you the letter she sent with it." The sun was suddenly much hotter, and Sandy—remaining strong—finished only the first page. "Why don't you just take it too? I'd like it back though." I guess Sandy had read my mind, because I had wanted to do just that, keeping anything that would, one last time, connect me with sweet Joane.

Sandy waited as I placed the envelopes in my car. As we turned around, I knew I wasn't going to make it. I was quietly sobbing as we approached the church. "I can't go back in there, Sandy. I just can't do it." Her arm gently on my shoulder comforted me. "Don't you want to just try? I'll wait with you." It took a few minutes, and as I felt myself regaining composure, we ventured back inside. The room was spinning, and this time, the noise was deafening. My heart was pounding and my resolve was ebbing. I found Danielle and apologized, "I'm not going to be able to stay, Danielle." I felt like I was betraying Joane, but

I couldn't risk being exposed for the weakling I felt I was and also the "secret lover" I had been to Joane. Irrational, I know, but somehow Danielle must have sensed it was more than just grief for her mother. "So, you're just going to leave me to cry alone?" she nervously chuckled. "I guess so," seemed too feeble, but it was all I could come up with at the moment.

On the drive home, at every stop sign and red light, I made attempts at reading Sandy's letter line by line but had reached my driveway before I could finish the first page.

Finally alone, with only Joane's memory, I finished Sandy's letter and slowly and carefully sliced open Joane's letter to me. Out of respect for Sandy's privacy and Joane's memory, I will never share those very personal letters publicly. However, I do think it prudent to comment on some of the points Joane shared with me. Her devotion to her family was typical of Joane's unconditional love. Yes, she was conflicted, but she knew that, as much as she loved me, she had responsibilities in the life she had chosen that superseded anyone else. She just couldn't let go of her "other love" either. It hurt no one but Joane, but, ultimately, she had to make that choice. Sandy was a good friend, with whom she could share her deepest feelings. Sandy was always there for her, as she had proven time and again. The most striking point that Joane made, which was very flattering and gratifying, is that, at times when she would tend to get depressed, the memory of our relationship and of my love for her kept her going. She remained faithful and true to her family through it all, not knowing when she wrote those letters whether she would ever see me again.

And indeed, the odds were against it. But love manifests itself in many different ways. Joane's love is a classic example of how love can survive or die, depending on whether one chooses to nurture it. I was fortunate to have known Joane and to have been the object of her love. In part, Joane ended her letter, "My love will always be with you, my love, and at death, bond even tighter…always yours, Joane."

I wrote Sandy, thanking her for her good friendship and her love for both Joane and me. I'm sure Joane would have wanted Sandy to read the precious missive her best friend had lovingly preserved all those years, so I carefully made a copy of Joane's letter and included it when I sent Sandy's original letter back to her.

An American Quaker and poet, John Greenleaf Whittier, wrote in the 19th century, "For of all sad words of tongue or pen, the saddest are these: 'It might have been!'" He was obviously addressing the issue of missed opportunities and possibly regrets. This sentiment was echoed a century later in a song by an unknown Canadian singer in late 1959. The artist was Joe London, and the song was entitled "It Might Have Been." Although altered, Whittier's words were further immortalized in this Canadian Top 40 hit, which incidentally never even cracked the top 100 songs in the U.S. that year. Neil Young recorded it several years later, but with no more success than the original. In 1969, The Hollies, another British group, recorded a song entitled "He Ain't Heavy; He's My Brother." The first line sums it up.

"The road is long…with many a winding turn."

Indeed it is, Joane. Indeed it is. We'll meet again…

CPSIA information can be obtained
at www.ICGtesting.com
Printed in the USA
LVHW082309100620
657786LV00028B/3130